FAITH, HOPE, LOVE

JOSEF PIEPER

FAITH

HOPE

LOVE

IGNATIUS PRESS   SAN FRANCISCO

Title of the German original:
Lieben, Hoffen, Glauben
© 1986 Kösel-Verlag GmbH & Co., Munich

Über den Glauben
© 1962 Kösel-Verlag GmbH & Co., Munich
English edition: *Belief and Faith: A Philosophical Tract*
Translated by Richard and Clara Winston
© 1963 Random House, Inc., New York
Copyright renewed, © 1991 by Random House, Inc.
This translation published by arrangement with
Pantheon Books, a division of Random House, Inc.

Über die Hoffnung, 7th edition
© 1977 Kösel-Verlag GmbH & Co., Munich
English edition: *On Hope*
Translated by Sister Mary Frances McCarthy, S.N.D.
© 1986 Ignatius Press, San Francisco

Über die Liebe, 7th edition
© 1992 Kösel-Verlag GmbH & Co., Munich
English edition: *About Love*
Translated by Richard and Clara Winston
© 1974 Franciscan Herald Press, Chicago

Printed in 1997, Ignatius Press, San Francisco
ISBN 0–89870–623–8
Library of Congress catalogue number 96–78013
Printed in the United States of America ∞

In memory of
Hildegard Pieper
†*June 25, 1984*

CONTENTS

FOREWORD

The earliest and the most recent of the works brought together here for the first time in one volume are separated by a temporal distance of thirty-seven years. And naturally there are also considerable differences in linguistic and intellectual character between the book on hope, published in 1935, and that on love, which appeared in 1972. These stem from the inner and external biography of the author. Some brief, prefatory remarks are therefore necessary.

When my manuscript "On the Meaning of Courage"—written down in anger at the beginning of 1934, in anger about the fact that no express counterpart had appeared to the words "heroic service", which were booming at that time, in the second year of the national socialist regime, from all the loudspeakers—when this work, declined by four or five of the publishing houses I was acquainted with, repeatedly came back to me like a boomerang, I sent it without a moment's hesitation, with the courage of despair, to Jakob Hegner in Leipzig, who, as the publisher of Claudel, Guardini and Bernanos, appeared to me to be entirely inaccessible. But to my surprise, in just a few days, the astonishing answer came that the book was accepted and would be printed that same year, which then actually happened. Far more astonishing still, however, was Jakob Hegner's additional and by no means "rhetorically" expressed question whether there were not seven such basic virtues.

He in any case was ready to publish two such works by me
every year—actually, an author interested him much more
than a single book. The vista suddenly opening up here
seemed to me like an absolutely unforeseeable stroke of
luck; and it was so indeed. In the summer of that event-
laden year 1934, with the wonderful letter from "my" publisher in my pocket, it did not take me long to consider
which should be the second virtue in the newly begun series: it could, of course, only be hope! The unconcerned
lack of hesitation with which I instantly set to work corre-
sponded, as I quickly began to feel, more to the state of
mind current in the thirties than to my level of knowledge
or powers of representation or intellect. After all, as an "un-
employed intellectual"—fortunately, or rather unfortunately,
completely free of any professional demands—I had a whole
autumn and winter long, with much effort and as a "labor
of love", but above all in undiverted surrender to the subject, to succeed in finishing the *opusculum* "On Hope". And
right on schedule came the slender Hegner volume, in the
typography and layout for which the publisher was justly re-
nowned.

How much I, basically unsuspecting, had fallen into a simply inexhaustible theme, which I had been capable of sketch-
ing only in outline at best, became clear enough to me quite
soon. In the new edition presented here, I have nevertheless
changed the original text only a little. But I would not like to
omit mention of particular later works, in which, prompted
by Gabriel Marcel and challenged by Ernst Bloch, I have
tried to supplement the first sketch considerably: namely, the
Paris lecture on the hope of the martyrs (which Teilhard de
Chardin vehemently attacked as "defeatist"[1]); the reflections

---

[1] *Sur l'Espérance des Martyrs*, in *Espoir humain et l'espérance chrétienne* (Paris,
1951).

from 1955 on the hiddenness of hope and despair;[2] but above all the Salzburg course "Hope and History".[3]

After the publication of my book on justice (1953), I had only the two most difficult of the seven treatises on the basic virtues left to write, the one on faith, the other on love. Meanwhile, by means of my *habilitation*, I had an opportunity at the university that had not been open to me until then: that of preparing what amounted nearly to a book in the form of lectures, therefore as an oral presentation, and to test it before a critical audience.

So I announced a semester course of lectures for the winter of 1955–56: "Faith as Philosophical Problem (Thomas Aquinas, J. H. Newman, K. Jaspers)". These were by all means to be philosophical, not theological, reflections—although I naturally remain convinced that philosophy and theology are to be differentiated, to be sure, but not dissociated. The writing by Karl Jaspers on "philosophical faith" always represents for me the adversarial view; I find its inner inconsistency both incomprehensible and characteristic of a certain type of modern thinking. After a second, entirely new lecture, recorded word for word, from the summer of 1961 ("Faith—Considered Philosophically"), the text of the book on faith was finally translated into the form of a written address and appeared as a book in 1962, with what was for me an important subtitle: "A Philosophical Treatise".

I more than once gave up in the face of the task of writing about the theme of "love", which I had, at any rate, put off to the end; and after a few years of futile attempts, I had finally resigned myself never to accomplishing an adequate presentation. Since it is told in detail in my autobiographical writings,[4] I need not relate once again in what unforeseen ways

---

[2] In: Josef Pieper, *Tradition als Herausforderung* (Munich).

[3] Munich: Kösel-Verlag, 1967.

[4] No one still remembers it: 3d ed. (Munich: Kösel-Verlag, 1979), 112f.

the book *On Love* came about after all. Incidentally, it seems to me today to be my most important book—perhaps because it cost me more effort than any of the others.

Arnulf Baring, who evidently knew this history of my effort, once asked me in a radio interview precisely what the difficulty was. The answer was not easy to formulate. Already during my work on the book about faith I had to some extent felt restricted by the definition of the notion "virtue"; this was also the reason why I insisted on calling the work a "philosophical treatise". Such a restriction, however, seemed to me quite impossible as regards the theme of "love"; in any event, I was absolutely against the concept. So I had the very clear, prodigious task of presenting what the German language, as distinct from many others, still calls by the single word "love" and of then discussing not only the "theological virtue" of *caritas-agape* but also eros, sexuality and even "love" of music and wine. In spite of all that, in the end, the difficulty—which almost forced me to abandon the project— then lay not only in bringing all that is homogeneous in all forms of love to a handy formula but also in making the real basis for this identity perceptible.

I trust that these preliminary remarks make clear that the works submitted here do not lay claim to being theological treatises in the strict sense.

                                                        J. P.

ON FAITH

He who wishes to learn
must believe
—Aristotle—

CONTENTS

I

The true meaning of root words is not easy to determine, despite the fact that they have "always" been present in language. It is well to distrust the perfection of excessively precise definitions.— The fundamental types of attitude: doubt, opinion, knowledge, belief.— Two elements of the concept of "belief": the content cannot be verified, and yet it is unreservedly accepted as true and real.— When there proves to be no substitute for a word, we know we are using it in the strict sense.— The complete concept in outline: Belief means to regard something as true on the testimony of someone else.

II

The conterminousness of the objective and the personal element: *aliquid et alicui credere.*— The decisive factor in human relationships is the appeal to the witness. Ostensible belief.— Belief in the strict sense can be neither demanded nor bestowed. To believe "in" someone.— The condition that must be fulfilled for belief to be a meaningful human act.

III

We can believe only if we want to. The determining factor is not the truth of the content but the sense that it is good to believe.— The function of the will in belief. Neither the act of belief itself nor the believed content is what is willed. The primary act of the will: to love. "We believe because we love." The believer affirms the witness and seeks communion with him, by virtue of which he then sees with the eyes of the knower.   35

IV

If there are no knowers, there also can be no believers. Belief is something secondary. On the other hand, imperfect access to reality is better than no access at all.— It must be possible to judge the credibility of the witness as well as the actuality and the meaning of his testimony. This knowledge, however, is to a considerable extent knowledge of persons.   42

V

Because belief springs from freedom, it is a particularly opaque phenomenon.— The conjunction of certainty and uncertainty. "Mental unrest" in spite of unconditional assent: *cum assensione cogitare*. Belief does not still, but kindles desire.— Firmness of the contact with reality nevertheless. Belief as "light".   49

VI

Belief as "acceptance of the principles of a religion" (Kant). *Res divina non visa*. The witness is God himself.— Disquisition on the philosophical, psychological, historical and theological views of belief.— Belief in revelation is not a development and continuation of "belief in general". The natural obstacles to belief in revelation. "Where knowledge suffices . . ."— Belief cannot be expected if God is not conceived as a personal Being capable of speech and if man is

ogy in the human realm: "I love you."— Belief means participation not only in the knowledge of God but in the divine reality itself.   82

I

WHO REALLY DETERMINES what is meant by "belief"?
Who is empowered to decide what should be the
"true" meaning of this and other root words in the language
of men? No one, of course. No individual, at any rate, no
matter how great his genius, can possibly determine and fix
anything of the sort. It is already determined in advance. And
all elucidation must start with this preexistent fact. Presumably Plato, Aristotle, Saint Augustine and Saint Thomas knew
precisely what they were doing when they started any discussion by querying linguistic usage: What do men mean
when they say "freedom", "soul", "life", "happiness", "love",
"belief"? Evidently these ancestors of Western philosophy
did not consider such an approach a mere didactic device.
Rather, they held the opinion that without such a link to
human speech as actually spoken, thinking would necessarily
be ethereal, insubstantial, fantastic.

Nevertheless, it would be wrong to imagine that determining what is truly meant by the living language of men is
an easily mastered task. On the contrary, there is much evi-

The motto [on p. 13 above] is taken from Aristotle's book *Sophistical Refuta-
tions*, chap. 2.2; 165b.

The German word *Glaube* may mean "belief" or "faith". In this translation we have usually rendered it by "belief"; but the reader should bear the
other possibility in mind if any phrases strike him as slightly strange. In quotations from Thomas Aquinas, *fides* has been translated by "belief" instead of
the more customary "faith" for the sake of consistency with the German
text.—TRANS.

dence that it is virtually impossible to exhaust the wealth of
meanings in words, especially root words, and to paraphrase
them precisely. Perhaps the individual mind is scarcely capable of holding their full richness of meanings in his consciousness. Then again, it seems to be the other side of the
coin that an individual ordinarily, when he uses words unself-
consciously, usually means *more* than he ever consciously realizes.

It may be that this sounds at first like a romantic exaggeration. But we can show that it is not. Everyone, for example,
thinks he knows precisely what so commonplace a word as
"resemblance" means. He will say, perhaps, that resemblance
is "agreement in several characteristics, in contradistinction
to likeness, which is agreement in all characteristics". And
what objections can be raised to so precise a definition,
which is, moreover, borrowed from a well-known philosophical dictionary?[1] Nevertheless, the definition is wrong,
or at least it is incomplete. An essential element of the meaning is lacking. That, to be sure, will be observed only by one
who examines the living usage of language. For a part of
living usage is not only what men actually say but what they
do *not* explicitly say. Another aspect of living usage is that
certain words cannot be employed in certain contexts. Thus
Thomas Aquinas once made the point[2] that we can meaningfully speak of a man's resemblance to his father, whereas it
is obviously nonsensical and inadmissible to say that a father
resembles his son. Herein it becomes apparent that the concept of "resemblance" contains an element of meaning that
has been overlooked in the apparently exact definition
quoted above ("agreement in several characteristics")—
namely, the element of descent and dependence. But who

[1] Johannes Hoffmeister, *Wörterbuch der philosophischen Begriffe*, 2d ed. (Hamburg, 1955), 19.
[2] I, 4, 3 ad 4; 1, d. 28, 2, 2.

would claim that this initially hidden aspect of the meaning had been present to his consciousness, explicitly and fully, from the very beginning?

We are therefore—let no one be surprised at this—electing a task that may possibly prove extremely difficult when we attempt to discover the full and undiminished meaning of a root word—the meaning, *nota bene*, that every mature person has in the back of his mind when he uses the word.

Such preliminary considerations are necessary lest we succumb to the lures of excessively precise definitions. For example, we are told that belief simply means "emotional conviction"[3] or else "practical" certainty about matters that cannot be justified "theoretically". Or it is said that belief is the subjectively adequate but objectively inadequate acceptance of something as true.[4] When we hear such suspiciously exact definitions, we would do well to receive them with a good deal of wariness and distrust.

But then, what do men really mean when they speak of belief? What is the true, rounded, complete signification of this concept? That is the first question we must take up in the following pages.

Someone gives me a news item to read that he himself thinks rather strange. After I have read it, he asks me: "Do you believe that?" What answer does he really want? He wants to hear whether I think that the fact given comports with the potentialities of the real world, what stand I take on it, whether I think it is *true*, whether I consider that it really

---

[3] Cf. David Hume, *An Inquiry concerning Human Understanding*, 5, 2.

[4] Kant defines belief as acceptance of something as true on "objectively" and "theoretically" insufficient grounds. So certain is he of this definition that he says he will not "waste time" on further explanation. Cf. *Critique of Pure Reason*, ed. R. Schmidt, Philosophische Bibliothek (Leipzig, 1944), 741f.

happened. It is obvious that there are various possible answers aside from yes or no. I might, for example, say: "I don't know whether it is true; to my mind, it might just as well not be." Or my reply might be: "I imagine that the report is accurate; it seems to me that it is probably right—although, as far as I can see, the contrary is not absolutely out of the question." It is also conceivable that I might reply with a firm: "No." This "no" in turn could have several meanings. It might mean that I think the news untrue, a mistake, a lie, a deliberately false trial balloon. On the other hand, my "no" might mean the following: "You ask me whether I believe it. No, I do not *believe* it, for I *know* that it is true. I have seen the incident reported here with my own eyes; I happened to be there."

Finally, there is the possibility that I might reply: "Yes, I believe that the report is true, that it happened as described." Perhaps I would be able to say that only after having quickly determined who the author of the story is or what newspaper printed it.

A first, approximate definition, then, would have to go as follows: To believe is equivalent to taking a position on the truth of a statement and on the actuality of the matter stated. More precisely, belief means that we think a statement true and consider the stated matter real, objectively existent.

The example just cited displays all the "classical" modes of potential attitudes: doubting, supposing, knowing, believing. How are they to be distinguished from one another? One distinction, for example, lies in assent or dissent. Supposing, knowing and believing are forms of assent. These in turn can be distinguished in terms of the conditionality or unconditionality of the assent. Only the knower and the believer assent unconditionally. Both say: "Yes, it is so and not different." Neither of the two attaches an overt condition to his "yes".

Finally, we could examine the various modes of potential

attitudes as to whether and to what extent they assume insight into the subject matter. On that score, we must distinguish between the knower and the believer. Assent on the basis of knowledge does not only presume familiarity with the subject—knowledge *is* that familiarity. Incidentally, refusal to take an unconditional position—the refusal implied in supposition or doubt—can be based precisely on familiarity with the subject. The believer, however, does not know the subject at all, although he regards it as true and real. Precisely this distinguishes the believer. But then we must ask: On what basis can he, like the knower, say without reservation or condition, "Yes, it is so and not different"? How is this possible if, as we have established, he is *not* familiar with the subject? This is precisely the point at which the difficulty is to be found—both the theoretical difficulty of illuminating the structure of belief as an act and the difficulty of justifying the act of belief as a meaningful and intellectually responsible act.

By way of preliminary, however, it seems essential for us to assure ourselves that both elements of meaning are actually present: unfamiliarity with the subject matter and yet, at the same time, unconditional conviction of its truth.

First: it is very easy to demonstrate that the believer is, as commonly understood, someone who possesses no exact knowledge of the thing he believes. When has an eyewitness ever begun his account of a happening with the words: "I *believe* it took place as follows . . ."? And no one who has arrived at a given result after careful investigation and after checking his reasoning can logically say: "I *believe* it is so." This negative proposition, at least, seems undeniable. And if we do not trust our own instinct about the use of words but seek some positive confirmation, we will find it in any standard dictionary. Thus we will find belief defined as follows:

"Confidence in the truth of a statement *without personal insight into the substance*";[5] "to be convinced *without having seen . . .*";[6] "conviction of the truth of a given proposition . . . *resting upon grounds insufficient to constitute positive knowledge*".[7]

The great theologians, too, attest to the same thing. *Creduntur absentia*, Augustine says.[8] That means that the formal subject of belief is what is not apparent to the eye, what is not obvious of its own accord, what is not attainable either by direct perception or logical inference. Thomas Aquinas formulates the same idea as follows: "Belief *cannot* refer to something that one sees . . . ; and what can be proved likewise does not pertain to belief."[9]

Naturally, this cannot mean that in the act of belief the believer simply takes leave of his own perceptions. A word must be said at this point to avert possible misunderstanding. Naturally it would not make sense to talk about "belief" if the subject for belief could be proved. Nevertheless, the believer must (for example) know enough about the matter to understand "what it is all about". An altogether incomprehensible communication is no communication at all.[10] There is no way either to believe or not to believe it or its author. For belief to be possible at all, it is assumed that the communication has in some way been understood.

In asserting this we are saying something whose full im-

---

[5] J. and W. Grimm, *Deutsches Wörterbuch*, article "Glaube", vol. 4, 1, 4, col. 7805.

[6] Trübner, *Deutsches Wörterbuch*, article "Glaube", 3:192.

[7] *The Century Dictionary* (New York: The Century Company, 1911), 1:513, col. 1.

[8] Letter 147 (to Paulinus). Migne, *Patrologia Latina* [hereafter PL] 33:599.

[9] 3, d. 24, 2, 1; cf. III, 7, 4.

[10] Cf. Alexis Decout, *L'Acte de foi. Ses éléments logiques. Ses éléments psychologiques* (Paris, 1947), 77, 79.

port will only be revealed in the specific area of *religious* belief. For what we are asserting is as follows: Even the revelatory pronouncements of God must, in order for men *to be able* to believe them, be "human" at least to the extent that the believer can grasp out of his own knowledge what they are about. Of course, human reason will never be able to fathom the event concealed behind theology's technical term "incarnation". Yet this event could never become subject to human belief if it remained utterly incomprehensible to men, if men had no means whatsoever of grasping what is meant by "incarnation". To put this in more "philosophical" terms: if God is conceived exclusively as "absolute Otherness", and if all direct analogies between the divine and human spheres are barred, then it is impossible to expect of men believing acceptance of any divine pronouncement; it is impossible to make "belief in revelation" comprehensible to men as a meaningful act. The great teachers of Western Christendom have expressed this idea many times. Thus Saint Augustine says that there is no belief without preceding knowledge and that no one can believe in God if he understands nothing.[11] And Thomas Aquinas states: "Man could not believingly assent to any proposition if he did not in some way understand it."[12]

But this remark is anticipation of our argument. What we are at present discussing is not the theological concept of belief but belief in general, taken in its most comprehensive but nevertheless strict and proper meaning. And an essential element of this meaning is the fact that the believer cannot know and verify out of his own knowledge the matter to which he assents.

There is a second vital element in the concept of belief: that the assent of belief is, as it were by nature, unqualified

---

[11] *De praedestinatione Sanctorum*, cap. 2, 5. PL 44:962f.

[12] II, II, 8, 8 ad 2.

and without reservation. Now this statement seems far less easy to substantiate. Living usage, it might be objected, rather suggests the reverse: that to say, "I believe it is so", implies a reservation. When we say that, we are clearly not making a simple asseveration; rather, we are implying that we are not wholly sure; we suppose, we think probable, we assume, we consider—and so on. (In fact—this by way of a digressive comment—everyday language recognizes a meaning of "believe" that is equivalent to "pretend". To "make believe" is to pretend that what is not true is true. And colloquially the meaning can be stretched even farther. "You cannot make me believe that" need not mean "You cannot convince me", but "You cannot fool me.") Linguistic usage, it would seem, contradicts the thesis that "belief" implies unqualified acceptance of something as true.

On this score, the following may be said. Every historical language that is the product of natural growth is characterized by something that does not occur in an artificial terminology: namely, *improper* use of words. "Improper" here means neither "vague" nor "meaningless" nor "arbitrary". Rather, it means to use words not in the strict and full sense that "properly" belongs to them. Impropriety in usage of a word can be recognized by one unmistakable sign: a word used in its improper sense can be exchanged for another without altering the meaning of the sentence. Thus, for example, in such cases the word "believe" can be replaced by

[13] Some writers have absurdly attempted to base a whole theory of the basic relationship between belief and knowledge on this improper meaning of the word "belief". For example S. Thompson ("A Paradox concerning the Relation of Inquiry and Belief", *Journal of Religion*, annual volume [Chicago, 1951]) has advanced the thesis that research assumes "belief" in the possibility of the fact being investigated. An archaeologist, he says, would not undertake to search for a lost city if he did not "believe" the possibility that it once actually existed in the given region. That is of course undeniable, but it is also utterly uninteresting since it has nothing whatsoever to do with the problem of "belief and knowledge".

"think", "assume", "consider probable", "suppose".[13] Contrariwise, we know a word is being used in its "proper" sense when any such substitution is impossible. We therefore must ask: In what context can the word "believe" not be replaced by any other?

Let us assume that I receive a visit from a stranger who says that he has just returned home from many years as a prisoner of war and tells me that he has seen my brother in prison camp; that this brother, missing for so long and believed dead, will probably soon be repatriated. Let us say that much of what he tells me fits into my own picture of my brother; thus there is the confirmation of internal probability. But I have no way at all of checking upon the decisive factor—whether my brother is still alive and what his state is. To a certain extent I can check on the credibility of the witness, and naturally I would do everything in my power to find out as much as possible about him. But sooner or later I shall inevitably be confronted with the decision: Am I to believe or not to believe the man's story; am I to believe *him* or not? In these interrogative sentences, it is quite clear that the word "believe" cannot be replaced by any other word. And that tells us that here "believe" is being used in its full, strict, proper sense.

Two things come to light immediately as corollaries of this argument. The believer, in the proper sense of the word, has—*first*—to do not only with a given matter, like the knower, but also with a given person: with the witness who affirms the matter and on whom the believer relies. *Secondly* (and this is the question we have been examining), belief in the proper sense really means *unqualified* assent and *unconditional* acceptance of the truth of something. Suppose that as the result of my pondering the matter I should say to the returned prisoner, now sitting at my table as my guest, that his account has greatly impressed me and that I am inclined to think it accurate, but since I do not have any means of checking. . . . If I were to say anything of the kind, I should have to be prepared for him to break in and say bluntly: "In other words, you don't believe me!" In order to soften the affront I might reply: "Oh, yes, I have full confidence in you, and I'm quite prepared to believe you, but of course I cannot be completely certain." If my visitor should insist that I do *not* really believe him—he would be entirely right. To say, "I believe you but I am not quite certain", is either to use the word "believe" in the improper sense or to be talking nonsense.

When the word "belief" is used in its proper sense, when no substitute for it is possible, then it signifies (in everyone's opinion, be it noted) an unrestricted, unreserved, unconditional assent. In respect to knowledge of the subject, the eyewitness and the knower are superior to the believer, but not in respect to undeterred firmness of assent.[14] "It is part of the concept of belief itself that man is certain of that in which he believes."[15] John Henry Newman, who, as is well known, was deeply interested all through his life in the structure of the act of belief, expressed the same thought in an almost challenging manner: "A person who says, 'I believe just at this moment . . . but I cannot answer for myself that I shall believe tomorrow,' does not believe."[16]

The question then arises all the more pointedly: How is it meaningfully possible for someone to say unconditionally: "It is thus and not different"? How can this be justified when the believer admittedly does not know the subject to which he thus assents—does not know it either directly, by his own perceptions, or indirectly, on the basis of conclusive arguments?

---

[14] "Perfectio intellectus et scientiae excedit cognitionem fidei quantum ad maiorem manifestationem non tamen quantum ad certiorem inhaesionem" (II, II, 4, 8 ad 3).

[15] "De ratione fidei est, quod homo sit certus de his, quorum habet fidem" (II, II, 112, 5 ad 2).

[16] John Henry Newman, "Faith and Doubt", in *Discourses to Mixed Congregations* (London, 1881), 216.

II

To believe always means: to believe someone and to believe something. "Ad fidem pertinet aliquid et alicui credere."[1] The believer—in the strict sense of the word—accepts a given matter as real and true on the testimony of someone else. That is, in essence, the concept of belief.

Strangely enough, in theological disputation the two elements of belief that we here present as linked—assent to the truth of a subject and assent to a person—have repeatedly been isolated and played off against one another, as though they were by nature incompatible. Martin Buber, for example, states that there are "two modes of belief",[2] the "Greco"-Christian mode and the Jewish mode. The first, he says, depends exclusively upon holding propositions to be true, whereas the second affirms a relationship of trust to God as a Person. It is not for me to define the nature of belief as it is conceived in religious Judaism. But the Christian concept of belief, at any rate, explicitly embraces both the material and the personal element. "Everyone who believes assents to the testimony of someone."[3] "Belief is always addressed to a person."[4] The first of these two sentences is by Thomas Aquinas; the second by Martin Luther—evidence

[1] II, II, 129, 6.

[2] Martin Buber, *Zwei Glaubensweisen* (Zurich, 1950).

[3] II, II, 11, 1.

[4] Cf. P. Dietz, *Wörterbuch zu Dr. Martin Luthers deutschen Schriften* (Leipzig, 1870), 2:128.

that on this score no difference of opinion existed between the Reformer and the last great teacher of a still undivided Western Christendom.

These twin elements, to believe *something* and to believe *someone*, are not to be taken as a structureless parallel, a mere coordinate existence of the two elements side by side. It may very well happen that one person can accept as true something another says without necessarily believing the other. For to believe means: to regard something as true and real on the testimony of someone else. Therefore, the reason for believing "something" is that one believes "someone". Where this is not the case, something other than proper belief is involved. A judge listening to the interrogation of members of a gang charged with some crime may very well be convinced that certain items in their statements are true; but the reason he thinks them true is not that he trusts the witnesses, that he assents to the witnesses as persons. His belief may be due to other causes—such as, let us say, a congruity between various independent statements. We might speak here of an assumption of probability, or perhaps even of a kind of knowledge. Such knowledge has been called *scientia testimonialis*, knowledge on the basis of the testimony of witnesses. But the phrase "on the basis of" may give rise to confusion. Strictly speaking, it is not the statement itself but the congruence of various testimonies that provides the basis for certainty. Thus this certainty has nothing to do with belief.

It presumably happens fairly often that something that in reality is not belief is nevertheless regarded as belief—possibly even by the "believers" themselves. Thus someone may accept the doctrines of Christianity as truth, *not* because they are witnessed and warranted by the revealing Logos of God, but because he is impressed by their "coherence", because the boldness and depth of the conception fascinate him, because those doctrines fit in with his own speculations on the mystery of the universe. This man would then regard the content of Christian religious doctrines as true, but "alio modo quam per fidem": in a different way from that of belief.[5] He might without any qualms consider himself a "believing Christian"; and others might likewise so regard him. Possibly the error would come to light only in a crisis; then it would become apparent that what was "collapsing" might have been various things: a kind of "philosophy of life", or "ideological" wishful thinking, or respect for tradition—but not at all belief in the strict sense.

If now we were to ask one who truly believes: "What do you really believe?" he would not need to name individual items of his creed; but if he wished to be perfectly precise, he would have to point to his authority and reply: "I believe what that person has said." In replying thus he would have named the essential common feature of all the individual items of his creed. He would be stating the reason for his accepting them as true. For that reason is merely the fact that someone said so. "In all belief, the decisive factor (*principale*) is who it is whose statement is assented to; by comparison the subject matter assented to is in a certain sense secondary." Thus Thomas Aquinas in his "Tract on Belief".[6]

If we pursue this consistently, it follows that belief itself is not yet "purely" achieved when someone accepts as truth the statement of one whom he trusts, but only when he accepts it *for the simple reason* that the trusted person states it.[7] That, of course, is an extreme position, which seems almost to verge upon unreality. What normally happens among human be-

[5] II, II, 5, 3; cf. II, II, 5, 3 ad 1.

[6] II, II, 11, 1.

[7] B. H. Merkelbach says in his *Summa Theologiae Moralis*, 2d ed. (Paris, 1935), 1:534: "Propriissime credimus ea quae nobis non sunt evidentia, sed quae non dubitando admittimus *unice propter testimonium* seu auctoritatem alterius . . . etiam si non appareat testimonium esse verum."

ings is that one person trusts and believes another but that he does not accept the other's statements *exclusively* on his word; rather, an element in his acceptance is their inner probability, their concordance with what he already knows, and so on. Nevertheless, at this juncture I wish to carry precise definition of the formal concept of belief to the extreme. For only at that extreme does another and hitherto hidden element come to light. For if that extreme case does occur (that someone should accept something unreservedly as true without any other supporting evidence, for the sole reason that someone else says so), then this wholehearted believer must logically accept as true *everything else* that his authority has said or will ever say in the future. We need only consider this proposition for a moment and it becomes clear beyond the possibility of doubt that in human relationships belief of this sort cannot exist. Belief of such an extreme sort, such as is involved in the expression "believe *in* someone", can neither be practiced by mature human beings nor be asked of them. (The immature child believes what his mother says for the sole reason that she says it. But the very fact that the child has no other reason for regarding things as true is, precisely, the measure of his immaturity.)

Here living language offers corroboration that has a certain topical significance. Let us assume that someone says, in all seriousness, that he believes "in" another person, and let us assume also that by this phraseology he means all that the words really signify (namely, that he is ready to accept as true and valid whatever this other person says and will say, even if such acceptance involves radical changes in his own life). It seems to me that if we make that assumption, the language itself—perhaps somewhat indistinctly, but nevertheless audibly enough—will impress upon us the fact that certain limits have been overstepped. The volume of the Grimms' *German Dictionary* containing the article on *Glaube* (belief) was first published in 1936. It oversteps the limits in the following definition:[8] "In the eighteenth century 'belief' was transferred from the sphere of the supernatural and religious with a special meaning to the area of the natural and this-worldly, and in the later usage usually signifies a strong emotional relationship to secular values, ideals, personalities, and so forth, which appear to be akin, in inner force and ethical content, to religious 'belief'." As evidence for this statement, the following linguistic examples are listed: "belief in oneself", "belief in humanity", "belief in Germany", "belief in the Führer". It seems to me that the sinister slogan that caps this series has here been placed in a manner as accurate as it is memorable within its "genealogical" context.

To repeat: wherever, in the relationships of men to men, "belief" in the strict sense is demanded or practiced, something essentially inhuman is taking place, something that is contrary to the nature of the human mind, something that is equally incompatible with its limitations and its dignity. The ancients expressed the same idea in their more temperate manner: "The cognition of one man is not by nature so correlated with the cognition of another man that the former may be governed by the latter."[9] That is to say: no mature man is by nature so spiritually inferior or superior to another that the one can serve the other as an absolutely valid authority.

It is fairly clear that this idea has a further drift. It tends to delimit the conditions in which belief in the full and strict sense can be meaningfully possible. One essential condition is this: that Someone exists who stands incomparably higher above the mature man than the latter stands above the immature man and that this Someone has spoken in a manner audible to the mature man.

[8] Vol. 4, 1, 4, col. 7816.
[9] 3, d. 24, 3, 2 ad 1.

Only on this assumption is it proper for a man simply to believe. Only then is it permissible; only then can belief be demanded of him. To be sure, if that is so, then belief is both demanded and necessary. If that condition is met, then belief is above all "natural" to man: that is to say, it is consonant with both his limitations and his dignity.

III

M AN CAN BE COMPELLED to do a good many things.
There are a good many other things he can do in a
halfhearted fashion, as it were, against his will. But belief can
never be halfhearted. One can believe only if one wishes to.
Perhaps the credibility of a given person will be revealed to
me so persuasively that I cannot help but think: It is wrong
not to believe him; I "must" believe him. But this last step
can be taken only in complete freedom, and that means that
it can also not be taken. There may be plenty of compelling
arguments for a man's credibility; but no argument can force
us to believe him.[1]

The unanimity of statements on this point is astonishing;
and the agreement ranges all the way from Augustine and
Thomas to Kierkegaard, Newman and André Gide. Augustine's phrase from the *Commentary on John* is famous: "Nemo
credit nisi volens": No one believes except of his own free
will.[2] Kierkegaard says that one man can do much for another, "but give him belief, he cannot".[3] Newman is forever
stressing, in one guise or another, the one idea that belief is
something other than the result of a logical process; it is precisely *not* "a conclusion from premises". "For directly you

---

[1] Christian Pesch, *Praelectiones Dogmaticae* (Freiburg, 1908–1916), 8:127f.

[2] The text runs: "Intrare quisquam ecclesiam potest nolens, accedere ad
altare potest nolens, accipere Sacramentum potest nolens: credere non potest
nisi volens." *In Johannis evangelium tract.* 26, 3. PL 35:1607.

[3] *Über den Glauben. Religiöse Reden*, trans. Theodor Haecker (Leipzig, 1936),
49.

have a conviction that you ought to believe, reason has done its part, and what is wanted for faith is, not proof, but *will*."[4] And André Gide? In the last jottings he published after his *Journals* we may read these sentences: "There is more light in Christ's words than in any other human word. This is not enough, it seems, to be a Christian: in addition, one must *believe*. Well, I do not believe."[5] Taken all together, these statements obviously mean the following: It is one thing to regard what someone else has said as interesting, clever, important, magnificent, the product of genius or absolutely "true". We may feel compelled to think and say any and all these things in utter sincerity. But it is quite a different matter to accept precisely the same statements in the way of *belief*. In order for this other matter, belief, to come about, a further step is necessary. A free assent of will must be performed. Belief rests upon volition.[6]

Indeed, this cannot be otherwise. When the knower says, "It is so and not otherwise", he may speak thus because the subject matter has been shown to him personally; the truth compels him to admit it. "Truth", after all, means nothing but the showing of what is. Precisely this self-demonstration of what is does *not* happen to the believer. It is not the truth, then, that compels him to accept the subject matter. Rather, he is motivated by the insight that it is good to regard the subject matter as true and real on the strength of someone else's testimony. But it is the will, not cognition, that acknowledges the good.[7] Thus, wherever belief in the strict

---

[4] Letter to Mrs. Froude dated June 27, 1848. See Wilfrid Ward, *The Life of John Henry Cardinal Newman* (New York, 1912), 1:242.

[5] André Gide, *So Be It, or The Chips Are Down* (New York: Alfred A. Knopf, 1959), 146.

[6] "[Fides] quae in voluntate est . . ." (Augustine, *De praedestinatione Sanctorum*, cap. 5, 10; PL 44:968). Cf. also II, II, 6, 1 ad 3.

[7] "Scientia et intellectus habent certitudinem per id quod ad *cognitionem* pertinent. . . . Fides autem habet certitudinem ab eo quod est extra genus cog-

sense is involved, the will is operative in a special fashion, the will of the believer himself. The will even takes precedence in the cognition of faith; it is the most vital element.[8] We believe, not because we see, perceive, deduce something true, but because we desire something good.

It is scarcely possible to make such a statement without at once being troubled by the thousand misunderstandings to which it gives rise—which, in fact, it encourages and provokes. I shall therefore plunge right in and discuss the most common of these misunderstandings.

If the believer is really led to believe "not by the reason but by the will",[9] then *what* is it that is actually willed; what does this volition aim at; what is its object? To this question the answer has been given: What is willed is the act of belief itself; the believer believes because he *wants* to believe. But this answer still throws no light upon the role played by the will as it is formulated in the Western doctrine of belief. From the psychological point of view, such a "will to believe" can of course exist. And pragmatism is by no means wrong when it asserts that believing is one of the needs of

---

nitionis, in genere *affectionis* existens" (3, d. 23, 2, 3, 1 ad 2).—"Quandoque . . . intellectus . . . determinatur . . . per voluntatem, quae eligit assentire uni parti determinate et praecise propter aliquid quod est sufficiens ad movendum voluntatem, non autem ad movendum intellectum, utpote quod videtur bonum vel conveniens huic parti assentire: et ista est dispositio credentis" (*Ver.* 14, 1).—"Alio modo intellectus assentit alicui, non quia sufficienter moveatur ab obiecto proprio, sed per quandam electionem voluntarie declinans in unam partem magis quam in aliam; et si quidem hoc sit . . . cum certitudine . . . erit fides" (II, II, I, 4).—"Bonum, quod movet affectum, se habet in actu fidei sicut primum movens" (*Ver.* 14, 2 ad 13).— "Intellectus credentis assentit rei creditae non quia ipsam videat . . . sed propter imperium voluntatis moventis intellectum" (II, II, 5, 2).— "Credere . . . non habet assensum nisi ex imperio voluntatis" (*Ver.* 14, 3).

[8] "In cognitione . . . fidei principalitatem habet voluntas" (*C. G.* 3, 40).

[9] "Intellectus credentis determinatur ad unum non per rationem, sed per voluntatem" (II, II, 2, 1 ad 3).

human nature. But it is nonsense to think that belief can be justified by the fact that it satisfies this need.[10] On the contrary, to take this view is to renounce the possibility of such justification; it is acceding entirely to the charge that belief is a wholly irrational matter, a form of intellectual untidiness that cannot pass muster or meet the test of the mind's obligation to face the truth.

We must also give short shrift to the notion that the will's precedence in the act of belief means that the believer is arranging his beliefs to conform with his deeper wishes. Thus, does one say, "I believe in eternal life", because one wishes for an eternal life? The doctrine of the precedence of the will cannot possibly mean that; we need waste no further words on such a conception. Nevertheless, there remains that old statement that the believer's mind is directed toward that which he hopes for and loves.[11] In the act of belief, therefore, the will may very well be engaged with the subject of belief. Before the human act of belief is possible, we must presuppose that the believer experiences the subject to be believed as something that really concerns him, as an object of hope, longing and love, and in that sense as a goal of volition. Nevertheless, it is not this kind of volition that is intended when it is said that the assent of belief is motivated by the will.

The question, therefore, still remains open: What is the aim of that volition which marks belief—if that volition is bound up with neither the act nor the content of belief? The answer is: The will of the believer is directed toward the person of the witness, toward the warrantor.

At this point, it is true, we find ourselves obliged to make a slight correction in our ordinary, narrowly activistic conception of volition. To will does not only mean "to decide . . .

---

[10] Cf. William James, *The Will to Believe* (New York, 1927), 59 and 91.

[11] "Per fidem apprehendit intellectus quae sperat et amat" (I, II, 62, 4).

for actions . . . on the basis of motives."[12] Volition is not merely the will to *act*; it is not directed solely toward something that is to be "brought about" and that consequently is not yet real. Rather, so say the ancients, volition has also the property of "wanting", affirming, loving, what already exists. Love is participation in and consummation of the beloved's being, as it is. It is, incidentally, not quite precise to say that in the traditional conception of volition love is one attribute among others; rather, love is conceived as the primal act of the will, as the fundamental principle of all volition and the immanent source of every manifestation of the will.[13]

Once more, then: Toward what does the believer direct his will when he believes? Answer: Toward the warrantor and witness whom he affirms, loves, "wills"—insofar as he accepts the truthfulness of what that witness says, accepts it on his mere word. This wholly free, entirely uncoercible act of affirmation, which is enforced neither by the power of self-evident truth nor by the weight of argumentation; this confiding, acknowledging, communion-seeking submission of the believer to the witness whom he believes—this, precisely, is the "element of volition" in belief itself.

The great German theologian Matthias Joseph Scheeben[14] has expressed this association in a long sentence that may strike one as somewhat schoolmasterly and old-fashioned but that is nevertheless a vital and extremely precise description:

> Assent of the intellect to the witnessed truth takes place only to the extent that the will . . . seeks and wishes to bring about consent or agreement with the judgment of the

[12] Johannes Hoffmeister, *Wörterbuch der philosophischen Begriffe*, 2d ed. (Hamburg, 1955), 670.

[13] "Amor est principium omnium voluntariarum affectionum" (*Car*. 2; cf. I, 20, 1).

[14] M. J. Scheeben, *Handbuch der Dogmatik*, ed. M. Grabmann, 2d ed. (Freiburg, 1948), 1:291, no. 633.

speaker, participation in and communion with his insight or, in other words, a spiritual union with him; the will seeks this union as a good and thus motivates the intellect to accept the insight of the witness as if it were its own—"so that the believer[15] stands in exactly the same relationship to that which the other knows, and which he does not know, as it does to that which he knows himself."

That is to say, the "good" toward which the will of the believer is directed is communion with the eyewitness or knower who says "it is so"; this communion comes to life and reality in that the believer, repeating this "it is so", accepts what the other says as truth—and accepts it *because* he says it. This idea has been summed up most cogently by John Henry Newman in his Oxford University addresses: "We believe because we love."[16]

Communion, spiritual union, love—these are, to be sure, grand words. And one might well ask with some misgiving whether they are not too grand, when, after all, what is involved is something so commonplace as men's trusting one another in ordinary human intercourse. Nevertheless, it becomes apparent that even so grand a word as "love" is not malapropos in talking of man's relationship to his fellowmen. Perhaps this becomes completely clear to us only when we consider the subject against the dark background of a contrasting reality. This does not call for any difficult intellectual operation; contrasting reality is by no means foreign to our experience. I refer of course to the life of our fellowmen under the conditions of tyranny. As we all know, under such conditions no one dares to trust anyone else. Candid com-

---

[15] At this point a quotation from Thomas Aquinas begins: ". . . ut stet illis quae alius scit et sunt sibi ignota, sicut his quae ipse cognoscit" (*In Trin.* 3, 1).

[16] J. H. Newman, "Love the Safeguard of Faith against Superstition", in *Oxford University Sermons* (London, 1880), 236.

munication dries up; and there arises that special kind of un-
healthy wordlessness which is not silence so much as muteness. This is what happens to human intercourse under the
peculiar pressures of dictatorship. Under conditions of freedom, however, human beings speak uninhibitedly to one another. How illuminating this contrast is! For in the face of it,
we suddenly become aware of the degree of human closeness, mutual affirmation, communion, that resides in the
simple fact that people listen to each other and are disposed
from the start to trust and "believe" each other. We do not
wish to rhapsodize about this, and grand words should always
be used with caution. Still, we do well to recognize that everyone who speaks to another without falseness, even if what
he says is not at all "confidential", is actually extending a
hand and offering communion; and he who listens to him in
good faith is accepting the offer and taking that hand. This
very advertence of the will, which, admittedly, we cannot
quite call "love", though it partakes somewhat of love's nature—this sense of mutual trust and free interchange of
thoughts produces a unique type of community. In such a
community he who is hearing participates in the knowledge
of the knower.

It is an axiom of theology that belief puts man into contact with the knowledge of God himself.[17] Something of the
same sort is vouchsafed everyone who believes a credible
witness: he is placed in a condition of seeing something that
would never be attainable by his own unaided sight, of seeing
with the eyes of him who sees directly. This miracle, however, is the fruit of that loving advertence. Not only is belief
based upon the turning of the will toward the witness; it is
that very turning of the will which makes belief.

---

[17] ". . . Fides, quae hominem divinae cognitioni conjungit per assensum"
(*Ver.* 14, 8).

IV

To BELIEVE MEANS: to participate in the knowledge of a knower. If, therefore, there is no one who sees and knows, then, properly speaking, there can be no one who believes. A fact everyone knows because it is obvious can no more be the subject of belief than a fact no one knows—and whose existence, therefore, no one can vouch for.[1] Belief cannot establish its own legitimacy; it can only derive legitimacy from someone who knows the subject matter of his own accord. By virtue of contact with this someone, belief is transmitted to the believer.[2]

There are several statements implicit in this proposition. To begin with: Belief is by its nature something *secondary*. Wherever belief is meaningfully held, there is someone else who supports the believer; and this someone else cannot be a believer. Before belief, therefore, come seeing and knowing. These take precedence over belief. Any serious examination of human modes of thinking and speaking will bear this out. The same obtains for the concept of belief in Occidental theology. Neither the theological nor the epistemological approach will permit us to elevate belief into something supreme and sublime that cannot be surpassed. Thus, Newman states rather sternly: "Faith, then, must necessarily be resolv-

[1] "Utroque . . . modo tollitur fides: tam scil. per hoc quod aliquid est totaliter manifestum quam etiam per hoc quod a nullo cognoscitur, a quo possit testimonium audiri" (III, 36, 2 ad 1).

[2] "Oportet cognitionem eorum, de quibus est fides, ab eo derivari, qui ea ipse videt" (*C. G.* 3, 154; cf. I, 12, 13 ad 3).

able at last into Sight and Reason; unless, indeed, we agree with enthusiasts."[3]

Therefore, when we rank belief as secondary to seeing and knowing, we are not going counter to the traditional doctrine of belief. Rather, we are completely in accord with that doctrine. "Visio est certior auditu", says Thomas;[4] seeing is surer than hearing. That is to say, in seeing for ourselves we are achieving more contact with reality and are in greater possession of reality than when we espouse knowledge based upon hearing.

This statement, to be sure, promptly calls for an important addition or, we might also say, a correction. The aphorism quoted from the *Summa theologica* was quoted only partially. The entire statement is as follows: "Ceteris paribus visio est certior auditu"; that is, *under otherwise similar conditions*, seeing is surer than hearing. That is to say: if both possibilities are equally available to us, if we have the choice, then we choose knowledge based on seeing and not knowledge based on hearing.

But perhaps man's situation is that he cannot choose, or, at any rate, not always. What is he to do when decision lies between *either* no access whatsoever to a given subject matter *or* knowledge on the basis of hearing; *either* incomplete knowing *or* no knowing at all? The fact remains, as we have said, that, *ceteris paribus*, seeing for oneself is surer than hearing. But what if seeing for oneself is impossible? Should we then, instead of accepting a less than complete access to reality as the best we can hope for, rather forgo all access, following the heroic maxim: "All or nothing"? That precisely is the question each man confronts when he has to decide between belief and nonbelief.

[3] J. H. Newman, "Faith and Reason", in *Oxford University Sermons* (London, 1880), 236.
[4] II, II, 4, 8 ad 2.

Let us take the case of a naturalist who around the year 1700 has set himself the task of describing the pollen grains of the flowers he knows. No doubt he would be able, with the naked eye and the aid of simple magnifying glasses, to find out a good deal by "seeing for himself". But suppose he is visited by a colleague who has seen such pollen at Delft under one of the first microscopes made by Antonie van Leeuwenhoek. Suppose this visitor tells him that the black dust that adheres to one's hand when one brushes a poppy is in fact a mass of geometric structures of extremely regular shapes that can be clearly differentiated from the pollen granules of all other flowering plants, and so on. Let us assume further that our naturalist has had no opportunity to look through a microscope himself and has never observed these things that his visitor reports. Granted these assumptions, would not our naturalist be grasping more truth, which means more reality, if he did *not* insist on regarding as true and real only what he has seen with his own eyes, if, on the contrary, he could bring himself to "believe" his visitor? In such a situation, what about the ranking of knowledge based upon seeing for oneself and knowledge based upon hearing? Does not hearing and believing take precedence?

Here is the point for us to present in its entirety the sentence of Thomas that we have hitherto abbreviated: "Under otherwise similar conditions, seeing is surer than hearing; but if the one from whom we learn something by hearing is capable of grasping far more than one could obtain by seeing for oneself, then hearing is surer than seeing."[5] Naturally, this sentence was originally formulated in regard to belief in the theological sense. But it is equally true of all kinds of belief; belief has the extraordinary property of endowing the be-

---

[5] "Ceteris paribus visio est certior auditu; sed si ille, a quo auditur, multum excedit visum videntis, sic certior est auditus quam visus" (II, II, 4, 8 ad 2).

liever with knowledge that would not be available to him by the exercise of his own powers.

A dictum from Hesiod's *Works and Days*[6] makes the very same point. As Hesiod puts it, being wise with the head of someone else is undoubtedly a smaller thing than possessing knowledge oneself, but it is far to be preferred to the sterile arrogance of one who does not achieve the independence of the knower and simultaneously despises the dependence of the believer.

Before we, as believers, accept the testimony of another, we must be sure that he has authentic knowledge of those things that we accept on faith. If he himself is, in his turn, only a believer, then we are misplacing our reliance. It becomes clear, therefore, that this reliance itself, which is the decisive factor in the act of belief, must be founded upon some knowledge on the part of the believer if it is to be valid. This is still another aspect of the proposition that belief rests upon knowledge.

To be sure, trusting reliance is by nature a free act. No argumentation, no matter how "compelling", can actually bring us to "believe" in someone else. Nevertheless, this act does not take place in a vacuum and without reason—without, for example, some conviction of the credibility of the witness on whom we rely. But this conviction in turn cannot possibly be belief; the credibility of the witness whom we believe cannot also be the subject of belief; this is where real knowledge is required. The matter is, to be sure, somewhat complicated.

Let us return to our example of the returned prisoner of

---

[6] *Works and Days*, 293ff. The passage is quoted by Aristotle (*Nicomachean Ethics*, 1, 2; 1095b) and also by J. H. Newman (*An Essay in Aid of a Grammar of Assent*, 342). Unfortunately, the vigor and vividness of Newman's version does not correspond with the original wording.

war. We can single out fairly clearly the element that requires belief. It is the information that my brother is alive. Let us say I have assured myself of the reliability and credibility of the witness by checking up, by sharp observation and direct experience. On the other hand, the credibility of the man might be underwritten for me by someone else, by one of my friends, say, who I discover knows my informant very well. In such a situation it would once again be an act of belief that assured me of my visitor's credibility. Nevertheless, it is clear that the conviction "My brother is alive", not only has a different content and has come about in a different way from the conviction "My informant is trustworthy", but also that these two acts of belief are based upon two altogether different testimonies from two different witnesses. In short, we see that the premises of belief cannot be the object of that same belief.

The real implications of this thesis dramatically come to light in the theological realm. We might imagine the following dialogue: "On the basis of what, really, are you convinced that there is an eternal life?"—"On the basis of divine revelation; he who is the absolute Knower and the absolute Truth has said so, and I *believe* him."—"On the basis of what are you so sure that anything like God exists and that he is absolutely knowing and truthful?" We obviously cannot simply respond: "I believe it." To put the matter more cautiously, there must at least be a possibility of responding: "I know it."

But the following question might also be asked in that dialogue: "On the basis of what are you certain that God has spoken at all and that he has actually said there is eternal life?"

Here, again, we could not legitimately respond with a simple profession of belief.

If man is prohibited from obtaining by his natural powers some kind of knowledge that God exists, that he is Truth itself, that he actually has spoken to us and that this divine speech has said and meant thus and so—then belief in revelation is likewise not possible as a meaningful human act (by a *human* act theology also understands the act of "supernatural", "infused" faith, for we ourselves are the ones who do the believing!). To put this as sharply as possible: If *everything* is said to be belief, then belief has been eliminated.

This very thing underlies the old idea of the *praeambula fidei*; the premises of belief are not a part of what the believer believes.[7] They pertain rather to that which he knows, or at least must be able to know. It is another matter that in the ordinary course of events, only a few really know what is in itself knowable. In any case this does not detract from the validity of the proposition: "Cognitio fidei praesupponit cognitionem naturalem."[8] Belief does not presuppose knowledge based upon belief in its turn dependent upon someone else, but rather knowledge out of one's own resources.

Nowhere, to be sure, will we find it written that this *cognitio naturalis* must always or primarily be derived by means of rational deduction. "Credibility", for example, is a quality of persons and can only be known in the same manner as we apprehend the other personal qualities of a person. In this realm, of course, syllogistic argumentation plays only the most minor part. When we direct our gaze upon a human being, we engage in a rapid, penetrating and direct cognition of a unique kind. Certainly we bring nothing of the sort to our examination of facts of nature, however earnest and searching this may be. On the other hand, such "intuitive"

---

[7] "Deum esse et alia hujusmodi, quae per rationem naturalem nota possunt esse de Deo . . . non sunt articuli fidei, sed praeambula ad articulos" (I, 2, 2 ad 1; cf. 3, d. 23, 2, 5 ad 5).

[8] *Ver.* 14, 9 ad 8; I, 2, 2 ad 1.

knowledge may be neither verifiable nor provable. Socrates declared that he could recognize a lover at once. *By what signs* do we recognize things of that sort? No one, not even Socrates, has ever been able to answer this question in a way that can be checked and demonstrated. Yet Socrates would stoutly insist that this knowledge was no mere impression but objective, true knowledge, that is to say, knowledge that had risen out of contact with reality.

Of course, we do not intend in the least to deny the necessity and the importance of rationally demonstrative argumentation (for the existence of God, say, or for the historical authenticity of the Bible), especially in the realm of religious truth. But it is equally evident to me that we might say: Whoever undertakes to defend belief against the arguments of rationalism should prepare himself by considering the question: "How do we apprehend a person?"[9]

[9] Jean Mouroux, *Ich glaube an Dich. Von der personalen Struktur des Glaubens* (Einsiedeln, 1951), 36.

V

N O ONE WHO BELIEVES *must* believe; belief is by its nature a free act. However convinced we are of the credibility of a witness, it is not enough to compel us to believe; and however incontrovertible the content of a truth may appear to the knower, it is *not* so to the believer. The believer, therefore, in that he believes, is always free. Because this is so, moreover, belief is a particularly opaque phenomenon. Not only religious belief in revelation but also the credence men pay to one another is by nature adjacent to and akin to mystery, because it springs from freedom.

The believer, therefore, has an alternative choice: he might choose to nonbelieve. But since his "certainty" presupposes that he has already settled on a single possibility, it is plain that the *certainty of the believer* must possess a special quality.

There are quite a few definitions of "certainty". The whole lot of them, it seems to me, may be reduced to two basic modes. The first conceives of certainty as a "firm assent, that is, assent excluding all doubt and regarded as ultimate".[1] It is immediately apparent that part of the nature of belief, not only of religious faith, is to be entirely certain in that sense. The concept itself excludes the possibility that belief and uncertainty can coexist side by side.

The second, equally common definition holds that certainty is a "firm assent founded on the evidentness of the

[1] Walter Brugger, *Philosophisches Wörterbuch* (Freiburg, 1947), 132.

matter".[2] Here the "evidentness" of the matter means nothing more nor less than its obviousness, which for the person involved springs from a clear cognition of this same matter. According to this definition, no believer, of course, can possess certainty—for belief means: to accept as true and real a matter that is *not* in itself obvious.

This curious coexistence of certainty and uncertainty, which not only describes but actually constitutes the psychological situation of the believer, must be considered more closely. Thomas Aquinas has coined a terse formulation for the duality of the matter:[3] in belief, he says, there is "aliquid perfectionis et aliquid imperfectionis", an element of perfection and an element of imperfection. The perfection inheres in the firmness of the assent, the imperfection in the fact that no vision operates—with the result that the believer is troubled by a lingering "mental unrest".[4]

The Latin word that we here translate as "mental unrest" is *cogitatio*. It is worthwhile to consider for a moment the meaning of this word, which we may think we are quite familiar with. So central is this term to the whole issue that tradition has included it in the briefest formula for the concept of "belief" we have; to wit: "cum assensione cogitare".[5] If we wished to translate this into English as: to "think" with assent, the phrase would be not only far too vague and colorless but would obviously fail to embrace the meaning of this precise formulation. Thomas himself explicitly intends it

[2] Ibid.

[3] "Fides habet aliquid perfectionis et aliquid imperfectionis: perfectionis quidem est ipsa firmitas, quae pertinet ad assensum; sed imperfectionis est carentia visionis, ex qua remanet adhuc motus cogitationis in mente credentis" (*Ver.* 14, 1 ad 5).

[4] "Motus cogitationis in ipso remanet inquietus" (*Ver.* 14, 1 ad 5).

[5] This formulation is first found in St. Augustine (*De praedestinatione Sanctorum*, cap. 2, 5). Thomas explicitly builds his analysis of the act of belief upon it; cf. II, II, 2, 1.

as a definitive characterization of the structure of the act of belief.[6] It is therefore vital to see just what is meant here by *cogitare* and *cogitatio*. What is meant is searching investigation, probing consideration, conferring with oneself before deciding, being on the track of, a mental reaching out for something not yet finally found.[7] All of these processes, taken together, may be subsumed within the term "mental unrest".

It is therefore the linking of final assent with a residual *cogitatio*, that is, the association of rest and unrest, that distinctively characterizes the believer.

There is a single act that is quite free of this mental unrest. That is assent on the basis of immediate insight. If the matter is present to the sight, there can be no uncertainty; the *observer* is entirely satisfied and at rest. On the other hand, it is obvious that *doubt* and *opinion* are necessarily accompanied by "mental unrest". But what is the state of affairs with *knowledge* based on logical conclusions? The final proposition of a proof is "known". The discursive movement back and forth, the "unrest" of argumentation, has already taken place; when the conclusion is reached, all that belongs, so to speak, to the past. Nevertheless this unrest remains latent in the results of knowing; it is continuously present as a condition. In *belief*, however, both elements—the assent and the mental unrest—are *ex aequo*,[8] equally valid, coeval and equally potent. "The movement [of the mind] is not yet stilled; rather there remains in it a searching and a pondering of that which it believes—although it nevertheless assents to what is believed

---

[6] "In hoc intelligitur tota ratio hujus actus qui est credere" (II, II, 2, 1).—"Com assensione cogitare separat credentem ab omnibus aliis" (3, d. 23, 2, 2, 1).

[7] "Cogitatio proprie dicitur motus animi deliberantis, nondum perfecti per plenam visionem veritatis" (II, II, 2, 1).—"Cogitatio . . . proprie in inquisitione veritatis consistit, quae in Deo locum non habet" (I, 34, 1 ad 2).

[8] "In fide est assensus et cogitatio quasi ex aequo" (*Ver.* 14, 1).

with the utmost firmness [*firmissime*]."[9] The "although" suggests the somewhat violent character of the connection. What we have is not really a compound, rather an antithesis: unstilled, persistent thinking *in spite* of unshaken assent.

It is astonishing to see with what outspoken candor a theologian such as Thomas Aquinas describes this element of uncertainty in the act of belief. In contrast to insight and knowledge, he says, it is part of the nature of belief to leave doubts possible.[10] This possibility is based on the fact that the believer's intellect is not really satisfied; rather, the mind, insofar as it believes, is operating not on its own but on alien soil.[11]

"Doubt" and *cogitatio* are, of course, not the same thing. Doubt restricts the unconditionality of assent; but what we have here called "mental unrest" is set in motion precisely because the assent of belief is unconditional and without reservation. We must discuss this matter in more precise and concrete terms.

Before the returned prisoner of war brought me news about the brother I had thought dead, no unrest really existed; instead, my mind had come to terms with the finality of resignation. But my peace is suddenly shattered by these tidings. I am first and foremost confronted with the question of whether or not I should believe it. But this is a different kind of unrest from the sort we have just been discussing. For this unrest is *abolished* as soon as I come to my decision to

---

[9] *Ver.* 14, 1.

[10] "In credente potest insurgere motus de contrario hujus quod firmissime tenet" (*Ver.* 14, 1).—"Credenti accidit aliquis motus dubitationis ex hoc quod intellectus ejus non est terminatus secundum se in sui intelligibilis visione" (3, d. 23, 2, 2, 3 ad 2).

[11] "Quantum . . . est ex seipso, non est ei [scil. intellectui credentis] satisfactum, nec est terminatus ad unum; sed terminatur tantum ex extrinseco. Et inde est quod intellectus credentis dicitur esse captivatus, quia tenetur terminis alienis et non propriis" (*Ver.* 14, 1).

regard the news as true; such unrest is cast off at the instant that I "believe". (Incidentally, it would also be eliminated by the decision *not* to believe.) Only now, however, along with the assent of belief itself, a new sort of unrest is aroused, is indeed caused by the assent. Once I regard the news as unconditionally true, I am tormented by the need to form a picture of the reality that is both revealed and concealed by the news. And at the same time I know that I shall never succeed in doing that. Precisely this is the "mental unrest" that the conviction of the truth of what is believed in itself evokes and that is therefore an inescapable accompaniment of the act of belief. There is no alternative; the believer is bound to be restive in this sense. "The cognition of belief does not quiet the craving but rather kindles it."[12]

But once again we must recall to mind the *ex aequo* reverse of the coin: that the firmness of the believer's assent to the truth of what he believes is neither affected nor restricted in the slightest by that "mental unrest"—insofar as real belief is involved. By this firmness we mean not only that "willed" adherence to a decision once taken which is dependent purely upon volition but also the calm sense of contemplating that reality which is both concealed and revealed in the testimony of the witness. For what the act of belief truly aims at is reality and not a message or a report; "it [the act of belief] does not stop at something that is said but at something that is."[13] The believer partakes truly of this reality; he touches it, and it becomes present to him—all the more so the more he is capable, by loving identification with the witness, of seeing with the latter's eyes and from his position.

---

[12] "Cognitio . . . fidei non quietat desiderium, sed magis ipsum accendit" (*C. G.* 3, 40).

[13] "Actus . . . credentis non terminatur ad enuntiabile, sed ad rem" (II, II, 1, 2 ad 2).

Thus the great teachers have had no scruples, on occasion, about breaking down the linguistic barriers they themselves have set up and calling belief "cognition", "insight" and "knowledge",[14] or even speaking of the "*light* of belief", by which "one sees what one believes."[15]

To be sure, the certainty of the believer cannot possibly stretch farther than the insight and reliability of the witness on whom he depends. If, therefore, we read again and again in the old theory of belief that the certainty of belief transcends the certainty of knowledge and insight by an infinite amount,[16] we must consider what grounds there are for this statement. The reason for that transcendent certainty does not lie in the fact that certainty of *belief* is involved but rather that the believer has to do with a witness whose insight and truthfulness infinitely exceed all human measures. Belief is more certain than any imaginable human insight—not insofar as it is belief, but insofar as it properly rests upon *divine speech*.

---

[14] *Ver.* 14, 2 ad 15.

[15] "Lumen fidei facit videre ea quae creduntur" (II, II, 1, 4 ad 3).

[16] 3, d. 23, 2, 2, 3.

VI

THOSE WHO SPEAK without qualification of "belief" or a "believing" person are usually using the word in its exclusively *religious* sense. "Preferably", Kant states, belief amounts to "the acceptance of the principles of a religion".[1]

Yet we must not imagine that we can step from our proceeding discussion of the meaning of belief straight to the meaning of the religious concept of faith. True, this concept is not an altogether "new" and "different" one. All the elements of meaning in the word "belief", as we have so far analyzed them, continue to pertain. Belief still means: to accept something unconditionally as real and true on the testimony of someone else who understands the matter out of his own knowledge. Similarly, all we have so far said concerning the importance of the function of belief in the affairs of our fellowmen continues to hold true. Any healthy human society depends upon the ability of its members to communicate and to believe. However, to say all this is not to say that *religious* belief is either meaningful or necessary. We have not yet proved that religious belief is legitimately possible at all. For such proof some further conditions must be met, conditions that can scarcely be taken for granted. On the contrary, it almost appears as if man's tendency is, precisely, *not* to meet these conditions, insofar as the problem is left to him. To repeat: what is re-

[1] *Die Religion innerhalb der Grenzen der bloßen Vernunft*, ed. K. Vorländer, Philosophische Bibliothek (Leipzig, 1950), 182.

quired here is not simply a further step along a prepared path but a leap.

First of all, however, we must state more precisely what we mean by the concept of "religious belief". The Kantian definition ("acceptance of the principles of a religion") is indisputable but vague. Thomas comes closer to the mark when he says that faith refers to the reality of God insofar as it is inaccessible to human knowledge.[2] However, even this statement fails to do justice to the crucial factor. For we have already demonstrated that the crucial factor of belief never consists in the matters that are believed. The believer, of whatever sort, is not primarily concerned with a given matter but with a given someone. This someone, the witness, the authority, is "the principal thing",[3] since *without* his testimony the matter would not be believed at all. Herein lies the decisive difference between religious belief and every other kind of belief: the Someone on whose testimony the religious believer accepts a matter as true and real—that Someone is God himself. The telling difference, therefore, is that in a manner scarcely to be encountered anywhere else in the world[4] the content of the testimony and the person of the witness are identical. God himself reveals to men the *res divina non visa*, that is to say, his own Being and works, which are normally hidden from man; and men believe the self-revealing God. "Cui magis de Deo quam Deo credam": Whom should I sooner believe in regard to God than God?[5]

---

[2] "Objectum fidei est res divina non visa" (III, 7, 3).—"Est autem objectum fidei aliquid non visum circa divina" (II, II, 1, 6).

[3] "Quia . . . quicumque credit, alicujus dicto assentit, principale videtur esse . . . in unaquaque credulitate ille cujus dicto assentitur" (II, II, 11, 1).

[4] On this see the remarks in chap. 9, pp. 84–85.

[5] Ambrose, Second Letter to Emperor Valentinian, PL 16:1015.

It was Saint Ambrose who coined that statement and Saint Augustine who expanded upon it. In its latter form it has become a textbook maxim.[6] Three distinctions are made: *Deo credere, Deum credere, in Deum credere.* "*Deo credere* means: to believe that what God says is true . . . ; thus we also believe a man, whereas we do not believe 'in' a man. *Deum credere* means: to believe that he is God. *In Deum credere* means: believingly to love, believingly to go to him, believingly to cling to him and be joined to his members." Thomas Aquinas has written a commentary on this text[7] and lays considerable stress upon the unity of the three aspects. These are not three different acts, he says, but one and the same act,[8] in which man believes God (*Deo, Deum*) and believes in God (*in Deum*).[9] This, then, is the basic structure of the act of religious faith. With this in mind, let us look further into the matter.

We shall continue to regard the subject from the philosophical point of view, as we have done heretofore. This is a *philosophical* essay. That means, first of all, that it deals with something other than theology. By theology we mean the effort to interpret the documents of sacred tradition and the revelation embodied in that tradition. A theological theory of belief, then, would remain within the context of those documents. Its first task would be to examine those documents for what they have to say about belief. For example, there would be a discussion of belief in its relation to incarnation, grace, baptism, church or belief as a foretaste of the

---

[6] Augustine, *Enarr. in psalmos* 77, 8 (PL 36:988); *In Johannis evangelium tract.* 29, 6 (PL 35:1630); *Sermo de Symbolo,* cap. 1 (PL 40:1190). The idea was taken up by Peter Lombard in his *Sentences,* which for centuries was *the* theological textbook of the West (cf. *Liber sententiarum* III, dist. 23, cap. 4).

[7] 3, d. 23, 2, 2, 2; cf. also II, II, 2, 2.

[8] II, II, 2, 2 ad 1.

[9] 3, d. 23, 2, 2, 2 ad 1; cf. *Ver.* 14, 7 ad 7.

future vision of God to be vouchsafed us when we leave this world behind—and so on. A philosophical essay on belief, however, does not take up such subjects.

Another fruitful approach might be a *psychological* examination of belief as a psychic act to be described empirically, arising as a regular thing within a certain nexus of motivations. Then again, there is also the possibility of considering the phenomenon of belief from the viewpoint of *religious history*. The *philosophical* approach, however, is something altogether unlike any of these. It differs from the "scientific" mode of the psychologist and historian chiefly in not attacking the subject under discussion from any one, explicitly stated, special aspect but in investigating its ultimate meaning from every conceivable point of view against the horizon of total reality. The philosophical thinker considers the meaning and site of "belief" within the whole extent of human reality. He differs from the theologian as follows: The theologian's eye is fixed upon the documents of sacred tradition, which it is his office to interpret. The philosopher's eye, on the contrary, is, ideally speaking, fixed upon the reality that is empirically encountered. Since, however, in keeping with his task, he must examine every conceivable aspect of his theme, it would be unphilosophical to exclude from his range of vision any attainable information on reality, whether this information be provided by one or another of the sciences or by theology. This should suggest clearly enough what a demanding task the philosophical thinker has assumed—a task full of difficulties and controversies. It might almost be called a hopeless task, if philosophizing itself were not an act of hope.

We have already implied that religious faith is not simply a kind of continuation, elaboration or further development of "belief in general". Similarly, we can assent to everything that has so far been said about belief and nevertheless be faced with an insuperable difficulty the moment we are asked to accept *religious* belief as something meaningful or actually necessary. The difficulty is even greater when we are asked to put such belief into practice existentially.

The obstacle that must be leaped rather than climbed consists in the difficulty of understanding why man's nature and situation should be such that he cannot make do with what is naturally accessible to him. Why should man be dependent upon information that he himself could never find and that, even if found, is not susceptible to rational examination? To be sure, no believer can ever directly examine the validity of what he believes. Still, belief in religious revelation is peculiar in that the reason for this nonexaminability lies both in the nature of the message and in the nature of the recipient. This nonexaminability is fundamental to the entire concept and cannot be done away with. No man, no matter how brilliant or how saintly, can undertake to evaluate the tidings that God has become man in order to enable us to participate in the life of God. He cannot test this message against reality. That is manifestly impossible.

And yet that is only one element in the "outrageous" summons to believe in such things as the Incarnation of God. We are not only summoned to accept as real and true a set of facts that we can in no way examine; we are also referred to a witness who never meets us directly, as do our human interlocutors, but who, nevertheless, demands of us the kind of absolute and unconditional assent that we are prepared to give in no other case.

Even this simple description of what takes place in the act of belief in religious revelation brings clearly to the fore the terms to which we must subscribe and the difficulty of the whole matter. The hurdle is very high, and yet we are supposed to leap it. Nowadays, says Romano Guardini, the question at issue is not so much whether this or that tenet of faith is true; rather, it has become hard for men to grasp "how the demand to believe can with any justification be made at all".[10]

"Where knowledge suffices we have no need of belief"— that is a proposition[11] that at first sounds highly plausible. But the question is, by what marks do we recognize where knowledge suffices and where it does not? Naturally no one can say whether something suffices without simultaneously considering what it is to suffice for. If anyone should therefore ask whether what is naturally knowable should not be sufficient for man, he can answer adequately only if he has first formulated what he considers a meaningful human life to be, that is to say, a life in keeping with man's true nature and also with his real situation in the world.

Anyone, for example, who is convinced that man by nature lives within the field of force of an absolutely superhuman reality and that admonition and instruction can be imparted to him from there—or, to put it differently, anyone who acknowledges divine speech directed toward man as something possible or even likely—has by that token already said that his own natural knowledge is, *if* God has really spoken to man, not "sufficient" for a truly human life. Conviction of the possibility of revelation therefore includes not only a particular conception of God but also a particular conception of the metaphysical nature of man.

It is clear that revelation is inconceivable if God is not conceived as a personal Being capable of speech. Yet as soon

[10] R. Guardini, "Der Glaube in der Reflexion", in *Unterscheidung des Christlichen* (Mainz, 1935), 245.

[11] This is a remark of Goethe's that, however, has been quoted incompletely. The complete sentence reads: "Where knowledge suffices, we have no need of belief; but where knowledge does not prove its virtue or appears insufficient, we should not dispute the rights of belief." To J. D. Falk on January 25, 1813 (*Werke, Briefe und Gespräche* [Zurich: Artemis-Ausgabe, 1949], 22:680).

as natural man is seriously faced with this conception of God, he finds something shocking in it. As C. S. Lewis says in his *Miracles*,

> It is always shocking to meet life where we thought we were alone. "Look out!" we cry, "it's *alive*." . . . An "impersonal God"—well and good. A subjective God of beauty, truth and goodness, inside our own heads—better still. A formless life-force surging through us, a vast power which we can tap—best of all. But God Himself, alive, pulling at the other end of the cord, perhaps approaching at an infinite speed, the hunter, king, husband—that is quite another matter. . . . There comes a moment when people who have been dabbling in religion ("Man's search for God"!) suddenly draw back. Supposing we really found Him? . . . Worse still, supposing He had found us?
>
> So it is a sort of Rubicon. One goes across; or not. But if one does, there is no manner of security against miracles. One may be in for *anything*.[12]

To that I have only this to add: If God is conceived as a personal Being, as a Someone rather than a Something, and a Someone who can speak, then there is no safety from—revelation.

This, however, is not the only premise that must be absorbed if faith in religious revelation is to be at all attainable as a living human act. Man must also have understood himself as a being by nature open to the divine speech, capable of being reached by it. I do not merely mean the openness of the human mind to the obvious reality of the world, for that is a faculty of all beings that have minds. Mind, indeed, can actually be defined as "receptivity to Being". And this cognitive apprehension of reality can be considered as a

---

[12] C. S. Lewis, *Miracles* (New York: Macmillan Company, 1947), 113–14.

form of hearing divine speech, since things, by virtue of
their origin in the creative Logos of God, themselves possess
"verbal character".[13] I am referring here, however, not to
openness to this "natural" revelation of God in the created
world, but to the power to apprehend a new and direct
form of divine speech that surpasses what has already been
"said" in the natural world. This latter form alone can be
called "revelation" in the strict sense. And openness to this
also must be understood as a faculty inherent in the human
mind by nature; otherwise we cannot say that belief is
something that may rightfully be demanded of men. That
special openness, to be sure, is inherent in the human mind,
not on the basis of its spirituality, but on the basis of its
creatureliness. To be a creature means: to be continually receiving being and essence from the divine Source and Creator and, in this respect, therefore, never to be finally
completed. Unlike the works made by man, which at some
given moment are "finished", creaturely things remain
indefinitely malleable because they can never become independent of the force of the Creator who communicates being to them. They do not cease to be clay "in the potter's
hand"; they remain by nature, by virtue of their creatureliness, continually in expectation of a new intervention by
God.[14] This intervention may take place in the form of that
vital communication which theology calls "grace", or in the
form of revelation.

It is rather important to see that receptivity to a possible
revelation is itself *not* something "supernatural". Rather, it
belongs to the human mind's natural state of being. For the
same reason the soul is *by nature* capable of receiving the
"supernatural" new life of grace ("naturaliter anima est

[13] R. Guardini, *Welt und Person* (Würzburg, 1940), 110.

[14] It is this ontological presence that is meant by the technical term *potentia
oboedientialis*.

gratiae capax").[15] It is important to see that, because it then follows that belief in revelation itself is in a certain sense natural.[16] Not only can man be expected to believe; but *not* to believe would be downright contrary to human nature—*if* God has spoken to man in an audible fashion. Unbelief, insofar as that means the refusal to believe God's audible speech, is violating more than an edict "within theology"; it is violating a standard that is set by the natural existential situation of man in the world. Unbelief contradicts what man is by nature.[17]

To be sure, it is one thing to acknowledge this idea of the natural receptivity of the mind *in abstracto*, as a tenet of philosophical anthropology. It is quite something else again to put it into practice. And, of course, belief in revelation, as a living act, can come about only if a man's self-understanding goes beyond mere conceptual thinking, if it shapes and governs the inner style of life; if, in other words, the receptivity inherent in the created mind is "realized" existentially. For that

[15] I, II, 113, 10. In the *sed contra* of this article Thomas quotes the saying of Augustine: "*To be able* to have belief, as *to be able* to have charity, belongs to the nature of man; but having belief, as having charity, belongs to the grace conferred upon the believer" (*De praedestinatione Sanctorum*, cap. 5, 10; PL 44:968).

[16] There exists also an exaggerated conception of the supernaturalness of belief. It is true, of course, that under the influence of belief we become aware of things that our natural reason does not recognize. Nevertheless, the results are a far cry from the situation that would obtain were the eye suddenly enabled not only to perceive sensuously but also to know conceptually; for then the nature of the sense organ would simply be abolished. The nature of intellectual cognition is not in the least abolished when our mind "believes God as a pupil believes his teacher" (II, II, 2, 3). A sense simply cannot "learn" to think conceptually. But what the human reason "learns" by believing the Word of God does not surpass its natural powers; for it belongs to the nature of mentality to have a direct relationship, an ontological openness to the original Source of all things, *immediatum ordinem ad Deum* (II, II, 2, 3).

[17] "Infidelitas . . . est contra naturam" (II, II, 10, 1 ad 1).

to happen, the complete, boundless energy of the heart is needed, along with extreme seismographical sensitivity and alertness. For there is an infinitude of hidden, often barely discernible modes of shutting the doors of the mind and heart. Undoubtedly there exists, for example, a lack of receptivity that is accompanied by no express gestures of refusal or rejection, which is simply *inattention*. Gabriel Marcel contends that the conditions of modern life not only favor but almost compel such inattention, which makes belief in practice rather improbable.[18] Yet Pascal, too, was aware of this very problem. Witness this aphorism in the *Pensées*, which suggests how easily a man can shut himself off from the whole of truth virtually with a clear conscience: "If you do not take the trouble to know the truth, there is enough truth at hand so that you can live in peace. But if you crave it with all your heart, then it is not enough to know it."[19] It is no excessively difficult matter to content oneself with what one already knows ("where knowledge suffices . . ."); but those who truly throw their souls open to the whole of truth expect, since they nowhere see the whole, that there will always be an additional new light beyond what they already know.

Those who are thus concerned for the whole of truth may find themselves obliged to exercise a highly special mode of critical caution, which, however, may be regarded as just the opposite, that is, as the expression of an altogether uncritical mentality. Those who accept nothing as true and valid that has not withstood their own exacting investigation are generally regarded as critical observers. But what about the person who, fearing that by such a procedure he may overlook some element in the whole of truth, prefers to accept less complete certainty rather than incur a possible loss of contact

[18] Gabriel Marcel, *Être et avoir* (Paris, 1935), 311.
[19] Pascal, *Pensées*, no. 226 (according to the numeration of Léon Brunschvicg).

with reality? Can he not also claim to be thinking critically?[20] It is certainly a debatable question which of two medical procedures is the more "critical" when sheer saving of life is at stake: a procedure that accepts only absolutely tested methods, or one that considers every method that offers some reasonable promise of success, even though it may be based only on a presumption. (And surely we may say that divine speech addressed directly to men is not going to be trafficking in trivialities, that the "saving of life" is truly at stake.) At any rate, the person who is primarily concerned with missing nothing, with omitting no chance to arrive at the whole of such vital truth, can scarcely be charged with being of "uncritical mind" if he prefers "not [to] wait for the fullest evidence . . . and . . . show his caution, not in remaining, uninfluenced by the existing report of a divine message, but by obeying it though it might be more clearly attested."[21]

As might be expected, the intellect bent on critical autonomy will take such a course only with reluctance. Nevertheless, this resistance should not be quickly branded as arrogance. The matter is highly complex, and we do not clarify it much by apodictic simplifications.

The salient fact remains that man does not stand, toward the self-revealing God, in the situation of an independent partner, equal in rank, who may be "interested" or not as he pleases. If a man becomes aware of certain teachings, or of certain data that purport to be the Word of God—then he cannot possibly assume the right to remain "neutral for the present". This is a point to which John Henry Newman[22] repeatedly adverts. Men, he says, are greatly inclined to "wait

---

[20] Cf. Josef Pieper, "Über das Verlangen nach Gewißheit", in *Weistum, Dichtung, Sakrament* (Munich, 1954), 41ff.

[21] J. H. Newman, "Faith without Sight", in *Parochial and Plain Sermons* (San Francisco: Ignatius Press, 1987), 239.

[22] J. H. Newman, *An Essay in Aid of a Grammar of Assent* (London, 1892), 425f.

quietly" to see whether proofs of the actuality of revelation will drop into their laps, as though they were in the position of arbitrators and not in that of the needy. "They have decided to test the Almighty in a passionless judicial fashion, with total lack of bias, with sober minds." It is an error as common as it is fatal, says Newman, to think that "truth may be approached *without homage*".[23]

---

[23] J. H. Newman, "Faith and Reason", in *Oxford University Sermons* (London, 1880), 198.

VII

I N THE COURSE OF HIS WORK Karl Jaspers has developed a concept of belief that, in spite of ultimate divergence, seems so closely akin to the one outlined here that we must briefly discuss it. This discussion is of some importance because Jaspers appears to speak on this point as representative of a whole type of contemporary thought that is engaged in dispute with the Christian tradition.

First: Jaspers evidently makes use of the term *belief* as a precise name for what he has in mind. He defines belief as "the certainty of truth that I cannot prove in the same way as scientific knowledge of finite things may be proved."[1] He asserts that this belief links man "with the ground of Being";[2] that it is "the substance of a personal life",[3] "the fulfilling and motivating element in the depth of man",[4] "the foundation . . . of our thinking"[5] and "the indispensable source of all genuine philosophizing".[6]

Secondly: If we ask what Jaspers singles out as matters that are to be accepted as true and real on the basis of such belief, we receive such answers as the following: "the idea of one God";[7] "that the Unconditioned exists as the basis of ac-

[1] *Der philosophische Glaube*, 2d ed. (Munich, 1948), 11.
[2] *Vom Ursprung und Ziel der Geschichte* (Munich, 1949), 272.
[3] *Existenzphilosophie* (Berlin and Leipzig, 1938), 79.
[4] *Ursprung und Ziel*, 268.
[5] *Philosoph. Glaube*, 10.
[6] *Existenzphilosophie*, 80.
[7] *Philosoph. Glaube*, 82.

tion";[8] "the unclosed nature of the created universe";[9] "the ultimate and only refuge with God";[10] "man can live under guidance by way of God";[11] "the reality of the world has a dwindling actuality between God and existence."[12]

Thirdly: After having read such sentences with complete assent, though perhaps with some surprise that they are presented as *philosophical* utterances, we begin to feel uncertainty when Jaspers declares that they are by no means "to be taken as communication of any content". Indeed, he says, at that point there begins "the error in the statement of philosophical dogmas".[13] "Belief does not mean a specific content, does not mean a dogma."[14] Jaspers here seems to be concerned with preventing the object of belief from being imprisoned in any rigid didactic formula—in which effort he is undoubtedly right. The object of belief cannot be delimited and fixed precisely, its content comprehensively described, as is the case with demonstrable items of knowledge. Nevertheless, it is scarcely possible to deny that in those dogmas some content is stated and communicated!

Fourthly: The fundamental fallacy of Jaspers' conception, however, comes fully to light when we pose the question that is decisive for all belief: *Who* really is believed; who is the Someone on whose testimony propositions "that I cannot prove"[15] are nevertheless accepted as true? There is no unequivocal answer to this question in Jaspers' works. Moreover, the question itself is not even expressly discussed. And in evading the question, Jaspers' reasoning founders upon a

[8] Ibid., 31.
[9] Ibid., 82.
[10] Ibid.
[11] *Einführung in die Philosophie* (Munich, 1953), 83.
[12] Ibid.; similarly in *Philosoph. Glaube*, 29.
[13] *Einführung*, 92.
[14] *Ursprung und Ziel*, 268.
[15] *Philosoph. Glaube*, 11.

serious error. True, Jaspers speaks quite clearly of that "trust without guarantee"[16] that makes belief what it is; true, he acknowledges what is virtually the same thing, the necessity for authority: "Even the philosopher must somewhere yield precedence to authority, though where its rule begins and ends cannot be fully determined"; "philosophical belief, incomprehensible to itself, demands at one point uncomprehended authority."[17] This, however, is where we must take issue. For the possible embodiment of this authority is left completely vague. To whom is that "trust without guarantee" to be vouchsafed?[18] Moreover, contrary to everything we might expect, Jaspers abruptly states with great sharpness that the philosopher must "cling to no authority, nowhere receive truth as a dogma, nor owe his salvation to any historically handed-down revelation".[19] No such submission, he declares, can be asked of the mature mind, because it would mean "destruction of his freedom and his dignity".[20] Which is nothing less than an express negation of belief itself.

(Incidentally, Jaspers lists the reasons that have been advanced in favor of submission to authority; none of these reasons, he contends, is convincing because each of them "denies freedom".[21] He names the following reasons:

Man is too weak to be able to be thrown on his own resources; authority . . . is a blessing to him; without the firm support of authority man would succumb to a casual subjectivity; as man becomes aware of his insignificance, he puts himself under the rule of authority; the tradition of author-

[16] *Von der Wahrheit* (Munich, 1947), 789.
[17] Ibid., 866.
[18] *Philosoph. Glaube*, 88. *Philosophie* (Berlin, 1948), 259.
[19] *Wahrheit*, 965.
[20] *Philosophie*, 263.
[21] Ibid., 265.

ity has existed for thousands of years. This alone is a testimony of its truth.[22]

We might possibly take up these points one by one, in order
to see whether they hinder man's freedom. But it is plain that
none of these reasons prompts the Christian to believe and
that the sole reason that actually does prompt him does *not*
deny freedom. This sole reason is: that God has spoken.)

If we consider the single strands that Jaspers has attempted to
intertwine in his conception of "philosophical belief", we
find ourselves somewhat perplexed, even as we are impressed
by the seriousness of his confrontation with the question. His
conception is, of course, far more highly differentiated than
our résumé of it suggests; but in summary its basic tenets
have perhaps come into clearer focus. And what is revealed is
a deep split in Jaspers' position. His stern rejection of belief as
incompatible with the freedom and dignity of the mind simply cannot stand side by side with the almost beseeching gesture with which he reminds us of the necessity of belief
(lacking belief, man is utterly "at the mercy of thought,
opinion, ideas, doctrines, whence come violence, chaos and
ruin").[23] And when Jaspers explicitly accepts ideas that are
included in the *corpus* of Christian revelation ("we philoso-
phize out of the biblical religion and there apprehend irreplaceable truths"),[24] the fact nevertheless remains that he just
as explicitly refuses to accept these doctrines as "revelation",
that is to say, on the testimony of God. Again, we must repeat
the dictum of Thomas Aquinas, for it seems to apply precisely to Jaspers: "Ea quae sunt fidei alio modo tenet quam
per fidem";[25] he regards much of what is said in Christian

---

[22] Ibid.
[23] *Ursprung und Ziel*, 268.
[24] *Philosoph. Glaube*, 69.
[25] II, II, 5, 3.

doctrine as true and to be honored; but he does so in a fashion different from that of belief.

In this, however, Jaspers represents a mental type that has become prevalent over much of the territory of the old Western world, threatened as it is by secularization. That type is characterized by two principal traits: first, by reluctance to abandon the content of traditional religious faith, "irreplaceable truths"; second, by the incapacity to accept that content on the basis of belief in the revelation—though that belief alone has made these truths accessible to us and is their ultimate bulwark.

We all know that we can hardly begin to talk about the "modern spirit" without hearing the term "unbelief" crop up early in the discussion. We should be reminded, however, that the great tradition of Western theology recommends extreme caution in the use of this word. Above all, we should clarify what precisely is meant by "unbelief" (as sin). It happens very often that a person hears the tidings of the faith but is not reached by them (which may very well be caused by the internal style of those tidings). The message is simply not perceived as something that can really concern the hearer; and in that case, of course, no belief arises. But such nonbelief cannot be termed "unbelief". In another instance, the content of the tidings may be well grasped; but for a wide variety of reasons it does not occur to the hearer that they can possibly be a supernatural message, divine speech, "revelation" in the strict sense of that word: and therefore no genuine belief comes into being. But once more "unbelief" would not be the right term for this lack of belief. Nor can we call unbelievers those who refuse to become involved at all and will not give their mind to considering the credibility of the testimony. Such refusal may be indefensible; it may be wrong; but it is not identical with unbelief.[26] Unbelief in the precise sense of the term is only that mental act in which someone deliberately refuses assent to a truth that he has recognized with sufficient plainness to be God's speech.[27]

One may ask whether unbelief in this sense ever occurs. To this we must reply that in actuality the usual counterpoise to belief seems to be less sheer unbelief than that inveterate inattentiveness of which we have already spoken. There is no sense in attacking this inattentiveness as "unbelief". Certainly it is not going to be conquered by such misnaming. Little is accomplished by vague lamentations over contemporary unbelief. We must take into account the extreme complexity of the matter. One root of the complexity lies in the fact that man "can also affirm God by way of partially *false* concepts".[28] Thus, French theology has recently reformulated and justified anew the old idea that it is quite possible "to affirm God in truth while at the same time *denying* him on the plane of a given set of notions".[29]

There is another aspect of the matter that should be repeatedly recalled to mind: that the "knower" naturally finds it especially hard to believe. This is why Thomas Aquinas placed him at the side of the martyr.[30] He who has attained to a certain stage of critical consciousness cannot exempt himself from thinking through the opposing arguments raised both by "philosophers" and "heretics". He must confront them. For this reason, Thomas says, the critical thinker

---

[26] "Voluntas non inquirendi de fide non est voluntas non credendi" (B. H. Merkelbach, *Summa Theologiae Moralis*, 2d ed. [Paris, 1935], 1:571f).

[27] Ibid.

[28] Jean Mouroux, *Ich glaube an Dich* (Einsiedeln, 1951), 82.

[29] Ibid., 45. Mouroux, referring to the commentary on Thomas by Cajetan and to the great Spanish baroque theologian Juan de Lugo, says that in these works "nothing new is expressed".

[30] II, II, 2, 10 ad 3.

who is at the same time a believer is to be compared with the martyr who sheds his blood, who refuses to abandon the truth of faith in spite of the "arguments" of violence.

The truth of faith cannot be definitively proved by any rational argument. The fact constitutes the believer's predicament. Hence the old rule of thumb: "The Christian who wishes to conduct a disputation on his belief should not attempt to prove his belief but to defend it."[31] The inward predicament of the believer is also of the same nature. Ultimately, the only possible opposition the believer can offer to his *own* rational arguments is defensive; he cannot attack, he can only hold firm. And the question arises whether, for a time at any rate, this holding firm may not inevitably take the form of silent defenselessness, as in the case of the martyr.

[31] *Rat. fid.*, cap. 2.

VIII

H E WHO CONCEIVES of God as a Someone capable of
speech, and of man as a being by nature receptive to
God, necessarily regards "revelation" as possible, perhaps
even to be expected. Nevertheless, he need not necessarily
think that it actually has taken place. It is obviously one thing
to consider something possible and another to consider it a
real happening. But belief in revelation can be supported
only on the ground that God has actually spoken in a manner
audible to man. And this fact, for its part, must be naturally
knowable; man cannot in turn be asked to believe it.

It is sheer waste of time to discuss the actuality of a divine
revelation with someone who, on the basis of his conception
of God and man, denies its very possibility. And even one
who considers divine speech directly addressed to man as
something in the order of things and to be expected must
still confront the question: In what form could such a divine
communication have taken place, and how could it be distinguished, how recognized? Once again, in order for belief to
take place as a conceivable human act, we must clear an intellectual hurdle. That hurdle is, understandably, a peculiarly
difficult one for modern man. The difficulty is by no means
deliberately invented, reprehensible and "his own fault";
rather, it is bound up with the transformation that has taken
place in man's conception of the natural world and its dimensions. Our knowledge of the reality of creation, as
against ancient and medieval conceptions of the cosmos, has

been profoundly corrected and enriched. "There came a voice from heaven" [*vox facta est de caelo*] was for Dante and his contemporaries a vivid conception that they saw no need to challenge. Contemporaries of Einstein, however, cannot give the same credence to the simple statement, when even the material reality of the world has grown harder and harder to fathom. "We can no longer experience God as operating in our world with the same naïve trust as was possible in earlier times."[1] And contemporary theology, we must concede, has provided few intellectual tools with which to conquer the legitimate difficulty that has thus arisen.

Karl Rahner called "amazement at the silence of God" and "the absence of God in the world" a "genuine and powerful experience". Those who have had this experience, he says, have tended to give it an atheistic interpretation, "looking upon it as evidence of the non-existence of God", whereas it is simply "the experience that God does not fit into the world picture".[2] Christian metaphysics, he continues, has always *known* this "but . . . has *lived* it too little".[3] Moreover, "the vulgar version of Christianity has failed to deal with" the element of truth in that "troubled atheism".[4] The task before us, he contends, is to "accept" that experience and "not to repress it with the premature, cheap apologetics of an anthropomorphic 'belief in God' ".[5]

All this helps to explain the ever-increasing difficulty men have in conceiving of audible speech of God, directed straight to them—that is to say, "revelation" in the strict sense—as a concrete event taking place here and now. But this situation also holds forth a rare challenge. The time has

---

[1] Karl Rahner, *Schriften zur Theologie*, vol. 3 (Einsiedeln, 1956), 462.

[2] Ibid., 461.

[3] Ibid., 460.

[4] Ibid., 461.

[5] Ibid., 462.

come to discard ideas that are no longer viable and to reconstruct faith along lines that will be acceptable to the modern consciousness.

Thomas Aquinas has described the event of revelation in a manner that, it seems to me, might do as well for us today as it did for his contemporaries, despite the transformation in men's picture of the world. There is nothing "medieval" in his formulation; above all, it is completely untinged by the notion that God is a Being living in the "apartment next door". Revelation, he tells us in the *Summa contra Gentiles*,[6] is simply the communication of a spiritual inner light whereby human cognition is enabled to observe something that would otherwise remain in darkness.

In immediacy and clarity this image leaves nothing to be desired. Nevertheless, it conveys the fact that this process of communication is a mysterious one, whose initial phase may not be grasped by the pictorial imagination. Yet it is during that phase that the real drama of revelation takes place: the sudden, flashing illumination; the wind's stirring the still motionless surface of water, which straightway receives this "inspiration" and passes it on to infinity. The innermost core of the event we call revelation is the divine act of communication itself. That, however, remains of necessity inaccessible to all human apprehension and utterly remote from the pictorial imagination.

But "communication" is not complete when something has been said; the message must be heard and received by the person for whom it is meant. Only then has true communication come about. The light communicated by revelation is intended for "man". And "man" means *all* men. The divine

[6] "Revelatio fit quodam interiori et intelligibili lumine mentem elevante ad percipiendum ea, ad quae per lumen naturale intellectus pertingere non potest" (*C. G.* 3, 154; cf. *Ver.* 12, 1 ad 3).

light is conveyed to the "inspired" first recipient and is there-
after passed from one man to the next. This process, the dif-
fusion of the event of revelation, is less inscrutable than the
initial flash of revelation itself. It lies within the scope of our
imaginations. Moreover, we see how this pattern of emana-
tion from a single point-source corresponds to the patterns
of spiritual life as manifested throughout history.

In all other cases when mankind acquires new, hitherto
unknown truths, what happens is that an elect individual or
one endowed with genius observes a new aspect of reality or
a hitherto undiscovered portion of the real world and that his
new knowledge is then passed on to others: by communication, publication, teaching, tradition. All subsequent versions
show clear gradations of greater or lesser closeness to the
original find. Thus, only a very few persons are capable of
sharing in the understanding of Einstein's unified-field
theory out of their own knowledge; a somewhat larger circle
can grasp the more or less precise paraphrases at second hand;
while "the public" has only very vague notions of what
Einstein actually meant—which in no way implies that the
public cannot participate, in a completely legitimate fashion,
in the truth of the prime discoverer.

If, then, we encounter this same dispensation and pattern
wherever "sacred tradition" claims to preserve and present
what Plato calls "a message handed down to us from a divine
source",[7] there is no reason to be surprised. On the contrary,
that is quite what we should expect.

What we have said above about the public's participation
in the unified-field theory has its parallel in the realm of belief in revelation. This calls for some careful thought. Although, of course, greater or lesser proximity to the source
is not, in the latter realm, determined only—nor even pri-

[7] *Philebus* 16, c. 5–9.

marily—by intellectual capacity, the realm of belief, too, has its "multitude", corresponding to "the public", who "comprehend" the tradition only within limits. Nevertheless—and this is the critical factor—they can truly partake of the truth of the divine Word as it was imparted to the first inspired recipient. "Implicit faith"—the *fides implicita* of the Schools—is acknowledged and practiced everywhere. In theology, to be sure, the concept of *fides implicita* has given rise to vehement dispute; it is no very long way from it to the opprobrious epithet "blind faith".[8] The German word for this is *Köhlerglaube*—charcoal burner's faith—and goes back to the story of the charcoal burner who met a learned scholar on the bridge at Prague and was asked what he believed. "I believe what the Church believes", the charcoal burner responded. It seems to me that this much-ridiculed man gave an answer by no means nonsensical and contemptible. On the contrary, his reply was intelligent, to the point and precise and would be perfectly acceptable in all other fields. If, for example, I were asked my opinion on the structure of the cosmos or the nature of matter, I would reply with a reference to modern physics. It is true that I have only a vague knowledge of its conclusions; but, by subscribing to the opinions of men like Planck, Bohr, de Broglie and Heisenberg, I truly share in those conclusions, although the exact manner of my sharing may be rather hard to define. In precisely the same way, *fides implicita* can enable the simplest mind, the one farthest removed from the original light, as well as the only half-instructed, to "belong" and to have a share in the revealed truth—by virtue of his believing tie to one who knows at first hand—which in this case means not only to the first recipient of the divine

[8] Martin Luther, *Warnungsschrift an die zu Frankfurt am Main, sich vor Zwinglischer Lehre zu hüten* (1533). Quoted from *Deutsche Thomas-Ausgabe*, vol. 15 (Heidelberg, 1950), 440f.

speech but to its Author himself. The great teachers of Christendom, at any rate, never hesitated to postulate the unity of true believers and gave the broadest interpretation to this concept. They have asserted, for example, that whoever in the pre-Christian and extra-Christian worlds has accepted the wisdom warranted by sacred tradition, whoever has accepted the tenet that God, in a manner pleasing to him, will be a liberator of men, has believed *implicite* in Christ.[9]

We can therefore conceive of the process of revelation, the actual reaching out of divine speech to historical man, as proceeding along such lines. Yet we are still faced with the difficult question of how and by what means a given claim to be divine revelation can, so to speak, present its credentials—not so much to the first recipient, for it may be assumed that he has found himself in a situation admitting of no doubt, but to all the others who through him have been informed of the message entrusted to him. How, in a word, do we recognize that something that lays claim to being revelation is really of divine origin? If there is no way to answer this question by the methods of rational argumentation, then there can be no such thing as genuine belief, since this is defined as accepting God's word as the warranty for the truth. Belief would become an altogether arbitrary matter.

This, of course, is not the place even to attempt a detailed answer. But we can speak here of a few of the conditions that must be met if such an attempt is not to be a hopeless undertaking from the start.

To begin with, it may be assumed that any appeal to "classical" arguments (miracles, prophecies, authenticity of the biblical accounts, the "Church" as a historical phenomenon,

[9] II, II, 2, 7 ad 3; *Ver.* 14, 11 ad 5.

and so on) will lead to nothing unless we first recover the living realization of how and why "revelation" is possible at all and to be expected. In other words, we must first engage upon some meditation concerning the metaphysical situation of man as a creature.

Furthermore, we are not dealing here with the apprehension of facts of nature but with the illumination of a particular and fundamental facet of existence. Hence the investigator must be prepared to offer a receptivity and attentiveness extending to the depths of his soul, a lack of bias that goes far beyond "scientific objectivity". Such openness cannot be taken for granted, of course. In fact, it is constantly endangered by the multifarious interests of the human person anxious to preserve his independence.

It is (thirdly) virtually impossible for the question at issue to be decided by the means of cognition available to the isolated individual. This is rather a task that must be attacked in a concerted fashion. All possible techniques of intellectual cooperation must be utilized. All that men have learned about group effort to achieve knowledge must be brought into play.

Naturally a project of this sort would not preclude the infinite variety of possible means of certainty that exist alongside the "objective" approach and that have great weight for certain persons while they may mean nothing to others. In all belief the person of the witness is "the main thing"; and each person's apprehension has its special modes, just as the decision on belief always has its place in the personal history of the believer himself. Thus it can happen that one man, while contemplating the cathedral of Rouen, is suddenly flooded with the certainty that this "fullness" must be the sign of divine revelation;[10] while another, as Simone Weil reports con-

[10] George Klünder, "Die Kirche ist die Fülle", in *Bekenntnis zur katholischen Kirche* (Würzburg, 1955), 70f.

cerning herself,[11] may accept the truth of Christ on the simple evidence of the rapture flooding the face of a young communicant. Who is to pass judgment on the legitimacy of such "arguments"?

To be sure, there are also such representative figures as Saint Augustine or Pascal, whose paths, though highly personal, have stood for those of many others—for a whole generation, for a century, for the kindred in spirit of all times and places. One of the greatest of such figures is, it seems to me, John Henry Newman, who in his formal writings and letters traced, with a completely "modern", self-critical keenness, the separate stages of his own acquisition of certainty—a process, incidentally, whose beginning was marked by a curious prayer that the young Oxford fellow intoned along with his group of friends: he prayed that if he should be led to the conclusion that truth resided with the Catholic Church, then might God sooner permit him to die than to be compelled to act in conformity with so terrifying an insight.[12]

[11] Cf. John M. Oesterreicher, "The Enigma of Simone Weil", in *The Bridge: A Yearbook of Judaeo-Christian Studies*, ed. J. M. Oesterreicher (New York: Pantheon Books, 1955), 1:123.

[12] John Moody, *J. H. Newman* (Berlin, 1948), 72f.

IX

Is it good for man to believe? Would he be cheating himself of an essential wealth of existence if he were to refuse to believe?

If this question is referred solely to the relationships of men among one another, it can scarcely be answered with a clear yes or no. A community in which men did not dare talk to one another with impunity or to meet each other in ordinary situations with trust and belief would be something inhuman. In such a community men would be robbed of the uniquely human possibility of one man's participating, by listening, in another's possession of reality. The wonderful opportunity provided by communication would be forfeited. Deadly silence would convert community living into a parched wasteland. Such a situation is by no means unreal, as everyone knows; there can indeed exist "a boundless muteness . . . in the heart of the clamorous times".[1] Yet our experience with this very situation teaches us that it is not wise, under all conditions, to believe one's human interlocutor. Such belief is "good" only to the extent that what he says truly throws open to the believer a new aspect of reality, one that would otherwise remain inaccessible.

On the other hand, it seems abundantly clear that such precautions do not apply to religious belief. Man can scarcely find anything better and more meaningful to do than "be-

[1] Konrad Weiß in an unpublished posthumous fragment, "Logos des Bildes".

82

lievingly to unite with the knowledge of God".[2] So it is. Nevertheless, we may appreciate the full implications of this apparently so obvious thought only when we consider not only the fact of revelation but also its *content*.

What is this content? Of what does the divine speech speak? We can answer this question only by referring to Christianity, the historical form that belief in revelation has taken—the only form, incidentally, within the area of our present world-European civilization, that has made such a claim for itself. What, then, is the object of the divine revelation revealed in Christ? Only theology can say, of course. But we are not plunging into theology, I think, if we simply take note of what theology says.

According to the theologians, the essence of the Christian faith can be summed up in two words. Those two words are Trinity and Incarnation. The "universal teacher" of Christendom has said that the whole content of the truth of Christian faith can be reduced to the dogma of the trinitarian God and the dogma that man participates in the life of God through Christ.[3]

(The outsider, who has the impression of a bewildering multiplicity of dogmas and ideas, will ask himself: What about all the rest; what about the knotty problems of sacraments and sacramentals, hell and "purgatory", veneration of Mary, cult of saints, visions, "apparitions", and so on? As regards the last two items—which, in fact, can occasionally obscure a view of the essentials—it should be clearly understood that they fall outside the category of things that we are required to accept on the testimony of God. Even the

---

[2] *Ver.* 14, 8.

[3] Duo nobis credenda proponuntur: scil. occultum Divinitatis . . . et mysterium humanitatis Christi" (II, II, 1, 8).—"Fides nostra in duobus principaliter consistit: primo quidem in vera Dei cognitione . . . ; secundo in mysterio incarnationis Christi" (II, II, 174, 6).

Church's "acknowledgment" of certain apparitions means no more than the following:[4] first, that nothing about these phenomena offends against the faith or the ethical principles of life; and secondly, that there are sufficient signs attesting that these things may be considered true and genuine *fide humana*, on *human* testimony; for which reason, thirdly, it is not right simply to despise them. But all the rest—the dogma of the sacraments, of the Blessed Virgin, of the last things—can really be reduced to the two tenets named by Thomas Aquinas. This matter, however, can be conveyed only to one who already believes.)

Such is the character of this basically unitary content of divine revelation that the reality it affirms is, in a peculiar fashion, identical with the act of revelation and also with the witness. Earlier in this book[5] it was said that this is a situation almost without parallel anywhere else in the world. The "almost" was intended to leave room for the possibly sole exception, for the situation in which a person turns to another and says: "I love you." That statement, too, is not primarily supposed to inform another person of an objective fact separable from the speaker. Rather, it is a kind of self-witnessing; and the witnessed subject matter is given reality solely by having been spoken in such a manner. In keeping with this condition, the only way the partner can become aware of the love that is offered is by taking what is said into himself, by listening. Of course, the state of being loved can simply happen to him, as to an immature child; but he can truly "know" it only by hearing the verbal avowal and "believing" it; only then will the other's love become truly present to him; only then will he truly partake of it.

---

[4] B. H. Merkelbach, *Summa Theologiae Moralis*, 2d ed. (Paris, 1935), 1:519.
[5] Cf. chap. 6, pp. 55ff.

On a higher plane, the very same rule applies to divine revelation. In speaking to men, God does not cause them to know objective facts, but he does throw open to them his own Being. The subject matter that forms the essential content of revelation—that man has been elected to participate in the divine life; that that divine life has been offered to him, in fact, already given—this subject matter owes its reality to nothing but the fact that it is pronounced by God. It is real in that God reveals it. The situation is not that the "Incarnation" exists "anyhow" as a fact and is subsequently made known by the revelation. Rather, the Incarnation of God and the revelation in Christ are one and the same reality. For the believer there is once more the experience that he, in accepting the message of the self-revealing God, actually partakes of the divine life therein announced. There is no other way in which he could partake of it save by belief. It is imparted to him—here the word "impart" is restored to its original meaning. Divine revelation is not an announcement of a report on reality but the "imparting" of reality itself. That imparting takes effect, however, only upon the believer.

Only now can we answer the question of whether it is "good" for man to believe. And the answer will have to run somewhat as follows: If God has really spoken, then it is not only good to believe him; rather, the act of believing generates those things that in fact are goodness and perfection for man. Receptively and trustfully hearing the truth, man gains a share not only in the "knowledge" of the divine Witness, but in his life itself.

ON HOPE

Although he should kill me,
I will trust in him.
—Job 13:15—

CONTENTS

I

Pastoral melodramatics have robbed the reference to man as a "pilgrim on this earth" and to his earthly life as a "pilgrimage" of its original significance and virility as well as its effectiveness. It no longer clearly mirrors the reality it is intended to convey. Its original meaning has been overgrown with a welter of extraneous aesthetic connotations; it has been all but buried under a veil of discordant secondary meanings, the false sentimentality of which actually destroys the joy that contemporary man—above all the younger generation and, perhaps, precisely the best of them—would have experienced in striving toward the reality that is ultimately reflected in the metaphor.

Nevertheless, this reality is part of the very foundation of being in the world for the Christian: the concept of the *status viatoris* is one of the basic concepts of every Christian rule of life.

To be a "viator" means to be "one on the way". The *status viatoris* is, then, the "condition or state of being on the way". Its proper antonym is *status comprehensoris*. One who has comprehended, encompassed, arrived, is no longer a *viator*, but a

For the thoughts expressed in this section, I am indebted above all to the study of the works of Saint Thomas Aquinas. Of the monographs available to me, first mention must be made of the excellent *Commentary on the Six Questions on Hope* (II, II, 17–22) by the Dominican J. Le Tilly, in the French edition of the *Summa Theologica* (Paris: Éditions de la Revue des Jeunes, 1929).

comprehensor. Theology has borrowed this word from one of Paul's epistles: "Brethren, I do not consider that I have laid hold [*comprehendisse*] of [the goal] already" (Phil 3:13). To be on the way, to be a *viator*, means to be making progress toward eternal happiness; to have encompassed this goal, to be a *comprehensor*, means to possess beatitude.[1] Beatitude is to be understood primarily as the fulfillment objectively appropriate to our nature and only secondarily as the subjective response to this fulfillment. And this fulfillment is the Beatific Vision.

The concepts *status viatoris* and *status comprehensoris* designate the natural states of being of all creatures—above all, of man. Nearly every theological statement about men (or angels) refers more or less explicitly to one or the other of these concepts; and it is astonishing how many basic concepts of theology have a meaning in reference to the state of being on the way that is different from their meaning in reference to the state of total possession.

It would be difficult to conceive of another statement that penetrates as deeply into the innermost core of creaturely existence as does the statement that man finds himself, even until the moment of his death, in the *status viatoris*, in the state of being on the way.

Although it is almost literally as high as heaven above the enlightened despair of secular man, the meaning this statement has acquired in popular piety—that the human soul comes, after the unrest of earthly life, into the peace of its heavenly home—is, nonetheless, but the easily remembered, figurative formulation of a metaphysical concept that is only partly comprehensible to the popular mind, clarification of which can lead the human spirit to the deepest knowledge of its own existence.

[1] III, 15, 10.

The state of being on the way is not to be understood in a primary and literal sense as a designation of place. It refers rather to the innermost structure of created nature. It is the inherent "not yet" of the finite being.

The "not yet" of the *status viatoris* includes both a negative and a positive element: the absence of fulfillment and the orientation toward fulfillment.

Fundamental to and constitutive of the negative side of the *status viatoris* is the proximity to nothingness that is the very nature of created things. The creature's relationship to nothingness has its roots in the primordial fact that whatever has been created has been created out of nothing. This is evident in the reverse side of human freedom, in the possibility of sinning; for sin is nothing other than a turning aside to nothingness. "In the natural course of events, the possibility of sinning cannot be taken from the creature endowed with intelligence; for by the very fact that it stems from nothingness, its power can revert to non-being."[2] Dissolution of the *status viatoris* and entrance into the *status comprehensoris* means that this power of the creature freely to turn toward nothingness is "linked" (*ligatur*)[3] to pure being by a grace-filled union. Freedom to sin is turned into the greater freedom of not being able to sin.[4]

The positive side of the concept of being on the way, the creature's natural orientation toward fulfillment, is revealed, above all, in man's ability to establish, by his own effort, a kind of justifiable "claim" to the happy outcome of his pilgrimage. This ability is none other than the possibility of meritorious action, which has the character of genuine "progress". (This does not alter the fact that "meritorious" action presumes the preexistence of something that cannot

---

[2] 2, d. 23, 1.
[3] Ibid.
[4] I, 62, 8 ad 3.

be "merited".) The *status comprehensoris* fulfills the "claim" of these "merits"; in consequence, the possibility of meritorious action ceases to exist just as does the freedom to sin. In the transition from the state of being on the way to that of *status comprehensoris*, then, the *status viatoris* is dissolved in both its negative and its positive aspects: the possibility of turning toward nothingness is abolished by union; the claim to and the orientation toward fulfillment are abolished by the reality of fulfillment.

The *status viatoris* comes to an end at the moment when uncertainty comes to border on certainty. This moment puts its seal not only on fulfillment but also on nonfulfillment. Even the decision in favor of nothingness becomes definitive at this time. The state of being on the way is dissolved in either case; even "Satan immediately lost the *status viatoris* by his sin."[5]

Eternal damnation is the irrevocable fixing of the will on nothingness, just as the *status comprehensoris* is the *confirmatio in bono*, the "fastening" of the will on the highest being. In damnation, the positive side of the *status viatoris*, the orientation toward fulfillment, is definitively cut off and destroyed; thus isolated, the negative side becomes an absolute value. The inner "not yet" that once characterized the creature's nature is changed into a characteristic inner "not".

The "way" of man leads to death. Since man, by his sin, came under the law of death at the beginning of his history, his life has become an incipient death.[6] The "way" of man leads to death as its end but not as its meaning. The meaning of the *status viatoris* is the *status comprehensoris*.

[5] *Mal.* 16, 5.
[6] Augustine, *De peccatorum meritis et remissione* 1, 16.

For man, then, the *status viatoris* lasts as long as he lives in the body; the *status viatoris* ends when he ceases to live in the body. For that reason, man's "way" is "temporality". Time, in fact, exists only in reference to the transitoriness of man. The union of his spirit with his body is the foundation of his union with time; spirit itself, including man's spirit, is "above time".[7] In death, since man then leaves the *status viatoris*, he also steps out of time. This does not mean, however, that he enters into the realm of God's own eternity.[8]

Present-day existential philosophy, which regards human existence exclusively in its temporality as a "being in time", is right to the extent that it opposes an idealistic doctrine of man in which the *status viatoris* seems transformed, against its nature, into a permanent likeness to God. But to the extent that this existential philosophy conceives of man's existence as essentially and "in the foundation of its being temporal" (Heidegger), it too fails to comprehend the true nature of its subject. Anyone, in other words, who seeks to understand temporality without restriction as the necessary mark of human existence will find hidden from him not only the "life beyond" time, but also the very meaning of life in time. Idealism fails to recognize the nature of human existence because it "omits" the *status viatoris*; existentialism fails to recognize the true nature of human existence because it denies the "pilgrimage" character of the *status viatoris*, its orientation toward fulfillment beyond time, and hence, in principle, the *status viatoris* itself.

Even the angels, whether blessed or fallen, were once, in the strict sense, *viatores*, "on the way". But their "way" was not "temporality" (which, again, does not mean they shared in

---

[7] I, II, 53, 3 ad 3.
[8] I, 10, 5.

the eternity of God). For the angel, the *status viatoris* was a single instant—"instant", too, refers to time, but we are unable to think in anything but a temporal mode—an instant in which the angel was able to make an intellectual decision for or against God. From the first moment of his existence, the angel stood "at the end of his pilgrimage";[9] the duration of a single unpropitious act of decision separated him from his goal. For the angel, this act put an end to the *status viatoris*.

Saint Thomas says that God decided on a "longer way" for men than for angels because, in the graduated order of their natures, man is more distant from God, "magis a Deo distans".[10]

The concept of the *status viatoris* designates, in a special sense, the inner structure of man's creatureliness.

The creatureliness of man reveals itself above all in the deep differentiation of being with regard to God that expresses the fundamental principle of the "analogy of being". This differentiation of being consists primarily in the fact that God is he who is absolute being, in the fullness of whose being essence and existence are one; whereas man is not ipso facto his own essence; his essence is "in the process of becoming". This becoming-ness of the creature is especially evident in the concept of the *status viatoris*; in the "not yet" of man's being on the way, the whole span of the creature's "becoming-ness" (Przywara) is revealed, as in a concave mirror, between the shores of being and nothingness.

To be a creature means "to be imprisoned in nothingness" (Heidegger); even more, it means being grounded in absolute

---

[9] *Quol.* 9, 8 ad 2.
[10] 2, d. 7, 1, 2; cf. 2, d. 23, 1, 2 ad 2; I, 62, 5 ad 1.

being and having an existential orientation toward being, toward one's own being and, at the same time, toward the Divine Being.[11] And this is as it should be: "Just as they have their source in nothingness, so created beings could sink back into nothingness if that were pleasing to God";[12] but "He created all things that they might be" (Wis 1:14). Among the numerous objections that Saint Thomas raises against his theses in the *Quaestiones disputatae*, there is one that might stand word for word in the tomes of nihilistic existential philosophy today: "Proprius motus naturae ex nihilo existentis est ut in nihilum tendat": the proper movement of a being that stems from nothingness is to tend toward nothingness.[13] To this objection the "universal teacher" of the Church responds as follows: The orientation toward nothingness is not the proper movement of natural being, which is always directed toward a good (but "good" means "existence"); the orientation toward nothingness comes into existence precisely through the rejection of this proper movement.[14] Despite every possibility of falling into nothingness, the proper orientation of the "way" is toward being—to such an extent that, to be possible, even the decision in favor of nothingness would have to wear the mask of a decision for being.

The whole span of creaturely existence between being and nothingness can never be understood, then, as though the relationship to nothingness were simply to be assigned equal rank with the relationship to being—or were even to be ranked before or above it. The "way" of *homo viator*, of man "on the way", is not a directionless back-and-forth between being and nothingness; it leads toward being and away from nothingness; it leads to realization, not to annihilation,

[11] *Pot.* 5, 4.
[12] *Pot.* 5, 4 ad 10.
[13] *Pot.* 5, 1, obj. 16.
[14] *Pot.* 5, 1 ad 16.

although this realization is "not yet" fulfilled and the fall into nothingness is "not yet" impossible.

For the individual who experiences, in the *status viatoris*, his essential creatureliness, the "not-yet-existing-being" of his own existence, there is only *one* appropriate answer to such an experience. This answer must not be despair—for the meaning of the creature's existence is not nothingness but being, that is, fulfillment. Nor must the answer be the comfortable certainty of possession—for the "becoming-ness" of the creature still borders dangerously on nothingness. Both—despair and the certainty of possession—are in conflict with the truth of reality. The only answer that corresponds to man's actual existential situation is hope. The virtue of hope is preeminently the virtue of the *status viatoris*; it is the proper virtue of the "not yet".

In the virtue of hope more than in any other, man understands and affirms that he is a creature, that he has been created by God.

II

I T WOULD NEVER OCCUR to a philosopher, unless he were also a Christian theologian, to describe hope as a virtue. For hope is either a theological virtue or not a virtue at all. It becomes a virtue by becoming a theological virtue.[1]

Virtue is not the tame "respectability" and "uprightness" of the philistine but the enhancement of the human person in a way befitting his nature. Virtue is the *ultimum potentiae*,[2] the most a man can be. It is the realization of man's potentiality for being. Virtue is the perfecting of man for an activity by which he achieves his beatitude.[3] Virtue means the steadfastness of man's orientation toward the realization of his nature, that is, toward good.

Theological virtue is an ennobling of man's nature that entirely surpasses what he "can be" of himself. Theological virtue is the steadfast orientation toward a fulfillment and a beatitude that are not "owed" to natural man. Theological virtue is the utmost degree of a supernatural potentiality for being. This supernatural potentiality for being is grounded in a real, grace-filled participation in the divine nature, which comes to man through Christ (2 Pet 1:4).

First, then, that steadfast orientation toward fulfillment which we call "theological" virtue has its source in a truly

[1] I, II, 62, 3 ad 2.
[2] *Virt. card.* 3.
[3] I, II, 62, 1.

divine substance in man, in grace.[4] Secondly, it is aimed directly at supernatural happiness in God, who is known in a supernatural manner. Finally, it is only through divine revelation that the existence, origin and object of this theological virtue are known to us.

When we say, then, that hope is a virtue only when it is a theological virtue, we mean that hope is a steadfast turning toward the true fulfillment of man's nature, that is, toward good, only when it has its source in the reality of grace in man and is directed toward supernatural happiness in God.

Justice, for instance, is already a true virtue, a clear tending toward good, even outside the supernatural order. When justice ceases to be directed toward good, it ceases to be justice. Hope, on the other hand, can also be directed—even in the natural sphere—toward what is objectively bad and yet remain real hope. Natural hope lacks the distinctive quality of virtue: "quod ita sit principium actus boni, quod nullo modo mali"—that it is so ordered to good that it cannot possibly turn toward evil.[5]

Obviously, hope experiences this firmness of orientation toward good above all as a God-given turning to God, that is, as a theological virtue.

Hope, like love, is one of the very simple, primordial dispositions of the living person. In hope, man reaches "with restless heart", with confidence and patient expectation, toward the *bonum arduum futurum*, toward the arduous "not yet" of fulfillment, whether natural or supernatural.

As we have said above, the patient expectation of the emotional-intellectual hope of natural man does not include, of

---

[4] Ibid.
[5] *Virt. comm.* 2.

itself, that certainty of being ordered toward true good that is the definitive mark of true virtue. But this natural expectation—as adaptable matter, as receptive *materia*—tends by its very nature to be stamped with the formative standard of virtue so that it may itself, by reason of this standard, gain a share in the orientation toward good.

As *materia*, the disposition of sensuous-intellectual hope that aspires to the "not yet" of man's natural fulfillment is ordered to two virtues in particular: magnanimity (*magnanimitas*) and humility.[6]

The proper impulse of natural hope, as such, is toward the virtue of magnanimity. Humility is the protective barrier and restraining wall of this impulse.

Magnanimity, a much-forgotten virtue, is the aspiration of the spirit to great things, "extensio animi ad magna".[7] A person is magnanimous if he has the courage to seek what is great and becomes worthy of it. This virtue has its roots in a firm confidence in the highest possibilities of that human nature that God did "marvelously ennoble and has still more marvelously renewed" (Roman Missal).[8] Thus magnanimity incorporates into itself the aspiration of natural hope and stamps it according to the truth of man's own nature. Magnanimity, as both Thomas and Aristotle tell us, is "the jewel of all the virtues",[9] since it always—and particularly in ethical matters—decides in favor of what is, at any given moment, the greater possibility of the human potentiality for being. It is good to think that, in this way, every virtue is borne along on a current that receives and guards the courageous unrest of our natural hope.

[6] II, II, 161, 1.
[7] II, II, 129, 1.
[8] II, II, 129, 3 ad 4.
[9] II, II, 129, 4 ad 3.

Humility, which is only apparently the opposite of magnanimity,[10] is not, in any sense, a forgotten virtue, but it is one that is often misinterpreted and misunderstood. To anticipate the grossest misunderstanding, humility is not only not itself an external attitude; it is also not bound to any external attitude. Humility rests on an interior decision of the will.[11] Furthermore, humility is not primarily an attitude that pertains to the relationship of man to man: it is the attitude of man before the face of God.[12] Humility is the knowledge and acceptance of the inexpressible distance between Creator and creature. It is, in a very precise sense, as Gertrud von le Fort once said, "man's true and proper worth before God". Man's worth, as that of a being possessed of a soul, consists solely in this: that, by his own free decision, he knows and acts in accordance with the reality of his nature—that is, in truth.

But let us return to our subject: humility and natural hope. It is the function of humility to be the negative measure of instinctive-natural hope. Magnanimity directs this hope to its true possibilities; humility, with its gaze fixed on the infinite distance between man and God, reveals the limitations of these possibilities and preserves them from sham realization and for true realization.

The proper ordering of natural hope is born, then, from the interaction of magnanimity and humility.

This explains the fact that these two natural virtues, magnanimity and humility, are the most essential prerequisites for the preservation and unfolding of supernatural hope—insofar as this depends on man. Together they represent the most complete preparedness of the natural man, whose existence is "postulated" by grace.

[10] II, II, 129, 3 ad 4.
[11] II, II, 161, 1 ad 2.
[12] II, II, 161, 1 ad 5.

On the other hand, the culpable loss of supernatural hope has its roots in two principal sources: lack of magnanimity and lack of humility. This remains to be discussed.

The supernatural life in man has three main currents: the reality of God, which surpasses all natural knowledge, manifests itself to faith. Love affirms—also in its own right —the Highest Good, which has become visible beneath the veil of faith. Hope is the confidently patient expectation of eternal beatitude in a contemplative and comprehensive sharing of the triune life of God; hope expects from God's hand the eternal life that is God himself: "sperat Deum a Deo".[13]

The existential relationship of these three—faith, hope, love—can be expressed in three sentences. First: faith, hope and love have all three been implanted in human nature as natural inclinations (*habitus*) conjointly with the reality of grace, the one source of all supernatural life. Second: in the orderly sequence of the active development of these supernatural inclinations, faith takes precedence over both hope and love; hope takes precedence over love;[14] conversely, in the culpable disorder of their dissolution, love is lost first, then hope, and, last of all, faith.[15] Third: in the order of perfection, love holds first place, with faith last, and hope between them.[16]

It remains, now, to shed further light on the relationship between hope and love by means of a distinction—a distinction, namely, between the perfect love of friendship (*amor amicitiae*) and the imperfect love of "concupiscence" (*amor*

---

[13] Cajetan, *Commentary* on II, II, 17, 5; no. 7.
[14] I, II, 62, 4.
[15] *De spe* 3 ad 11.
[16] *Virt. card.* 3.

concupiscentiae), that is, between a love that loves the beloved
for his sake and one that loves him for its own sake.

The virtue of hope is associated primarily with that *im*perfect love of God that desires God, the Highest Good, only for
its own sake. Indeed, it belongs to the concept and nature of
hope that one can hope only for oneself (and for him whom
one loves, for the "other self").[17] Nevertheless, this imperfect
love of hope—Francis de Sales calls it *amour d'espérance*—is
the not-to-be-undervalued precursor of the perfect love of
friendship (*caritas*), by which God is affirmed for his own
sake. And the perfect love of God, which is the theological
virtue of love and, at the same time, the mother and root of
all Christian virtues, flows back again on hope to mold and
enhance it.[18]

"Thus the theological virtues flow back upon themselves
in a sacred circle: one who is led to love by hope has thereaf-
ter a more perfect hope, just as he also believes now more
strongly than before."[19]

The assumption that the existence of a "concupiscent" love
of God that is referred by hope to oneself, and hence that
hope itself, is no more than an "interested" and "mercenary"
love unworthy of the truly perfect Christian (as though man
could possibly be "disinterested" in the fulfillment of his
own nature in God—for what else is "heaven" all about?)
belongs, it would seem, to those inevitable temptations to
pride by which even the strongest souls are endangered. The
Council of Trent has spoken authoritatively on this subject:
"If anyone says that the faithful ought not to expect and
hope for eternal happiness from God for the sake of his
mercy and the merits of Jesus Christ . . . , let him be anath-

[17] *De spe* 3.
[18] I, II, 62, 4.
[19] *De spe* 3 ad I.

ema."[20] Two hundred years earlier, Saint Bonaventure had written in his *Commentary on the Sentences of Peter Lombard*: "There are many who look for beatitude but worry little about themselves and much about God."[21]

It is very difficult to keep in mind the fundamentally incomprehensible fact that hope, as a virtue, is something wholly supernatural. Certainly, man's innate capability plays a role in the gaining of that for which he hopes, that is, of eternal happiness. "But the very habit of hope [*ipse habitus spei*], by virtue of which one expects happiness, stems, not from merit, but solely from grace."[22] In his excellent study of the theological virtues, the holy Paschasius Radbertus, a great Frankish theologian of the Carolingian period, expressed this thought in the following words: "Christ is held by the hand of hope. We hold him and are held. But it is a greater good that we are held by Christ than that we hold him. For we can hold him only so long as we are held by him."[23]

(It follows, incidentally, from the supernatural character of hope that what we must say and write about this "infused" virtue differs from what we would say and write about courage, for instance, or justice. A discussion about hope can seek to achieve only indirectly what can rightly be expected from a presentation of the "acquired", and therefore "acquirable", virtues—namely, that it be, at the same time, an incentive to the virtue in question.)

The embodiment, at once symbolic and truly fundamental, of the supernatural life in man is the man Christ, "in whom dwells the fullness of the Godhead". He is also the embodi-

[20] Council of Trent, sessio 6, cap. 16, can. 26.
[21] 3, d. 26, 1, 1 ad. 5.
[22] II, II, 17, 1 ad 2.
[23] *De fide, spe et caritate* 2, 1.

ment of our hope: "Christ in you, your hope of glory!" (Col
1:27). (How does it happen that we are so prone to understand Holy Scripture in a vague approximation rather than in
the precise meaning of its passages? It is due in part, perhaps,
to a decline in the proper dogmatic interpretation of Scripture.)

Christ is the actual foundation of hope. In a striking sentence, the letter to the Hebrews speaks of the hope we have
"as a sure and firm anchor of the soul, reaching even behind
the veil, where our forerunner Jesus has entered for us"
(6:19). Thomas Aquinas comments: "Christ has entered for
us into the inner sanctuary of the tent and has there made
firm [*fixit*] our hope."[24]

Christ is, at the same time, the actual fulfillment of our
hope. This fact is expressed with singular clarity in the passage in which Saint Augustine undertakes to interpret the
scriptural text "Spe salvi facti sumus": In hope were we saved
(Rom 8:24): "But Paul did not say, 'we shall be saved', but
'we have already been saved'; yet not in fact [*re*], but in hope;
he says, 'in hope were we saved.'" "This hope we have in
Christ, for in him is fulfilled all that we hope for by his promise."[25] "As yet we do not see that for which we hope. But we
are the body of that Head in whom that for which we hope
is brought to fulfillment."[26]

This inherent linking of our hope to Christ is so crucial
that one who is not in Christ has no hope (1 Th 4:13).

The *Compendium of Theology*, of which Saint Thomas had
completed only about a third before his death, was intended
to present the whole doctrine of salvation in three parts
named after the three theological virtues. The second, largely

[24] *In Hebr.* 6, 4.
[25] *Contra Faustum* 11, 7.
[26] *Sermones* 157, 3.

unfinished part, which contains only a few chapters under
the title "On Hope", was to have been an explanation of the
Our Father. "Just as our Savior initiated and perfected our
faith, so it was salutary that he should lead us to living hope
by teaching us the prayer by which our hope is especially
directed to God."[27]

Prayer and hope are naturally ordered to each other. Prayer
is the expression and proclamation of hope; it is "inter-
pretativa spei";[28] hope itself speaks through it.

And all the prayers of the Church, "bolder [in their hope]
than all the great thoughts of the philosophers", have the
uniform conclusion: "per Christum Dominum nostrum"—
through Christ, our Lord. This fact links the present discussion with those that have preceded it.

It will, perhaps, not be superfluous to state here that the three
preceding sections present the central message of this book.
They contain the core of the theological doctrine of hope.
This core is the statement that hope, as the lasting elevation
of man's being, cannot exist except from, through and in
Christ.

As Bonaventure emphasized in his *Commentary on the Sentences of Peter Lombard*, the nature of the certainty that apper-
tains to hope is "hard to define".[29]

On the one hand, hope partakes of the unconditional certitude of faith,[30] on which it depends: hope is grounded
above all in the divine mercy and omnipotence, "through
which even one who does not possess grace can yet become
a partaker of it in order thus to achieve everlasting life; every-

---

[27] *Comp.* 2, 3.
[28] II, II, 17, 4.
[29] 3, d. 26, 1, 5.
[30] II, II, 18, 4.

one who has faith has also this certitude about the omnipotence and mercy of God."[31] Hope's unfailing certitude is
based on this fact, that is, on the genuinely grace-filled nature
of supernatural hope.

It is not certain, however, that man, of himself, will be able
to "persevere in hope". As long as he is in the *status viatoris*,
man, even the "perfect Christian", can, by turning aside to
nothingness, use his free will to destroy the supernatural life
that is in him and with it the hope of eternal life that is
rooted therein. "It is not the certainty of hope that is thus
denied",[32] but only the possibility of a subjective certainty of
salvation.

> Although all must place the firmest hope in God's help, no
> one must promise himself anything with absolute certainty.
> For God does, of course, perfect the good work he has be-
> gun by causing the will and the accomplishment if only they
> do not withdraw themselves from his grace. Yet those who
> believe themselves to stand should take care lest they fall and
> should work out their salvation in fear and trembling. . . .
> That is, they must fear, knowing that they have been born
> again unto the hope of glory, but not yet unto glory.[33]

However magnanimous he may be, natural man can never
hope for the eternal life of the Beatific Vision of God without falling into pride (and thus ceasing to be magnanimous).
Yet this supernatural fulfillment of man's nature, toward
which the theological virtue of hope is directed, is, all un-
noticed, the object of all natural hope. All our natural hopes
tend toward fulfillments that are like vague mirrorings and
foreshadowings of, like unconscious preparations for, eternal
life.

---

[31] II, II, 18, 4 ad 2.
[32] II, II, 18, 4 ad 3.
[33] Council of Trent, sessio 6, cap. 13.

In a certain sense, the virtue of hope brings order and direction in its wake even for man's natural hope, which is bound thereby to its proper and final "not yet": "In our orientation toward eternal life, we hope to receive help from God not only for spiritual but also for corporal deeds."[34] On the clear basis of this sentence from Saint Thomas Aquinas (in which he plainly says that it is permitted us to surround even the natural goods of life with supernatural hope, that is, with a hope directly infused by God), there become manifest—as faint foreshadowings, yet clearly visible to the devout eye—some of the basic structures on which the supernatural realm is built.

The ease with which an age living in the certainty of faith could combine natural with supernatural hope is almost incomprehensible to us today. It is very difficult for us to understand how unabashedly Dante, for instance, in the twenty-fifth canto of the *Paradiso* (Dante, in a dialogue with James, the Apostle of Hope, the "Baron" of heaven, unfolds in this canto of the *Divine Comedy* a whole theology of supernatural hope)—how unabashedly, I repeat, Dante, carried up to the "heavenly sphere of the fixed stars", gives free expression even to his earthly hope of returning to Florence in glory. ("If it should chance that e'er the sacred song / To which both Heaven and Earth have set their hand, / . . . Should touch the cruel hearts by which I'm banned / From my fair fold where as a lamb I lay, / . . . With altered voice, with altered fleece today / I shall return, a poet, at my font / Of baptism to take the crown of bay.")[35]

Supernatural hope, then, which embraces not only the firm expectation itself but also the living source of this expecta-

[34] *De spe* 1.
[35] *Paradiso* 25, 1–9.

tion, is able to rejuvenate and give new vigor even to natural hope. "Rejuvenate" is precisely the right word here. Youth and hope are ordered to one another in manifold ways. They belong together in the natural as well as in the supernatural sphere. The figure of youth is the eternal symbol of hope, just as it is the symbol of magnanimity.

Natural hope blossoms with the strength of youth and withers when youth withers. "Youth is a cause of hope. For youth, the future is long and the past is short."[36] On the other hand, it is above all when life grows short that hope grows weary; the "not yet" is turned into the has-been, and old age turns, not to the "not yet", but to memories of what is "no more".

For supernatural hope, the opposite is true: not only is it not bound to natural youth; it is actually rooted in a much more substantial youthfulness. It bestows on mankind a "not yet" that is entirely superior to and distinct from the failing strength of man's natural hope. Hence it gives man such a "long" future that the past seems "short" however long and rich his life. The theological virtue of hope is the power to wait patiently for a "not yet" that is the more immeasurably distant from us the more closely we approach it.

The supernatural vitality of hope overflows, moreover, and sheds its light also upon the rejuvenated powers of natural hope. The lives of countless saints attest to this truly astonishing fact. It seems surprising, however, how seldom the enchanting youthfulness of our great saints is noticed; especially of those saints who were active in the world as builders and founders. There is hardly anything comparable to just this youthfulness of the saint that testifies so challengingly to the fact that is surely most relevant for contemporary man: that, in the most literal sense of these words, nothing more

---

[36] I, II, 40, 6.

eminently preserves and founds "eternal youth" than the theological virtue of hope. It alone can bestow on man the certain possession of that aspiration that is at once relaxed and disciplined, that adaptability and readiness, that strong-hearted freshness, that resilient joy, that steady perseverance in trust that so distinguish the young and make them lovable.

We must not regard this as a fatal concession to the *Zeitgeist*. As Saint Augustine so aptly says: "God is younger than all else."[37]

The gift of youth that supernatural hope bestows on man leaves its mark on human nature at a much deeper level than does natural youth. Despite its very visible effect in the natural sphere, the Christian's supernaturally grounded youthfulness lives from a root that penetrates into an area of human nature that the powers of natural hope are unable to reach. This is so because the supernatural youthfulness emanates from participation in the life of God, who is closer and more intimate to us than we are to ourselves.

For this reason, the youthfulness of the individual who longs for eternal life is fundamentally imperishable. It cannot be touched by aging or disappointment; it proves itself above all in the face of the withering of natural youth and in temptations to despair. Saint Paul says, "Even though our outer man is decaying, yet our inner man is being renewed day by day" (2 Cor 4:16). But there are no other words in Holy Scripture or in human speech as a whole that let resound as triumphantly the youthfulness of one who remains firm in hope against all destruction and through a veil of tears as do those of the patient Job: "Although he should slay me, I will trust in him" (13:15).[38]

---

[37] *De genesi* 8, 26, 48.

[38] This text corresponds to the Latin Vulgate but not to the original Hebrew text.

This whole book about hope revolves around this sentence because I believe it is vitally important for an age from whose despair there seems to issue a forced and superficial cult of youthfulness to have a glimpse of the highest pinnacle to which the hope-filled youthfulness of those who entrust themselves to God can soar. Job's words cut the foundation, moreover, from under a misapprehension that can, in fact, be critical in a catastrophic age, namely, the mistaken assumption that the substance of natural hope can be encompassed by supernatural hope even from below (instead of from above); in other words, that the fulfillment of supernatural hope must occur through the fulfillment of natural hope. It might be well, at a time when temptations to despair abound, for a Christianity that labors hard to hold high the banner of hope in eternal life to help its "younger generation" to read and, above all, to understand Job's words at an early age.

Nonetheless, this chapter will conclude with the verses that occur at the end of the fortieth chapter, the famous chapter that contains the message of salvation, of the Book of Isaiah, the book of the hope and consolation of Israel—the verses that begin with the Advent *Consolamini*: "Be comforted, be comforted, my people" (Is 40:1). These verses—the German mystics would call them a *jubilus*—read as follows: "But they that hope in the Lord shall renew their strength; they shall take wings as eagles; they shall run and not be weary; they shall walk and not faint" (Is 40:31).

III

THERE ARE TWO KINDS of hopelessness. One is despair; the other, *praesumptio*.[1] *Praesumptio* is a perverse anticipation of the fulfillment of hope. Despair is also an anticipation—a perverse anticipation of the nonfulfillment of hope: "To despair is to descend into hell."[2]

By describing both despair and presumption as "anticipation", we disclose the fact that both of them destroy the pilgrim character of human existence in the *status viatoris*. For they are both opposed to man's true becoming. Against all reality, they transform the "not yet" of hope into either the "not" or the "already" of fulfillment. In despair as in presumption, that which is genuinely human—which alone is able to preserve the easy flow of hope—is paralyzed and frozen. Both forms of hopelessness are, in the last analysis, unnatural and deadly. "There are two things that kill the soul," Saint Augustine tells us, "despair and false hope."[3] And Am-

---

[1] Pieper takes exception here to the usual German translation of Latin *praesumptio* as *Vermessenheit* (overconfidence), preferring instead the linguistically and semantically more accurate translation *Vorwegnahme* (anticipation). As a cognate of the Latin *praesumptio*, English *presumption* is, of course, etymologically close to the Latin original. Semantically, on the other hand, it has acquired, in everyday speech, much of the meaning associated with German *Vermessenheit*. I have, nevertheless, retained it in translation because it is the term most generally used in this context in theological writings in English.—TRANS.

[2] Isidore of Seville, *De summo bono* 2, 14; cited in II, II, 20, 3.

[3] *Sermones* 87, 8.

brose says, "He seems not to be human at all who does not hope in God."[4]

Today when we speak of despair we are usually referring to a psychological state into which an individual "falls" almost against his will. As it is here used, however, the term describes a decision of the will. Not a mood, but an act of the intellect. Hence not something into which one falls, but something one posits.

The despair of which we are speaking is a sin. A sin, moreover, that bears the mark of special gravity and of an intensity of evil.

Hope says: It will turn out well; or more accurately and characteristically: It will turn out well for mankind; or even more characteristically: It will turn out well for us, for me myself. To these characteristic degrees of hope there correspond the degrees of despair. The most characteristic form of despair says: It will turn out badly for us and for me myself.

It is essential for both hope and despair, moreover, that these sentences not be understood in a merely "theoretical" sense. Both he who hopes and he who despairs choose these attitudes with their will and let them determine their conduct.

Both hope and despair are capable of varying degrees of depth. All manner of doubt can exist, as it were, closer to the surface above a hope that has its roots in the most interior depths of the soul. But these doubts do not touch the hope that is so deeply rooted; they have no ultimate significance. Similarly, an individual in the last stages of despair can, by reason of the natural and cultural forces in the penultimate

---

[4] *De Isaac et anima* 1, 1.

regions of his soul, appear to others and even to himself to be an "optimist". He has only to seal off the innermost chamber of his despair so radically that no cry of pain can escape to the outer world (and there are many indications that man in the modern world has become a true virtuoso in this respect).

The deepest and most authentic depth of hope was opened up to mankind by the original event of the redemption. Through this event, too, the possibility of despair was increased by one more abyss of darkness. Natural man can never say as triumphantly as can the Christian: It will turn out well for me in the end. Nor can the hope of natural man look forward to an "end" like that of the Christian. But neither can a heathen be tempted to the same depths of despair as the Christian—and, indeed, as the greatest Christians and the saints. For the same flash of light that reveals to the creature the supernatural reality of grace lights up also the abyss of his guilt and his distance from God.

It makes a great difference, then, whether it is a Christian or a heathen who says: It will turn out badly for mankind, for us, for me myself.

The Christian who despairs about eternal life not only destroys the pilgrim character of his natural existence but also denies the actual "way" to eternal happiness and fulfillment: Christ himself, who appeared in human form. "Despair has no foot on which to walk the way that is Christ", says Saint Paschasius Radbertus.[5] (How little the primitive etymology on which this formulation of the truth is based—*spes–hope* is linked to *pes–foot*—is able to conceal or detract from its impressiveness!) For the Christian, despair is a decision against Christ. It is a denial of the redemption.

[5] *De fide, spe et caritate* 2, 4.

In despair, the nature of sin per se becomes especially clear, namely, that it is in conflict with reality. Despair is a denial of the way of fulfillment—and this before the very eyes of him who is preeminently "the way" to eternal life.

It is not by chance, I think, that Thomas Aquinas, at the very beginning of the article entitled "Is Despair a Sin?", explicitly designates precisely this characteristic of sin (that it contradicts reality) as the foundation of his argument: "Every movement of the will that is in conformity with true insight is good in itself, but every movement of the will that is the result of a false judgment is evil in itself and is a sin."[6] Elsewhere he says, "If sin could truly not be forgiven, then it would not be a sin to doubt the forgiveness of sin."[7]

Despair is the state of being that is proper to the damned. And the despair of one in the *status viatoris* is, as we have said, a kind of anticipation of damnation.

The pain of despair lies in the fact that it denies the way to fulfillment, which the nature of him who despairs does not cease to desire. Like hope, despair presumes the existence of a desire: "That for which we have no desire can be the object neither of our hope nor of our despair."[8]

Despair is self-contradictory, self-divisive.[9] In despair man actually denies his own desire, which is as indestructible as himself.

Objectively speaking, despair is not the most serious sin. But it is the most dangerous of all.[10] It threatens man's moral ex-

[6] II, II, 20, 1.

[7] *Mal.* 3, 15.

[8] I, II, 40, 4 ad 3.

[9] In a play on the German word *Verzweiflung* (despair), Pieper suggests here that the *zwei* (two) in this word reflects the divisive effect of despair on the human spirit.—Trans.

[10] II, II, 20, 3.

istence, for man's self-realization is linked to hope. "It is not so much sin as despair that casts us into hell", says Saint John Chrysostom in his commentary on the Gospel of Saint Matthew.[11]

Since Peter Lombard composed his *Sentences*, the Church's theology has counted despair among the sins against the Holy Spirit. Despair moves thus into the vicinity of that dark mystery expressed by the Lord: "Whoever speaks against the Holy Spirit, it will not be forgiven him, either in this world or in the world to come" (Mt 12:32). I say deliberately no more than that despair moves "into the vicinity" of this mystery. For Saint Thomas refers this word of the Lord solely to a persistent, blasphemous resistance to grace, whereas he says of despair only that it is difficult for it to find forgiveness.[12] It is difficult for this reason: that despair, in that it "closes the door" (here again the picturesque Frankish idiom of Saint Paschasius Radbertus),[13] is by its very nature a denial of the way that leads to the forgiveness of sin.

"In both good and bad, one proceeds, as a rule, from what is imperfect to what is perfect."[14] A sin as "perfect" as despair is normally not the first sin to be committed, nor does it "just happen". Rather, the beginning and the root of despair is *acedia*, sloth.

There is hardly another concept that has become so demonstrably "at home" in the consciousness of the average Christian as that of *acedia*. (This fact is due in part to the usual translation of the word as *Trägheit*: "sloth",[15] which,

---

[11] 86, 4.

[12] *Mal.* 3, 15.

[13] *De fide, spe et caritate* 2, 6.

[14] II, II, 14, 4 ad I.

[15] In this and the following paragraphs, Pieper is pointing out the difference of meaning between Greek *acedia* and its usual German translation *Trägheit*. Since German *Trägheit* is generally equivalent to English *sloth* (i.e., disinclina-

while it coincides to some extent with the most immediate meaning of the Greek word *akedeia*, reflects only imperfectly and incompletely its true conceptual meaning.)

In popular thought the "capital sin" of sloth revolves around the proverb "An idle mind is the devil's workshop." According to this concept, sloth is the opposite of diligence and industry; it is almost regarded as a synonym for laziness and idleness. Consequently, *acedia* has become, to all practical purposes, a concept of the middle-class work ethic. The fact that it is numbered among the seven "capital sins" seems, as it were, to confer the sanction and approval of religion on the absence of leisure in the capitalistic industrial order.

But this is not just to render superficial and shallow the original concept of *acedia* as it exists in moral theology; it is to transform it completely.

According to the classical theology of the Church, *acedia* is a kind of sadness ("species tristitiae")[16]—more specifically, a sadness in view of the divine good in man. This sadness because of the God-given ennobling of human nature causes inactivity, depression, discouragement (thus the element of actual "sloth" is secondary).

The opposite of *acedia* is not industry and diligence but magnanimity and that joy which is a fruit of the supernatural love of God. Not only can *acedia* and ordinary diligence exist very well together; it is even true that the senselessly exaggerated workaholism of our age is directly traceable to *acedia*, which is a basic characteristic of the spiritual countenance of precisely this age in which we live. (The meaningless expression "Work and don't lose hope" offers some elucidation of

---

tion to labor), it has been possible to translate this passage as a contrast of meaning between the Greek and English terms without doing violence to Pieper's thought.—Trans.

[16] I, II, 35, 8; II, II, 35; *Mal.* 11; *Ver.* 26, 4 ad 6.

this relationship.) The indolence expressed by the term *acedia* is so little the opposite of "work" in the ordinary meaning of the term that Saint Thomas says rather that *acedia* is a sin against the third of the Ten Commandments, by which man is enjoined to "rest his spirit in God".[17] Genuine rest and leisure (*Muße*) are possible only under the precondition that man accepts his own true meaning.

In the classical theology of the Church, *acedia* is understood to mean "tristitia saeculi",[18] that "sorrow according to the world" of which Paul says, in the Second Epistle to the Corinthians (7:10), that it "produces death".

This sorrow is a lack of magnanimity; it lacks courage for the great things that are proper to the nature of the Christian. It is a kind of anxious vertigo that befalls the human individual when he becomes aware of the height to which God has raised him. One who is trapped in *acedia* has neither the courage nor the will to be as great as he really is. He would prefer to be less great in order thus to avoid the obligation of greatness. *Acedia* is a perverted humility; it will not accept supernatural goods because they are, by their very nature, linked to a claim on him who receives them. Something similar exists in the sphere of mental health and illness. The psychiatrist frequently observes that, while a neurotic individual may have a superficial will to be restored to health, in actuality he fears more than anything else the demands that are made, as a matter of course, on one who is well.

The more *acedia* advances from the region of emotion into that of intellectual decision, the more it becomes a deliberate turning away from, an actual fleeing from God. Man flees from God because God has exalted human nature to a higher, a divine, state of being and has thereby enjoined on man a

---

[17] II, II, 35, 3 ad 1; *Mal.* 11, 3 ad 2.
[18] *Mal.* 11, 3.

higher standard of obligation. *Acedia* is, in the last analysis, a "detestatio boni divini",[19] with the monstrous result that, upon reflection, man expressly wishes that God had not ennobled him but had "left him in peace".[20]

As a capital sin, sloth is man's joyless, ill-tempered and narrow-mindedly self-seeking rejection of the nobility of the children of God with all the obligations it entails. As a genuine possibility and necessity, however, this "being a child of God" is an irrevocable fact that no one can alter. And since this irrevocable fact, which is not to be compared with the external offer of some gift or other, is precisely the renewal of man's whole nature at the center of his being, *acedia* means, in the last analysis, that man will not be what God wants him to be—in other words, that he will not be what he really is.

Acedia is what Kierkegaard, in his book on despair (*Sickness unto Death*), has called the "despair of weakness", which he considers a preliminary stage of despair proper and which consists in the fact that an individual "is unwilling, in his despair, to be himself".

Though not the only offspring of *acedia*, despair is the most legitimate. Saint Thomas Aquinas has assembled the *filiae acediae*, the companions and peers of despair, in a demonic constellation[21] that it will be rewarding to consider for a moment. For, since this association is not accidental but is actually founded on their common origin, the knowledge of their relationship casts an illuminating light on the nature of despair.

In addition to despair, *acedia* gives birth to that uneasy restlessness of mind that Thomas calls *evagatio mentis*: "No one

[19] *Mal.* 8, 1.
[20] II, II, 35, 3.
[21] *Mal.* 11, 4; II, II, 35, 4 ad 2.

can remain in sadness";[22] but since it is precisely his most inward being that causes the sadness of one who has fallen prey to *acedia*, the result is that such a one struggles to break out of the peace at the center of his own being.

For its part, *evagatio mentis* reveals itself in loquaciousness (*verbositas*), in excessive curiosity (*curiositas*), in an irreverent urge "to pour oneself out from the peak of the mind onto many things" (*importunitas*), in interior restlessness (*inquietudo*), and in instability of place or purpose (*instabilitas loci vel propositi*).[23] All these concepts that are inseparably related to "uneasy restlessness of mind" (*evagatio mentis*) are to be met with again in Heidegger's analysis of "everyday existence" (which, however, is not concerned with the religious significance of *acedia*): "being's flight from itself", "loquaciousness", "curiosity" as concern about the "possibility of abandoning oneself to the world", "importunity", "distraction", "instability".

Evagatio mentis and despair are followed by a third offspring of *acedia*—a sluggish indifference (*torpor*) toward those things that are in truth necessary for man's salvation; it is linked by an inner necessity to the denial of man's higher self that springs from sadness and sloth. The fourth offspring is pusillanimity (*pusillanimitas*) toward all the mystical opportunities that are open to man. The fifth is irritable rebellion (*rancor*) against all who are charged with the responsibility of preventing man's true and divinized self from falling prey to forgetfulness, to "self-forgetfulness". The last offspring is *malitia*, malice par excellence, a conscious inner choice and decision in favor of evil as evil that has its source in hatred for the divine in man.[24]

[22] *Mal.* 11, 4.
[23] II, II, 35, 4 ad 3.
[24] *Mal.* 4, 14 ad 8.

We have said that slothful sadness (*acedia*) is one of the determining characteristics of the hidden profile of our age, of an age that has proclaimed the standard of a "world of total work". This sloth, as the visible mark of secularization, determines the face of every age in which the call to tasks that are genuinely Christian begins to lose its official power to bind. *Acedia* is the signature of every age that seeks, in its despair, to shake off the obligations of that nobility of being that is conferred by Christianity and so, in its despair, to deny its true self.

Is not the mere listing of the "offspring of sloth", of the siblings and peers of despair, a most striking confirmation of this diagnosis? Do we not read it with something approaching the shamefaced chagrin of a person who has been surprised in dishonest dealings? Does not the present era witness the ripening of all these fruits of despairing sadness?

These things are not said here for the sake of the easy and all too cheap pleasure of pointing out the weaknesses of our age. Moreover, temptations to *acedia* and despair are not temptations that lose their power if one averts one's eyes from them. Temptations to *acedia* and despair can be overcome only by the vigilant resistance of an alert and steady watchfulness.[25] Despair (except, perhaps, one's awareness of it) is not destroyed by "work" but only by that clear-sighted magnanimity that courageously expects and has confidence in the greatness of its own nature and by the grace-filled impetus of the hope of eternal life.

The root and origin of despair is the slothful sadness of *acedia*. But its "perfection" is accompanied by pride. Theology has pointed out often enough the relationship between pride and despair. When an individual whose despair springs ini-

[25] II, II, 35, 1 ad 4.

tially "from weakness" comes "to realize why he does not want to be himself, then it changes suddenly, and defiance steps in" (Kierkegaard).

Pride is the hidden conduit that links the two diametrically opposed forms of hopelessness, despair and presumption. At the nadir of despair, the self-destructive and perverse rejection of fulfillment borders on the most extreme form of the not less destructive delusion of presumption—the affirmation of nonfulfillment as though it were fulfillment.

IV

BY IMPLANTING IN MAN the new "future" of a practically inexhaustible "not yet", supernatural hope lays the foundation for a new youthfulness that can be destroyed only if hope is destroyed. In both forms of hopelessness—in despair as well as in presumption—the youthfulness of one who hopes is reduced, as it were, to nothingness, but in different ways: in the case of despair, by senility; in presumption, by infantility.

The "infantility" of presumption lies in its perverse anticipation of fulfillment. Because man comes to believe that he has actually attained the "arduous" goal that, in reality, lies still in the future, the tension of hope is relaxed in the middle of the "way" and passes into the peaceful certainty of possession.

Incidentally, presumption is less opposed to hope than is despair. For despair is the true antitype of hope, whereas presumption is but its *falsa similitudo*,[1] its fraudulent imitation. In much the same way, infantility has a false and merely "imitative" resemblance to true youthfulness, the proper antitype of which is aging.

The presumption that is opposed to the theological virtue of hope is the individual's perverted attitude toward the fact that eternal life is the meaning and goal of our earthly "way".

[1] II, II, 21, 3.

We are not speaking, then, of that other presumption that has to do with natural powers and goals. More than a hundred questions will intervene in the *Summa* before Thomas will devote two articles to this kind of presumption.[2]

The presumption of which we speak is, rather, an attitude of mind that fails to accept the reality of the futurity and "arduousness" that characterize eternal life. In conjunction with attainability, these two characteristics—futurity and "arduousness"—constitute the formal nature of the object of hope.[3] If one of these characteristics is missing or ceases to be genuine, hope is no longer possible. In other words, presumption destroys supernatural hope by failing to recognize it for what it is; by not acknowledging that earthly existence in the *status viatoris* is, in a precise and proper sense, the "way" to ultimate fulfillment, and by regarding eternal life as something that is "basically" already achieved, as something that is "in principle" already given.

The notion of overconfidence, of an overreaching of oneself,[4] that is never absent from the false anticipation that is presumption clearly indicates the negative relationship of presumption to reality. On the other hand, however, the sense of "titanic" and "idealistic" that resonates in these words can easily obstruct and cover one's sight of the true essential core of presumption as a sin against hope.

For the essential nature of presumption is, as Saint Augustine says, a "perversa securitas",[5] a self-deceptive reliance on a security that has no existence in reality. In the last analysis,

[2] II, II, 130.

[3] I, II, 40, 1.

[4] Pieper uses here the German words *ver-messenheit* and *sich ver-messen* (see note 1 in chap. 3), hyphenating them in order to give full weight to the prefix ("*ver-*"), which in German often signals a reversal or distortion of meaning.—TRANS.

[5] *Sermones* 87, 8.

what appears to be a "superhuman" element in the anticipation of fulfillment is, in reality, none other than a yielding to the, if not exactly "heroic", yet certainly not despicable weight of man's need for security. In the sin of presumption, man's desire for security is so exaggerated that it exceeds the bounds of reality. It is important to keep in mind what presumption really is.

Presumption reveals itself in two basic forms that correspond to the mutually opposed pretexts on which it bases its inordinate satisfaction.[6]

Theology calls the first kind of presumption "Pelagian". It is characterized by the more or less explicit thesis that man is able by his own human nature to win eternal life and the forgiveness of sins. Associated with it is the typically liberal, bourgeois moralism that, for no apparent reason, is antagonistic not only to dogma per se but also to the sacramental reality of the Church: solely on the basis of his own moral "performance", an "upright" and "decent" individual who "does his duty" will be able to "stand the test before God" as well.

Between this first basic kind of presumption and the second lies that pseudoreligious activism that believes it can construct, out of a thousand "exercises", a claim to the kingdom of heaven that is rightful and absolutely valid and able, as it were, to pit itself against God.

The second form of presumption, in which, admittedly, its basic character as a kind of premature certainty is obscured, has its roots in the heresy propagated by the Reformation: the sole efficacy of God's redemptive and engracing action. By teaching the absolute certainty of salvation solely by virtue of the merits of Christ, this heresy destroys the true pilgrim character of Christian existence by making as certain

---

[6] II, II, 21, 4.

for the individual Christian as the revealed fact of redemption the belief that he had already "actually" achieved the goal of salvation. It has often been observed how close—both logically and psychologically—this second form of presumption is to despair, on the one hand and, on the other, to the moral uninhibitedness of that "inordinate trust in God's mercy" that theology reckons, along with despair, among the "sins against the Holy Spirit".

Presumption has its source in a self-esteem that, while false, is somehow affirmed by the individual's own will; it consists in the will to achieve a certainty that is necessarily invalid because there is no valid ground for it. Even more specifically, this false esteem of oneself is a lack of humility, a denial of one's actual creatureliness and an unnatural claim to being like God.[7] Hope presupposes not only magnanimity but also humility. Saint Augustine says in his *Commentary on the Psalms* that only to the humble is it given to hope.[8]

Despair and presumption block the approach to true prayer. For prayer, in its original form as a prayer of petition, is nothing other than the voicing of hope.

One who despairs does not petition, because he assumes that his prayer will not be granted. One who is presumptuous petitions, indeed, but his petition is not genuine because he fully anticipates its fulfillment.

This sheds a new light on the words of Holy Scripture: "that they [the Lord's disciples] must always pray and not lose heart" (Lk 18:1). Explicit in these words is the never-ceasing necessity of a hope that is humble enough really to pray and, at the same time, magnanimous enough to wait cooperatively for the fulfillment of its prayer.

[7] Ibid.; *Mal.* 8, 2.
[8] 118, 15, 2.

In theological hope the "antithesis" between divine justice and divine mercy is, as it were, "removed"—not so much "theoretically" as existentially: supernatural hope is man's appropriate, existential answer to the fact that these qualities in God, which to the creature appear to be contradictory, are actually identical. One who looks only at the justice of God is as little able to hope as is one who sees only the mercy of God. Both fall prey to hopelessness—one to the hopelessness of despair, the other to the hopelessness of presumption. Only hope is able to comprehend the reality of God that surpasses all antitheses, to know that his mercy is identical with his justice and his justice with his mercy.

Presumption, however, is the lesser, and despair the greater, sin: "Because of his infinite goodness, it is more proper to God to spare and to show mercy than to punish. For the former belongs to him by reason of his nature, the latter only by reason of our sins."[9] In other words, the anticipation of fulfillment is not so contrary to man's real existential situation as is the anticipation of nonfulfillment. The ungrounded certainty of presumption is less contrary to human nature than is despair.

Nevertheless, it remains true that presumption is a sin in the real and strict sense; in its most extreme form, it is, indeed, a sin against the Holy Spirit.

That ultimate existential uncertainty, the root of which—so long as we remain in the *status viatoris*—is the ever-present possibility of voluntary defection, is inevitably present even in the lives of the saints. It is inseparable from the concept of being on the way. It is wholly impossible for "pilgrim man"—and hence cannot constitute a valid goal for him—to escape from this uncertainty into absolute certainty. Absolute

[9] II, II, 21, 2.

certainty is unattainable, even "in principle", for *homo viator*. What this realization amounts to is this: in the existential uncertainty that is his natural lot, man understands himself as a finite nature that does not have being from himself and therefore does not possess himself—that is, as a creature—and that takes refuge in the merciful power of God's decrees.

The uncertainty of human existence cannot be totally removed. But it can be "overcome"—by hope, and only by hope.

The precariousness of the "potentiality for being" that is a mark of creaturely existence is reflected in the fact that hope lives intimately with fear. This union of hope and fear is operative not only in the natural sphere but also—a concept that is full of mystery and difficult to comprehend—in the supernatural sphere. Theological hope is essentially linked to the fear that is counted among the seven gifts of the Holy Spirit: the "fear of the Lord".[10]

It is this fear that is excluded by the false certainty of presumptive anticipation.[11] And because presumption shuts out fear, it also shuts out the virtue of hope, which is based on the fact that fulfillment has "not yet" been accomplished and that nonfulfillment has "not yet" been excluded.

---

[10] II, II, 19, 9 ad 1.
[11] II, II, 21, 3 ad 3.

V

ONE OF THE LAST VERIFIABLE of the theses that define the image of man for our time holds that it is not seemly for man to be afraid.

Waters from two sources are mingled in this attitude. One is an enlightened liberalism that relegates fearfulness to the realm of the unreal and in whose worldview, accordingly, there is no room for fear except in the figurative sense. The other is an unchristian stoicism that is secretly allied with both presumption and despair and confronts in defiant invulnerability—without fear, but also without hope—the evils of existence, which it sees with admirable clarity.

The classical theology of the Church is equally removed from both the oversimplification of liberalism and the desperate rigidity of stoicism. It takes for granted that fears are a reality of human existence. And it takes equally for granted that man will respond to what is objectively fearful with fear.

However, the real concern of classical theology is with something quite different; hence it regards fear from a very different point of view. It inquires into the *ordo timoris*,[1] into the due order of fear—that is, into the various (negative) gradations of the objects of fear. It praises or blames, not fear itself, but the order or lack of order that is manifest in it.

[1] II, II, 125, 1 ad 1.

"Fear embodies the concept of sin insofar as it is opposed to the order of reason",[2] that is, insofar as it is opposed to the objective truth of reality. This is true, however, not only of fear but also of fearlessness. Among the sins opposed to the virtue of fortitude (and one cannot say this too emphatically: the virtue of fortitude!), Saint Thomas lists not only disordered fear but also unnatural fearlessness (*intimiditas*).[3]

In its concept of man, classical theology is aware of a fearlessness that bespeaks a lack of fortitude as well as of a fearfulness that is not only not "unworthy" but actually ethical; that accords with the nature of reality and with the spiritual dignity of man. On the basis of this theology one must assume, then, that something is not quite in order when a man is afraid of nothing and that the ideal of "stoic" invulnerability and fearlessness is based on a false interpretation of man and of reality itself.

Thomas Aquinas points, in particular, to three passages of Holy Scripture, which, incidentally, are scarcely known to contemporary Christianity, as proof that fearlessness as a fundamental attitude—which, in any event, can "be maintained" only through self-deception—is nothing short of unnatural. According to Thomas,[4] the first passage, which is from the book of Job, refers to fearlessness that has its source in a presumptuous pride of mind: "He was made to fear no one" (Job 41:24); the second passage[5] is from Sirach: "He that is without fear cannot be justified" (Sir 1:28); the third is from the book of Proverbs: "A wise man feareth and declineth from evil" (Prov 14:16).[6]

[2] II, II, 125, 4.
[3] II, II, 126.
[4] II, II, 126, 1.
[5] II, II, 126, 1 ad 1.
[6] II, II, 126, 1 ad 2.

In the present context, however, we are speaking of fear only "insofar as it somehow turns us to God",[7] that is, we are speaking of the "fear of the Lord". This is true also of what follows. If we consider the matter from a metaphysical rather than a psychological point of view, this fear is that "partial truth"—often so disguised as to be unrecognizable—that lies hidden in all the other fears and anxieties that plague mankind.

It is not easy for contemporary man to come to an understanding of what is really meant by the classical concept of "fear of the Lord" and "fear of God": too many liberal and stoic obstructions stand in the way.

From the beginning, one must keep firmly in mind that fear of the Lord is, in the undiminished and precise sense of the word, truly "fear". Fear of the Lord is not the same as "respect" for God. This popular misunderstanding and attenuation rob the concept of most of its original meaning. It is just as inexact—and opens the way to a similar misunderstanding—to interpret it as "reverence" or "awe". The fact that classical theology expressly teaches that fear of the Lord—although wholly directed to God—still is obviously not a fear "of" God, in the sense in which one might speak of the fear "of" some misfortune, is one indication among others of how far these euphemisms fall short of the true meaning of "fear of the Lord".[8] Such a distinction would be totally meaningless if fear of the Lord were understood as "reverence" or "respect"; for, formally speaking, acts of reverence and respect are referred to God in the same direct sense in which fear is directed to evil.

It remains, then, to inquire what it is that fear of the Lord fears.

[7] II, II, 19, 2.
[8] II, II, 19, 1.

It has become customary in our age to speak—and not always without self-complacency—of man's imperiled and threatened existence. But the words are seldom used to refer to the utmost and ultimate danger that threatens man's existence and before which every other threat of catastrophe and destruction, even on a planetary scale, and every other danger inherent in the struggle for existence are secondary and even unreal. This ultimate threat, which introduces into the very core of human existence the real possibility of a diminution and corruption of being, is none other than the *posse peccare*, the ability to commit sin. This statement must, of course, be freed from its exclusive moralistic connotation and linked once more to its original and deeper meaning—its reference to being itself.

It is to the fearfulness of this very real possibility, which is always rising anew from the ground of the creature's being—to the fearfulness of being separated by sin from the Ultimate Ground of all being—that the fear of the Lord, which is a true fearfulness, affords the only true answer.

No "heroism" can overcome this fear. Its object is inseparably and irrevocably linked to the nature of "pilgrim man's" existence. One can, perhaps, turn one's gaze from what gives rise to this fear; one can, perhaps and as it were, forget the fear of the Lord. But to do so is to forget oneself, to contradict the reality of one's own existence.

There are two ways of fearing the possibility of incurring sin: because of the sin itself or because of the punishment due it. The more genuine fear is the fear of sin as sin. But because punishment is not linked to sin by an "arbitrary ruling" of God and, as it were, *ex post facto*, but is directly linked to and proceeds from the very nature of sin, it follows that a fear that is initially linked to punishment can nevertheless be, in a genuine sense, a fear of sin.

Theology calls this true fear of sin a *timor filialis* or a *timor*

castus, a "filial" or "chaste" fear. (The latter designation origi-
nated with the Fathers of the Church and is no longer
wholly comprehensible to us today.) The other kind of fear is
called *timor servilis*, a "servile" fear.

"Servile" fear is an imperfect fear of the Lord. It has its
source—"All fear is born of love";[9] fear is "love in flight"[10]—
in an imperfect form of "concupiscent" love of God. The
timor servilis fears above all the loss of personal fulfillment in
eternal life—in other words, eternal damnation. Therein lies
the nature and substance of "servile" fear.[11]

Although it is something imperfect, this substance of "servile" fear, namely, the fear of eternal punishment, is nevertheless "good";[12] indeed, it is "from the Holy Spirit".[13] It can
pave the way for a true love of God (*caritas*);[14] and it is the
"beginning of wisdom" (Ps 111:10), for it disposes the soul
for wisdom.[15] Today, we can hardly bring ourselves to reflect
on these teachings. There are many reasons for this. In addition to the general inhibitions that have their source in liberalism and stoicism, which we have mentioned above, there is
also a more specific reason: above all, that the "last things"—
heaven and hell—have come to be, in the public consciousness and even among Christians, something not to be taken
seriously. Heaven has been reduced to a playground and the
angels to playmates of small children, whereas for Saint Thomas Aquinas the apparition of an angel had the character of
something elementally frightening and confusing—which
explained why an angel's first word to man was always "Be

[9] II, II, 126, 1.
[10] Augustine, *De civitate Dei* 14, 7.
[11] II, II, 19, 4 ad 3.
[12] II, II, 19, 4.
[13] II, II, 19, 9.
[14] II, II, 19, 8 ad 1.
[15] II, II, 19, 7.

not afraid."[16] In like manner, hell and the fallen angels have become less real to us because they have been stripped of their natural state as spiritual realities and thus of their ultimate awesomeness.

As a reason for turning to God, fear of eternal damnation belongs admittedly to an imperfect level of love of God. Yet, on this level of the interior life, it is the only possibility of an appropriate existential answer to one of the most central realities of human existence. It is impossible—again, at this level of love—"to overcome" one's anxiety in the face of eternal punishment; neither "a proper attitude" nor indifference nor optimism is sufficient for this purpose. In any event, even if it were possible, such a conquest could occur only in open conflict with the objective reality of being. The only victory over the fear of eternal damnation that is both genuine and appropriate to man's nature is advancement in love.

By that genuine love of God that affirms the Highest Good for its own sake, "servile" fear is transformed and raised to a fear that is both "filial" and "chaste".

It must be repeated here: "filial" fear is also genuine fear. In a certain sense, in fact, it incorporates the concept of fear more truly than does "servile" fear. For "filial" fear sees sin as sin; but sin is "evil" to a greater degree than punishment is.[17] Thus the fear of sin responds to a deeper imperilment of human existence than does the fear of eternal damnation. It has its dwelling closer to the innermost and most crucial core of man's intellectual and moral existence, whereas fear of eternal punishment seems to be ordered rather to the psychic and emotional spheres. The "servile" fear of damnation decreases as man's nature is the more deeply penetrated by his

[16] III, 30, 3 ad 3.
[17] *Mal.* 1, 5.

love of friendship with God,[18] that is, the more closely he is bound to the eternal ground of his being. Because it is true fear, "filial" fear, on the other hand, increases as the love of God grows in intensity. This fact may, at first glance, seem surprising, but its inner necessity is revealed as one's understanding penetrates more deeply. On the one hand, the very real possibility of sin is not excluded for "pilgrim man" even on the highest level of the love of God; a voluntary defection from God is always "wholly possible" (*omnino possibilis*)[19] for him as long as he has "not yet" attained the *status comprehensoris*. On the other hand, the orientation toward nothingness and the reduction to nothingness that is the true nature of sin is evident only to one who is a "friend of God"; only supernatural love of God—fear is "love in flight"—at once enables and compels the individual to fear the possibility of sin as greatly as its very genuine fearfulness demands.

In a different sense from the "servile" fear of eternal damnation, the "chaste" fear of a sinful turning away from God is also the "beginning of wisdom": the former prepares the soul for wisdom; the latter is the first fruit of wisdom itself.[20]

"Filial" fear, which is ordered to the perfect love of God, is numbered among the gifts of the Holy Spirit. It is a gift that entirely surpasses the potentialities of natural man.[21]

Ethical good is none other than the development and perfection of the natural tendencies of our nature:[22] it is man's natural fear of the diminution and annihilation of his being; its perfection lies in the fear of the Lord.

---

[18] II, II, 19, 10.
[19] II, II, 19, 11.
[20] II, II, 19, 7.
[21] II, II, 19, 9.
[22] II, II, 108, 2.

From this statement we may draw some noteworthy conclusions. If man's natural anxiety in the face of nothingness is not perfected by the fear of the Lord, it erupts "unperfected" and destructive into the realm of his intellectual and spiritual existence. The dominance of this "unperfected", destructive anxiety is a sign that an individual has voluntarily denied and rejected the fear of the Lord. The fear of the Lord, however, is characteristic of and intrinsic to every good human act; by the same token, it is somehow excluded and lost through every sin.[23] Hence "unperfected" anxiety is the mark and accompaniment of (objective) sin, that is, of what is contrary to reality. At this point, theology is once again in accord with the findings of modern psychiatry.

There is only one possible way in which man's natural anxiety in the face of nothingness can penetrate his intellectual and psychic life *without* immediately destroying it. This one way is the perfecting of natural anxiety by the fear of the Lord. Only the fear of the Lord contains in itself the ontological ground of all "health": it accords with reality.

Fear of the Lord and the theological virtue of hope are naturally ordered to one another; they complement one another.[24] Our hesitation in acknowledging this complementarity seems to find its counterpart and confirmation in the fact that even Saint Thomas, who changed his opinion in only a few recorded instances, stated this relationship of hope and fear of the Lord clearly and definitively only in the second part of the second major part of the *Summa*—something he had not done in the first part or in his earlier commentary on the *Sentences* of Peter Lombard.

The link between hope and fear is that "concupiscent" love which seeks God first for its own sake. This love, as we

[23] *Mal.* 8, 2 ad 5.
[24] II, II, 141, 1 ad 3.

have seen, is the foundation of hope, and fear is its "negative side". We can hope and fear only for ourselves (and for those we love).

"Servile" fear corresponds to that level of hope which has not yet been molded by *caritas*, by the true love of friendship for God. "Chaste" or "filial" fear is the "negative side" of the loving hope that is contained in the love of friendship.

Fear of the Lord assures the genuineness of hope. It eliminates the danger that hope may be turned into its *falsa similitudo*, its false image: into the presumptuous anticipation of fulfillment. Fear of the Lord keeps ever before the mind of one who hopes the fact that fulfillment has "not yet" been accomplished. Fear of the Lord is the constant reminder that human existence, although destined for and oriented toward fulfillment by the Highest Being, is, nevertheless, perpetually threatened in the *status viatoris* by the closeness of nothingness.

Paschasius Radbertus comments with an appositeness we can but admire: "Holy fear guards the summit of hope."[25]

In Holy Scripture (Ps 115:11), the same thought is expressed in language that is at once simple and elegant: "They who fear the Lord trust in the Lord."

---

[25] *De fide, spe et caritate* 2, 7

ON LOVE

Love is the prime gift.
Whatever else is freely
given to us becomes a
gift only through love.

CONTENTS

141

the "courage to be".— Benevolence is not yet love; kindness without love.— What is the source of our knowledge that it is "good" to be?— Love as choosing; nevertheless the universality of approbation. Jealousy.— Degrees of approval.— Affirmation of existence and appreciation of "qualities".   187

ward" is the beloved himself.— The unresolvable paradox of "selfless self-love". 233

VIII

The erotic love of man and woman as the paradigm of love in general.— Eros, as mediative and humanizing force, links sexuality and agape.— Eros and beauty. The nature of beauty as promise.— Eros: purest realization of yea-saying.— False apotheosis of eros.— Erotic love as symbol of God's love. 246

IX

The conviction that "everything belongs".— Sexual powers as a good taken for granted.— The susceptibility to misinterpretation of everything mediative, including eros.— The absolutizing of isolated sexuality: ever a possibility as a practice and an outlook.— What is meant by "unspoiled youth"? Sex seeks the neutrality of enjoyment, not personal union.— "The fig leaf moved up in front of the face".— The deceptive character of mere sexuality. Trivialization by making light of; sex without pleasure.— Compulsive nature of sex consumption; "totalitarian coldness".— Diabolism and "exorcism". The role of sophistry. 260

X

Some thoughts on friendship, maternal and paternal love.— Reenactment of the Creator's primal affirmation: the basis for an understanding of *caritas*.— Mother Teresa in Calcutta and her "hospital of the dying".— The novelty in this love. What is meant by "for Christ's sake"?— Loving one's fellowmen as "companions in future bliss". The common element in *caritas* and erotic love.— What is natural to love and natural in love is presupposed but also perfected. Perfection always means transformation as well. Fire as the symbol of love.   272

I

THERE ARE MORE THAN ENOUGH considerations that might keep us from committing ourselves to the subject of love. After all, we need only leaf through a few magazines at the barber's to want not to let the word "love" cross our lips for a good long time. But there is an equal danger lurking in an entirely different quarter, the "triumphal misunderstanding"[1] that unrealistically and exaggeratedly portrays love as pure "unselfishness" and, in so doing, makes the reality of love evaporate. Still and all, such scruples are primarily a matter of taste and impression. Only after we have overcome them do we find ourselves confronting the true difficulty: the sheer overwhelming vastness of the subject. Are we, in fact, dealing with only one subject? Does the noun "love" cover a single, or approximately single, area of meaning—or is it not rather something like an archipelago of extremely varied meanings with no discernible connection among them? Is there anything in common among what the entertainment industry calls "love", what is called *amour physique* in Stendhal's famous essay, and that "theological virtue" which is usually named together with faith and hope? Again, is not the kind of "love" mentioned in Plato's *Symposium* something entirely different? Moreover, no one questions our right to speak of "loving"

The motto is taken from Thomas Aquinas' *Summa theologica* (I, 38, 2): "Amor habet rationem primi doni, per quod omnia dona gratuita donantur."

[1] This accurate expression comes from Theodor W. Adorno's *Noten zur Literatur*, vol. 2 (Frankfurt, 1961), 7.

wine, nature, singing. And is there not an absolute abyss between all that and the Bible's statement that God is love?

If we consider the extensive vocabulary of other languages for
this area, we may well ask ourselves whether this difficulty exists
primarily for German, which is obliged to include widely different concepts within the single word *Liebe*. A famous German
classical scholar[2] has actually called his own language "poor" because it has only a single noun for things that "have nothing to
do with each other", whereas the Greeks, the Romans and the
speakers of the Romance languages have a good half dozen different words at their disposal for "love". One professor of philosophy has attempted to rectify the situation by proposing and
even carrying out the absurd suggestion that we at least distinguish between *love*[1] and *love*[2] (to be pronounced "love superscript one" and "love superscript two") but with the proviso that
these are not to be understood as "different aspects of one and
the same general 'love'".[3]

In reality the matter is far less simplistic than it may appear
at first glance. First of all, the German language, as soon as we
go beyond the confines of nouns and enter the realm of
verbs, proves to be not all that poor in vocabulary. Some of
the words, in fact, suggest a depth of meaning that is not
easily plumbed. What, for example, is the inner significance
of *einander leiden mögen*?—which means "to like", although
the literal sense is "to be able or willing to suffer someone".
(A somewhat similar meaning is found negatively in the English phrase: "He does not suffer fools gladly.")

Furthermore, in other languages also a single fundamental
word apparently underlies all the variety in vocabulary and

[2] Ulrich von Wilamowitz-Moellendorff. Anders Nygren used the phrase
quoted here as a motto in his two-volume work *Eros und Agape* (Gütersloh,
1930, 1937), 1:43.
[3] Johannes Rehmke, *Grundlegung der Ethik als Wissenschaft* (Leipzig, 1925),
98f., 114.

binds together all special meanings. In Latin, for example, and in the modern languages descended from it, this fundamental word is *amor*. "Omnis dilectio vel caritas est amor, sed non e converso";[4] this sentence simply confirms existing usage: that all *dilectio* (*dilection*; the word is now obsolete in English, although "predilection" survives) and all *caritas* (*charité*, charity) is fundamentally *amor* (*amour, amore, amór*). Thus we must once again wonder whether those seemingly disparate things referred to by the German word *Liebe* and the English word "love" really "have nothing to do with one another". Sigmund Freud, on the one hand, also speaks of the "carelessness" of language in applying the word *Liebe*.[5] But, on the other hand, he points out, "In all its whims linguistic usage remains faithful to some kind of reality."[6] Presumably, then, there may be a message hidden within the apparent or alleged "poverty" of the German vocabulary of love. It may be that the language itself is telling us not to overlook the underlying unity in all the forms of love and to keep this broad common element in mind in the face of all the misuses that result from narrowing down the concept.

Such misuses certainly occur in plenty. Apparently the basic words of any language, words that concern the central issues of existence, are particularly subject to perversion. André Gide at eighty, already too weary to continue his journals, wrote in one of his last notations a few weeks before his death, "Distinction, dignity, greatness—I am afraid and almost embarrassed to employ these words, so shamelessly have they been misused. . . . They might be called obscene words like, moreover, all noble words, starting with the word 'virtue'."[7] C. S. Lewis has actually called this tendency to invert

[4] I, II, 26, 3.
[5] *Gesammelte Werke* (London, 1940–), 14:462.
[6] Ibid., 13:122.
[7] *Ainsi soit-il ou les jeux sont faits* (Paris, 1952), 156.

the meanings of words of ethical praise into their opposite, a law: "Give a good quality a name and that name will soon be the name of a defect."[8]

This partly accounts for the shyness that appears to inhibit many persons from pronouncing the shamefully abused word "love". Instead, people prefer to speak of "humanitarianism" or "solidarity". But do not such terms mean something different from "love"? If it is possible to exchange or find substitutes for fundamental words, that is certainly not something that can be done arbitrarily; the process is not susceptible to an act of will, no matter how well founded. On the other hand, it seems perfectly possible to carry the misuse of such a word so far that it will be completely ruined and will simply disappear from usage. The semantic history of the German "love" vocabulary, by the way, offers two striking examples of such occurrences. These examples should provoke a good deal more thought than has hitherto been given to them.

Minne, for instance, is a word that was totally eliminated from living German speech because it had been so misused. In the works of medieval poets like Wolfram von Eschenbach and Walther von der Vogelweide, but also in general, nonpoetic usage, *Minne* was "the usual word for love".[9] Thus the German language originally had more than one noun at its disposal. In fact, *Minne* seems to have been the more exacting term, compared to *Liebe*.[10] It signified, according to the Grimm *Deutsches Wörterbuch*,[11] not only man's devoted love for God (*Gottesminne*), but the solicitude accorded those in need of help and the love between man and woman. But by the year 1200 Walther von der

[8] *Studies in Words* (Cambridge, 1967), 173.

[9] Hermann Paul, *Deutsches Wörterbuch*, 4th ed., rev. Karl Euling (Halle, 1935), 353.

[10] "Constant love is called *Minne*"—Ulrich von Lichtenstein. Cf. *Trübners Deutsches Wörterbuch*, vol. 4 (Berlin, 1943), 631.

[11] Vol. 6, col. 2239f.

Vogelweide was already complaining that "many a false coin is struck"[12] with the image of *Minne*. The word remained in use for quite a while; but the progressive vulgarization of its meaning eventually had the consequence that employing it "became impossible".[13] Then it was extinguished with a kind of fierceness; it was even replaced in already printed books by pasting the word *Liebe* over it.[14]

In Notker's German psalter, written around the year 1000, *Minne* held sway unassailed; for Luther, five hundred years later, the word no longer existed.[15] As the Grimm dictionary laconically observes, it has "been avoided since the sixteenth century and is now obsolete".[16] And so it has remained to the present day. None of the efforts of the romantics and none of the Wagner operas has succeeded in bringing the word back to living speech. Although a new German translation of Kierkegaard by Emmanuel Hirsch[17] attempted to render one of the two Danish expressions for love by *Minne*, that effort has remained an isolated bit of archaizing without any significance for actual contemporary German speech.

The second linguistic episode on which we would briefly report here is the attempt to introduce the word *caritas* into German usage—or, rather, the failure of this attempt. The episode shows how fruitless it is to try to control a living language and to overcome its supposed "poverty" by deliberate correction. In this case the intention was to set off the special aspect of love as a theological virtue in contrast to whatever else language calls by the name of "love". Granted, at this point another and even more far-reaching

[12] Cf. Fr. von Lipperheide, *Spruchwörterbuch* (Berlin, 1962), 620.
[13] Kluge-Götze, *Etymologisches Wörterbuch der deutschen Sprache*, 11th ed. (Berlin, 1934), 392.
[14] *Trübners Deutsches Wörterbuch*, 4:631.
[15] Ibid., 4:632.
[16] Vol. 6, col. 2241.
[17] Düsseldorf-Cologne, 1956–.

problem enters in, that of "language and terminology"—
the historically evolved word as distinct from the artificial
technical term. Of course, there can be no objection to using more or less artificial terminology in technical discus-
sions, in the interest of greater accuracy. Thus, for example,
there is nothing wrong with the theologian's use of the
term *caritas* in order to define more precisely the supernatural love of God and neighbor. And as long as this technical
expression is distinguished from ordinary speech and is kept
apart from it, everything is "quite all right". But if it is in-
troduced into general usage or adapted, it is flung into the
dynamic processes of living language and inevitably runs
the risk of semantic change, of a narrowing of meaning and
of becoming worn out. What is more, the danger to such
technical terms seems greater than to words that have
evolved naturally or have been created by poets in the spirit
of the language.

Precisely this is what happened when the word *caritas*
moved from a technical expression in theological discourse
to a quasi-German loanword, *Karitas*.[18] The meaning of
these two words has ceased to be identical. *Karitas* (much like
charity in English) now means, principally if not exclusively,
organized care for those in need, together with the necessary
apparatus (associations, offices, directors, and so on). Again
we must say that of course there can be no objection to this;
on the contrary, the shift in meaning in one sense expresses a
fine and praiseworthy thing. What is more, who would venture to deny that in most cases the love of God and love of
neighbor are at work, more or less hidden, in the administra-
tion of charity. Still, what theological precept has always

---

[18] The word *Karitas* first appears in the "Duden" in the ninth edition of
1915; the spelling with *K* is indicated as preferred, although *Caritas* is also
mentioned. This spelling was consistently used up to the 16th edition of 1967.
Karl Jaspers in his *Philosophie* also speaks exclusively of *Karitas*.

meant by *caritas* is something quite different and far more. When we give thought to this, it is no longer hard to see that Karl Jaspers should place "charity" and "love" in opposition and can speak of the possibility of "charity without love".[19] In the thirties there were efforts—probably under the influence of Anders Nygren's book *Eros und Agape*—to introduce the biblical Greek term *agape* into general usage in German. Had this been more successful, the word would sooner or later have probably suffered a similar fate.

But whether or not the immediately available stock of words is "poor" or "rich"—what is far more crucial is for us to grasp as much as we can of the multiplicity of the phenomenon we call "love". This can be done only by an interpretation of both our own language and of foreign languages, to the extent that they are accessible to us—which they may or may not be even when we "know" them. The fragmentary and haphazard nature of such attempts at interpretation is as self-evident as it is unavoidable. I am convinced that not even the matter that everybody means and "knows" in our own daily speech can be translated into exact, carefully considered phraseology without something's being omitted. In addition, we can scarcely count on perceiving the overtones and reverberations of living usage in other languages, not to mention "dead" ones. And of course we realize that no one ever obtains a working knowledge of more than a tiny fraction of the languages that have actually been spoken on our planet, including present-day living languages. Nevertheless, keeping in mind the incompleteness and the accidental character of our information, we may still say that we learn quite a good deal about the phenomenon of "love" by carefully considering the vocabulary associated with it.

[19] Karl Jaspers, *Philosophie*, 2d ed. (Berlin, 1948), 623ff.

Latin, the "ancient" language that up to the present day has made the most vital contributions to the vocabulary of the nations of Europe, had at least half a dozen words to signify love. *Amor* and *caritas* are generally known. But the Christian acts of love that nowadays are lumped under the heading of *caritas* ("charity") were called by the contemporaries of Saint Augustine acts of *pietas*, as he himself relates.[20] *Dilectio*, a fourth word, has already been mentioned in passing. But we must include in this same category not only *affectio* but also and rather unexpectedly *studium*. It has even been said[21] that this very word expresses an aspect of loving concern that was particularly characteristic of the Romans, namely, the desire to serve and to be "at the service of". This does indeed point out something seldom specified as part of love but that everyone agrees belongs to the full realization of love.

Pietas, too, it appears, points to an element in the whole picture of love that is not immediately apparent. Granted, it can scarcely be said that an essential (and therefore permanent) element of love is something like pity (from *pietas*!), although Arthur Schopenhauer so argued with a radicality that plainly distorted the actuality, "All true and pure love is pity."[22] But the Latin word does rightly suggest that real love "cannot be without mercifulness".[23]

The term *affection* introduces still another of the semantic elements in "love"; the word has passed into French and En-

---

[20] *City of God*, 10, 1.

[21] Carl Abel, *Über den Begriff der Liebe in einigen alten und neuen Sprachen* (Berlin, 1872), 11. The well-known phrase from Tacitus (*Annals* 1, 1), "sine ira et studio", likewise means approximately: without anger and *predilection*. And when Sallust (*De coniuratione Catilinae*, 51, 13) says that the powerful man may neither love nor hate, he too uses the word *studere* ("neque studere neque odisse").

[22] *Sämtliche Werke* (Leipzig: Insel-Ausgabe, n.d.), 1:493.

[23] Goethe in a letter dated January 2, 1800, to F. H. Jacobi, "that true appreciation cannot be without mercifulness".

glish virtually unchanged in appearance and meaning. The element is that of *passio*, which here means neither passion nor suffering but the passive nature of love. For despite the active grammatical form, everyone knows that loving is not exclusively, and perhaps not even primarily, something that we ourselves actively do. It is additionally and perhaps much more deeply something that happens to us. Goethe at sixty remarked in conversation, "Love is suffering. . . . You have to put up with it; you don't seek it."[24] Although he could claim a certain competence on the subject of love, this was probably something of an exaggeration. Yet the question remains: Who, strictly speaking, is the active subject when someone "pleases" us or when we find someone "enchanting"? Ordinary usage, at any rate, would scarcely term it truly human love if the "lover" displayed, no matter how heroically unselfish he might be, nothing but consciously directed (inner or outer) activity but not a grain of passivity, no sign of having been affected.

On the other hand, of course, no one fails to recognize that the passively blind process of spontaneously "being pleased" cannot be everything, that an element of probing judgment and selective preference enters in. Love that comes from the center of existence, engaging the whole human being, essentially implies *diligere* also. The word means electing and selecting. In Latin and the languages derived from it, *dilectio* (*dilection*) seems to be an indispensable word in the vocabulary of love—indispensable in defining the personal, mental quality of human love. In the purely sensual realm, *dilectio* naturally has no place, whereas the word *amor*, as Thomas[25] says, embraces the sensual and the mental, and even the spiritual and supernatural elements.

---

[24] To Riemer on July 11, 1810.
[25] 3, d. 27, 2, 1.

The word *caritas*, too, as its basic meaning indicates, pertains to an act that can be performed only in the mind, namely, evaluation.[26] (*Caritas*, incidentally, is not at all, as might be thought, a distinctively Christian coinage but also is part of living usage in classical Latin, for example, in Cicero.)[27] We use the related adjective *carus* to denote what is "dear" to us, what we are prepared to pay a high price for. This curious ambiguity occurs in many languages (in Latin, German, French and English, for example), identifying what is beloved with what is expensive. What this suggests is worth noting: for it brings up the question of whether union with the—really or only supposedly—beloved means enough to the lover for him to be willing to pay something for it and, if so, how much. Here, it seems to me, the essence of all true love, and particularly of the love for God (specifically called *caritas*), which so resists our probing, is actually expressed. We sometimes doubt whether we can possibly "love" God, since he is inaccessible to our emotions. But the word itself tells the questioner that *caritas* is not just something sentimental, nor does it primarily refer to a special intensity of feeling. Rather, it suggests the extremely "solid" and sober matter of evaluation and of readiness if need be to pay something for the union with God. This is the metallic core of *caritas*. The extent to which its radiations can reach out to and penetrate the realm of emotion and even of sensuality is frequently manifested, especially in those who have founded their lives upon *caritas* in the contemporary sense of charity. This is the reason, I think, that Saint Francis de Sales in the title of his

[26] Thomas Aquinas says that what the concept of *caritas* adds to that of *amor* is, as the word itself indicates, the appreciation of superior value (I, II, 26, 3).

[27] In Cicero, for example, we find the phrase "caritas generis humani" (*De finibus bonorum et malorum* 5, 23, 65). Cf. also *Partitiones oratoriae* 16, 56, and 25, 88.

magnificent treatise on divine love speaks neither of *charité* nor *dilection*. Instead he calls it, with an explicit justification,[28] *Traité de l'amour de Dieu*. And *amor* (*amour*) is, once again, nothing more nor less than the German word *Liebe* or the English word "love": the one word that includes all the dimensions. If Saint Francis really gives particular emphasis to any single aspect, it is to the aspect of being carried away, of being kindled to an ardor that actually has physical effects.

Like all living languages, of course, Latin tended to blur the neatly defined boundaries between the areas of meaning covered by different nouns. Saint Augustine, for example, had a fine sense of linguistic nuances and himself sometimes spelled out the differences (for example, between *amor* and *dilectio*).[29] Yet he was inclined to stress the common element underlying all the forms of love. In the Bible too, he remarks,[30] the words *amor*, *dilectio*, *caritas* basically mean the same thing. The Vulgate, in fact, translates the Greek words *agápe* and *agapán* without differentiation, it appears, by *amor*, *caritas*, *dilectio*, and by *diligere* as well as *amare*.[31]

Eros: this Greek word, which has been taken into all European languages, is far more ambiguous than it is usually represented to be. From even a casual reading of the Platonic dialogues, we begin to see how wide its range of meaning is. Affection kindled by physical beauty; intoxicated god-sent madness (*theia mania*); the impulse to philosophical contemplation of the world and existence; the exaltation that went with the contemplation of divine beauty—Plato calls all these things

---

[28] Francis de Sales, *Traité de l'amour de Dieu*, vol. 1 (Annecy, 1894), 73.

[29] *In Epistolam Johannis ad Parthos tractatus*, 8, 5; Migne, *Patrologia Latina* [hereafter PL] 35:2038.

[30] *City of God*, 14, 7. Cf. also *De Trinitate*, 15, 18; 32.

[31] Cf., for example, Jn 15:9; 16:27; Rom 5:5; 2 Pet 1:7.

"eros". In Sophocles, moreover, the word is used to mean approximately "passionate joy".[32] The fact that this passage introduces into the very meaning of *eros* the essential relationship of love and joy is an achievement that should never be forgotten or lost; we shall have occasion to speak of it again.

Philia, usually too narrowly translated by "friendship", seems, like its related verb *phileín*, to stress chiefly fellow feeling, the solidarity among human beings, and not only of friends but also of spouses, fellow countrymen and people in general. "It is my nature to join in love, not hate"—in this famous sentence of Antigone, she speaks neither of *eros* nor of *agape*; the word used is *phileín*.[33] *Agape* as a substantive first came into common usage in biblical Greek. Karl Barth conjectures that the New Testament (as was likewise the case, incidentally, with the Septuagint, the pre-Christian Greek translation of the Old Testament) might have taken up this term precisely because (somewhat along the lines of English "to like") it had been "a relatively colorless word".[34] Richard Reitzenstein, the philologist and historian of religion, says that in classical Greek *agape* was not reckoned "among literary words".[35] *Storgé*, for example, was "literary"; it meant principally familiar love; so was *philanthropia*, which meant primarily benevolent kindness but was also used for love between the sexes. We might also mention *philadelphia*, a late word for brotherly love, which, like *philanthropia*, entered the Greek of the New Testament.[36] But these are of no further concern to us. *Eros* and *agape* remain more important, as the

[32] *Aias*, 693. I owe this reference to the Greek–English dictionary of Liddell and Scott (Oxford, 1958), 695.

[33] Sophocles, *Antigone*, 523: *symphileín éphyn.*

[34] *Kirchliche Dogmatik*, vol. 4, pt. 2 (Zollikon-Zurich, 1955), 836.

[35] Quoted in Heinrich Scholz, *Eros und Caritas. Die platonische Liebe und die Liebe im Sinne des Christentums* (Halle, 1929), 112.

[36] *Philadelphia*: Rom 12:10; 1 Th 4:9; Heb 13:1; 2 Pet 1:7. *Philanthropia*: Titus 3:4.

words that with presumably mutually exclusive intent rally the sides and determine the character of the philosophical and theological disputation in which we mean to intervene vigorously in the course of the following pages.

But for the moment we must attempt to formulate a question whose answer, it is true, can become apparent only at the conclusion of this book. But the question itself comes to the fore now, arising from a peculiarity in the biblical use of *agape*. I am referring to what may be called the "absolute" use of this word, for instance, in the sentence: "He who fears is not perfected in love" (1 Jn 4:18). In love *with whom*, we are inclined to ask; or should it be: In the love *of whom*? Certainly a subject and also an object of love are intended. But the sentence is framed as if to imply that something like a new personal quality, the trait of "being in love", exists and fundamentally affects man's relationship to the universe. But, as we have said, the precise nature of this quality, and whether it may be posited as an actual potentiality of man, can best be dealt with at the end of our discussion. Perhaps it will turn out that an answer to this question *is* the conclusion of the book.

The reader who pauses at this point and looks back for a moment will possibly note a curious omission from our rapid inventory: Does *sex* really not have a place in the classical vocabulary of love? That would certainly be a matter for astonishment—all the more so since any "puritanical" taboos would scarcely have prevailed; we need only think of the blunt language of Aristophanes, Plautus, Terence, and so on. What then is the case? I shall limit myself to quoting an American writer, the author of important works of cultural anthropology, "The curious thing to our ears is how rarely the Latins speak of *sexus*. Sex, to them, was no issue; it was *amor* they were concerned about. Similarly, everyone knows the Greek word *eros*, but practically no one has ever heard of their term for 'sex.' It is *phýlon* . . . a zoological term."[37] With a glance at our contemporary situation the same writer advances the thesis: "We are in flight from eros—and we use sex as the vehicle for the flight."[38] But here we are already anticipating a subject that in any case must be discussed at length.

Our review of the *English* and *French* vocabularies need not be long—all the more so since (of course) the most important words of the Latin language recur in these languages, with slightly altered meanings (*amour, dilection, charité, charity, affection*). Still, we must mention a few points that enrich and complete the concept of "love".

For example, we very quickly encounter the English distinction between "to like" and "to love". A schoolboy, C. S. Lewis comments, is chided for saying of strawberries, "I love them."[39] But if he is "passionately fond" of them, usage permits the phrase. And yet it is not, strictly speaking, the intensity of the emotion that makes for the distinction. Rather, entirely different modes of emotion are involved. Moreover, "to like" can also be applied to a person, but "to love" refers to the more committed "real" love that is directed toward the other's self. It is, of course, perfectly possible to say of someone, "I like him, but I do not love him." In the context of our discussion, however, the converse and equally conceivable case is more important: that it is possible to love someone although there are many things about him that one does not "like". Hence the irrelevance of the argument that it is impossible to like everybody, so how can we possibly obey the commandment to love our neighbor. But then what is meant by loving? That is precisely our question.

---

[37] Rollo May, *Love and Will* (New York, 1969), 73.
[38] Ibid., 65.
[39] C. S. Lewis, *The Four Loves* (London, 1960), 19.

I have long been fascinated by two other aspects of the English vocabulary of love. One is the identity of the words "to like" and "likeness". To be sure, etymologists hold that the words are not at all identical, that they come from entirely different roots; and since I was unable to check this assertion, I let the matter rest. But then an excellent dictionary[40] called my attention to the fact that *amor* and *amare* have something to do "with the radical notion of likeness". More specifically, they are related to the Greek *háma* ("at the same time"), the Latin *similis* and English "same".[41]

Our concern here, as is the case with our whole effort to survey the vocabulary, is not with the etymological oddity. It is rather with what we can learn from these close relationships about the secret link between "love" and "likeness". The relationship is a more or less concealed one, and yet it does not surprise us. On the contrary, it brings to the fore a long suspected and almost consciously known semantic element: that "love" includes and is based upon a preexistent relation between the lover and the beloved; that, in other words, no one could love anyone or anything were not the world, in a manner hard to put into words, a single reality and one that can be experienced as fundamentally characterized by unity—a world in which all beings at bottom are related to one another and from their very origins exist in a relationship of real correspondence to one another. In short, we are confirmed in our sensing that love not only yields and creates unity but also that its premise is unity. Paul Tillich has actually included this state of affairs in his definition of love. Love, he says, is not so much the union of those who are

<hr />

[40] C. T. Lewis and C. Short, *A Latin Dictionary* (Oxford, 1958), 107.

[41] In the Polish–German border region there is (or was) a remarkable colloquial phrase that corroborates this assumption. The phrase is (or was): "Das ist sehr gleich"—literally: "That is very like." The meaning: "That is true and I like it." Cf. C. Abel, *Der Begriff der Liebe*, 42, n.

strangers to one another as the reunion of those who have
been alienated from one another. But alienation can exist
only on the basis of a preexisting original oneness.[42]

For a long time the original meaning of the phrase "to be
fond of" seemed to me another riddle of English usage. And
what was meant by "a fond look"? That, of course, is the
naïve question of a nonlinguist; still, among my English and
American friends I have found hardly any who could answer
it. It was therefore a surprise to me to learn that in Middle
English *fond* was spelled *fonned* and was thus a disguised past
participle derived from an obsolete verb that meant something like enchant or bewitch. To be fond of and fondness
therefore suggest "a kind of fascination of the mind"[43]—
which once again recalls the passive nature of love as something suffered. Once more the question arises: Are we, when
we love, not so much active ourselves as stirred, changed,
moved by something lovable? Is love primarily (or only
immediately, at the first moment) rapture over the beloved,
being rapt by the beloved? Etymologically, *rapture* means carrying someone away, forcibly transporting him out of himself.[44] That is pretty much a circumlocution for the meaning
of the Latin noun *affectio*.

In *French* this word *affection* actually seems to signify the
comprehensive category under which all the various forms
of love are subsumed. If we look up the word *amour* in a
French dictionary, we will find love "in general" characterized as an *affection profonde*, whereas erotic love in the narrower sense is defined as a *sentiment d'affection* of one sex for
the other.[45]

[42] *Love, Power, Justice* (New York, 1954), 25.

[43] *Begriff der Liebe*, 17.

[44] *The Century Dictionary and Cyclopedia* (New York, 1911), 8:4963.

[45] Cf., say, Littré's *Dictionnaire de la langue française*, 1956 ed.

To conclude this inevitably more or less haphazard inquiry into vocabulary and usage, let me add two remarks about *Russian* (for which I am wholly dependent upon information from others). They concern two remarkable, so it seems to me, peculiarities in the Russian language's vocabulary of love.

First of all, Russian has a word (*lubovatsia*) that seems to mean approximately "to love with the eyes":[46] a form of loving that becomes a reality through seeing. The perspectives that unexpectedly come to mind seem infinite. Plato and all philosophies derived from him maintain that the quality that makes a thing the object of possible love is *beauty*. "Only the beautiful is loved"; "we cannot help loving what is beautiful"—these are two statements by Saint Augustine.[47] If this is true, and if the old definition is also right: *pulchrum est quod visu placet*, to be beautiful means to be "pleasing to sight"[48]— then evidently there can be no true love without approving contemplation, without a looking that as yet is not tinged with the desire to possess. And it is the achievement of the Russian language to bring this aspect of the phenomenon of love to consciousness by having a special term, a word that in itself is lovable, for the concept "to love with the eyes".

The second Russian peculiarity pierces even more deeply into the matter. Usage involves not only what is actually said but also the impossibility of employing a word in certain contexts—linguistic taboos, as it were. In this connection it has been pointed out, on the basis of an analysis of Latin usage, that it evidently never occurred to the Romans that the gods could "love" men.[49] Now, although the dictionaries

---

[46] Abel, *Begriff der Liebe*, 31.

[47] *Confessions*, 4, 13; *On Music*, 6, 13.

[48] The German word *schön* (beautiful) is connected with *schauen* (to see); its literal meaning is "worth seeing".

[49] This would greatly distinguish them from the Greeks. Plato, at any rate, expressed the conviction that the world and man sprang from the goodness of the Creator, who was without jealousy. Cf. *Timaeus*, 29 d.

published within the country after the October Revolution of 1917 repress the fact,[50] the Russian language has a word (*blágost*) for this very concept: the love of God for men! So here is still another semantic element that must be considered by anyone hoping to grasp the concept and, above all, the reality of "love" in its full breadth and depth.

[50] I owe this information to my colleague Professor Hubert Rösel.

II

I F, ACCORDING TO THE MANY VOICES of language, love is
both something that we "practice" and do as conscious
actors and also something that comes over us and happens to
us like an enchantment; if, on the one hand, it is an emotion
directed toward possessing and enjoying and, on the other
hand, a gesture of self-forgetful surrender and giving that
precisely "does not seek its own advantage"; if it is a turning
toward someone, possibly God or other human beings (a
friend, a sweetheart, a son, an unknown who needs our help),
but possibly also toward the manifold good things of life
(sports, science, wine, song); if, finally, it is an act that is as-
cribed to God himself and even in a certain sense is said to be
identical with him ("God is love")—if all this is so, does it
not seem rather improbable that any kind of common element can be assumed to lie behind all these phenomena? In
other words, is there any meaning at all to the universal question: What is the "nature" of love? On the other hand, we are
inclined to feel from the start that the fact of there being one
single word for all this cannot be entirely without some
foundation in reality. But if the recurrent identity underlying
the countless forms of love does exist, how can it be more
exactly described?

My tentative answer to this question runs as follows: In
every conceivable case love signifies much the same as approval. This is first of all to be taken in the literal sense of the
word's root: loving someone or something means finding

him or it *probus*, the Latin word for "good". It is a way of turning to him or it and saying, "It's good that you exist; it's good that you are in this world!"

To avert possible misunderstandings we must elaborate, and almost correct, this definition. I do not mean that the act of love necessarily involves any such bare statement, although that is quite possible. The approval I am speaking of is rather an expression of the *will*. It signifies the opposite of aloof, purely "theoretical" neutrality. It testifies to being in agreement, assenting, consenting, applauding, affirming, praising, glorifying and hailing. Distinct as the difference in intensity is between mere agreement and enthusiastic affirmation, there is one common element in all the members of this series—which, of course, could easily be extended. All the members are, without exception, forms of expression of the will. All of them mean: I want you (or it) to exist! Loving is therefore a mode of willing. If we are somewhat taken aback at this point, to put it mildly, that is due to the narrow conception of willing impressed upon us by certain philosophical and psychological doctrines. We have been taught to restrict the concept of willing to the idea of willing *to do*, in compliance with a much-quoted definition stating that "real willing" means "deciding in favor of actions on the basis of motives".[1] Such activistic restriction has, quite characteristically, also been applied to the concept of knowing—as though knowing consisted solely in the "rational work" of logical thinking and not just as much in the form of "simple intuition", in which we are immediately certain of precisely the fundamental subjects of thinking, such as existence.[2] Thinking is "discursive"—still on the "course" to its

---

[1] Johannes Hoffmeister, *Wörterbuch der philosophischen Begriffe* (Hamburg, 1955), 670.

[2] Cf. Josef Pieper, *Leisure, the Basis of Culture*, rev. ed. (New York, 1964), 9ff.; *Happiness and Contemplation* (New York, 1958), 74, 80.

own proper result; it is, we might put it, knowledge of what is absent. But what the thinking mind is still seeking the intuiting mind has already found; it is present to it and before its gaze; its eye "rests" upon it. Seeing, intuiting, in contrast to thinking, has, it has been said,[3] no "tension toward the future".

Precisely in the same way there is a form of willing that does not aim at doing something still undone and thus acting in the future to change the present state of affairs. Rather, in addition to willing-to-do, there is also a purely affirmative assent to what already is, and this assent is likewise without "future tension"; "le consentement est sans futur".[4] To confirm and affirm something already accomplished—that is precisely what is meant by "to love". It is true that the will, as Thomas Aquinas once remarked, is usually called a "striving force", *vis appetitiva*. "But the will knows not only the act of striving for what it does not yet have but also the other act: of loving what it already possesses and rejoicing in that."[5] A French commentator on Thomas actually distinguishes, in keeping with this pronouncement, between the will as a "force of love" (*puissance d'amour*) and the will as a force for deciding upon choices.[6]

But this equating of willing and loving is not only to be found in the speculations of a more or less specialized literature; it also occurs in ordinary speech. For example, Jerome's Latin Psalter undoubtedly represents Occidental linguistic usage just as much as it helped create that usage. Many times[7] Jerome puts it that God "wills" man (Ps 18:19), "The Lord has brought me forth into a broad place. He delivered me

---

[3] Dietrich von Hildebrand, *Transformation in Christ* (New York, 1948), 96.

[4] Paul Ricoeur, *Philosophie de la volonté*, vol. 1 (Paris, 1963), 322.

[5] *Pot.*, 3, 15 ad 14.

[6] *Somme théologique*, vol. 1, *La Charité* (Paris, 1967), 277f.

[7] For example: Ps 22:9; 41:12.

because he willed me." "Quoniam voluit me." That is quite
legitimately rendered in the translation of the Benedictines
of Beuron Abbey,[8] "Because he loves me". Martin Buber in
his translation of the psalms also plays upon the erotic meaning of love, "He has fetched me out into the broad places; he
unlaces me, for he has pleasure in me."

But it does not suffice to say that aside from willing-to-do
there is "also" love as one among several possible forms of
willing, just as alongside of thinking there is "also" seeing as a
mode of knowing. Rather, in the great tradition of European
thinking about man it has always been held that just as the
immediate certainties of seeing are the foundation and prerequisite of all intellectual activity, so also love is the primal
act of willing that permeates all willing-to-do from its very
source. It is asserted that all volitional decision has its origin
in this fundamental act, that loving is the underlying principle of willing and comes first both in temporal succession
and order of rank. Not only, it is held, is love by its nature the
earliest act of will,[9] and not only is every impulse of the will
derived from love,[10] but love also inspires, as the *principium*,[11]
that is, as the immanent source, all specific decisions and
keeps them in motion.

It is immediately apparent that here we are asserting something that strikes at the root of the whole structure of existence. For if it is true that all beings at the core are nothing
but will,[12] and if the will, of all the forces of the psyche, is the

[8] This has recently been included in the German edition of the Jerusalem
Bible (Freiburg, 1968).

[9] "Primus . . . motus voluntatis et cuiuslibet appetitivae virtutis est amor"
(I, 20, 1).

[10] "Omnis actus appetitivae virtutis ex amore seu dilectione derivatur" (I,
60, prologue). Cf. also I, 20; *C. G.* 1, 4, 19.

[11] *Car.* 21: "principium omnium voluntiarum affectionum".

[12] Augustine, *City of God*, 14, 6.

dominant and most powerful force,[13] then love as the primal act of the will is simultaneously the point of origin and the center of existence as a whole. What kind of person one is will be decided at this point.[14] "Ex amore suo quisque vivit, vel bene vel male"—Whether for good or evil, each man lives by his love.[15] It is his love and it alone that must be "in order" for the person as a whole to be "right" and good. There is, says Augustine,[16] a very brief definition of virtue (and "virtue" means nothing but "human rightness"): "Virtus est ordo amoris."

Now, however, we are not speaking of virtue and of rightness but of the fact that love is an act, in fact the primal act, of the will. But what is it that I really "will" by loving? What do I want when I turn to another person and say: It's good that you exist? It is clear, as has already been noted, that this can be said and meant with very different kinds of orchestration. *In concreto* many different degrees of intensity are conceivable. Still, even the weakest degree evidently testifies to approval of the mere existence of the other person; and that certainly is no small thing. We need only try to answer with complete sincerity the test question: Do I really in my heart of hearts have "nothing against" (this being probably the minimal degree of approval) the existence of this particular, unique associate, neighbor or housemate? And to move from that to: "How wonderful that you exist!" In saying that, what do I really have in mind? What am I really getting at? What precisely is it that I am "willing"?

Such writers as Thomas Aquinas, Ortega y Gasset, Vladimir Soloviev and Maurice Blondel have replied to this ques-

---

[13] Thomas Aquinas, II, II, 34, 4.

[14] "Talis est quisque, qualis eius dilectio" (Augustine, *In Epistolam Johannis ad Parthos* 2, 14; PL 35:1997).

[15] Augustine, *Contra Faustum* 5, 10; PL 42:228.

[16] *City of God* 15, 22.

tion with astonishing unanimity in basic intent, although the radicality of some of their statements sometimes makes their point too strongly and renders their answers of dubious value if not downright wrong. Thomas Aquinas in his now famous beginner's textbook avers: The first thing that a lover "wills" is for the beloved to exist and live.[17] "The 'I' who loves above all wants the existence of the 'You'."[18] The somewhat forgotten phenomenologist and logician Alexander Pfänder, a magnificent analyst of the mental processes, calls love "an act of partisanship for the existence of the beloved"[19] and even "a continual affirmative keeping the beloved in existence";[20] the lover "confers upon the beloved the right to exist on his own authority".[21]

It is true that we read these last two sentences with a feeling of uneasiness; something seems to be wrong. Is this not sentimentally overestimating the powers of a loving person? Ortega y Gasset, although basically intending to make the same point, puts it much more precisely and circumspectly: As lovers, he says, we "continually and intentionally give life to something that depends on us."[22] The lover "refuses to accept the possibility of a universe without it."[23] Maurice Blondel boldly asserts: "L'amour est par excellence ce qui fait

---

[17] "Primo vult suum amicum esse et vivere" (II, II, 25, 7). Thomas does not even shrink from the conclusion that this assent of the will extends, for one who loves out of supernatural *caritas*, even to the demons, to the fallen angels! We want (*volumus*), he writes in the same *Summa theologica*, in the treatise on *caritas*, that those spirits may be sustained and preserved in what they are by nature (II, II, 25, 11).

[18] Maurice Nédoncelle, *Vers une philosophie de l'amour et de la personne* (Paris, 1957), 15.

[19] "Zur Psychologie der Gesinnungen", *Jahrbuch für Philosophie und phänomenologische Forschung*, 1 (1925), 368.

[20] Ibid., 370.

[21] Ibid., 369.

[22] *On Love* (New York, 1957), 20.

[23] Ibid.

être"[24]—love is above all what "makes be", that is, what makes something or someone exist. But again we can accept this sententious phrase only if we understand it as bespeaking the lover's *intention*.

By far the most extreme formulation of the idea that is struggling to emerge through all these different phrases is to be found in Vladimir Soloviev's essay "On the Meaning of Sexual Love",[25] in which he describes love as a force that excludes death, protests against it and actually denies it. I confess that I react to such a statement with perplexed astonishment. Perhaps we may say that true love makes us realize, more directly than any theorizing can, that the beloved as a person cannot simply drop out of reality, and even— though this to be sure will be evident only to the believer— the beloved will be physically resurrected and live forever, through death and beyond it. This, at any rate, is the way I have always understood Gabriel Marcel's moving words: "To love a person means to say: You will not die."[26] This is certainly "partisanship for the existence of the beloved";[27] a more intense partisanship cannot be conceived. But does it make sense to say of human love, as Vladimir Soloviev does, that it excludes death and that the inevitability of dying is "incompatible with true love"?[28] That, it seems to me, is crossing a boundary that might almost be called the border with madness.

In a trenchant and witty phrase, Nietzsche has said, "There is always some madness in love; but there is also always some

---

[24] *Exigences philosophiques du Christianisme* (Paris, 1950), 241.

[25] *Deutsche Gesamtausgabe der Werke von Vladimir Solowjew*, ed. Wl. Szylkarski, vol. 7 (Munich, 1953).

[26] *Geheimnis des Seins* (Vienna, 1952), 472.

[27] Pfänder, *Psychologie der Gesinnungen*, 368.

[28] *Sinn der Geschlechterliebe*, 235.

sense in madness."[29] Thus, at least a grain of truth may be detected in all these hyperboles, even in Soloviev's concept. Starting from such different bases, all these attempts to describe phenomenologically what love is really about ascribe to it the power to sustain existence (keeping the beloved in being; conferring the right to exist; giving existence; and even annulment of death and mortality). Certainly the fact that they all agree on this should cause us to reflect. Granted, these statements tend rashly to overlook the limits imposed upon finite man. Nevertheless, they all bring into the range of vision an aspect of reality that is worth considering. More precisely, two aspects are involved.

First, let us remember that "the most marvellous of all things a being can do is to be."[30] Existence itself, "la présence effective dans le monde",[31] this simple "act" of being in existence—this being that is so completely incomprehensible and subject to no definition whatsoever, is conferred upon us and all other beings by love and by love alone. And precisely this is what we know and corroborate when we ourselves love. For what the lover gazing upon his beloved says and means is *not*: How good that you are *so* (so clever, useful, capable, skillful), but: It's good that you are; how wonderful that you exist!

Second, the other element in these claims that remains true in spite of the seeming frenzy of the statements is this: that in fact the most extreme form of affirmation that can possibly be conceived of is *creatio,* making to be, in the strict sense of the word. "Creation is the comparative of affirmation."[32]

---

[29] *Also sprach Zarathustra* I, in *Gesammelte Werke* (Munich: Musarion-Ausgabe, 1922), 13:46.

[30] Étienne Gilson, *History of Christian Philosophy in the Middle Ages* (London, 1955), 83.

[31] In an interview in the weekly *Action* (December 29, 1944). Cf. also Jean Paul Sartre, *L'Existentialisme est un humanisme* (Paris, 1946), 18.

[32] Georg Simmel, *Fragmente und Aufsätze* (Munich, 1923), 24.

And I am convinced that no one more fully appreciates this, no one is more persuaded of it beyond all argumentation and proof, than the true lover. He "knows" that his affirmation directed toward the beloved would be pointless were not some other force akin to creation involved—and, moreover, a force not merely preceding his own love but one that is still at work and that he himself, the loving person, participates in and helps along by loving. Granted, such intimations would immediately lose all credence if they seriously tried to attribute to any human being, no matter how passionate or heroic a lover he might be, any really creative power in the strict sense. It is God who in the act of creation anticipated all conceivable human love and said: I will you to be; it is good, "very good" (Gen 1:31), that you exist. He has already infused everything that human beings can love and affirm, goodness along with existence, and that means lovability and affirmability.[33] Human love, therefore, is by its nature and must inevitably be always an imitation and a kind of repetition of this perfected and, in the exact sense of the word, *creative* love of God. And perhaps the lover is not unaware of this before reflecting at all. How otherwise, for example, can we understand what is perhaps too rarely considered: that even the very first stirrings of love contain an element of gratitude? But gratitude is a reply; it is knowing that one has been referred to something prior, in this case to a larger frame of universal reference that supersedes the realm of immediate empirical knowledge.

Now, however, the "but" must follow the "yes". Yes, all human love is an echo of the divine, creative, prime affirmation by virtue of which everything that is—including therefore what we *in concreto* love—has at once received existence and goodness. *But*: if all goes happily as it should, then in

---

[33] "Amor Dei est infundens et creans bonitatem in rebus" (I, 20, 2).

human love something *more* takes place than mere echo, mere repetition and imitation. What takes place is a continuation and in a certain sense even a perfecting of what was begun in the course of creation.

III

BUT THEN, if a human being already exists anyhow, could we not say that it does not matter whether a lover finds this fact wonderful and affirms it? Does it really add or take away anything that someone says, "It's good that you exist"?

It is clear that in asking this question, which sounds so extremely "realistic", we are basically asking what is the "function" of love within the whole of existence; what is it supposed to do and accomplish in the world. It is one and the same question that we have to answer at this point. But in order to answer this it admittedly does not suffice to analyze, no matter how precisely, the lover's intention and what is "really" willed and meant by the one who feels loving concern. We must move across to the other shore, that is, we must examine the matter from the point of view of the person who happens to be loved. What is really taking place on his side? Soberly considered, what does it mean for a person that another turns to him and says (or thinks, or experiences), "It's good that you exist"?

On this matter let me first give the floor to Jean Paul Sartre, a writer from whom we should have expected a radically different answer from the one he actually gives. According to the "theory" he has systematically developed, every human being is in principle alien to every other, who by looking at him threatens to steal the world from him; everyone is a danger to everyone else's existence, a potential executioner. But fortunately, the creative artist in Sartre, or simply the brilliant observer and describer of human reality, repeatedly rises up against merely intellectual theses. And the artist in him, altogether unconcerned about his own "philosophy", will then say things like this: "This is the basis for the joy of love . . . : we feel that our existence is justified."[1] As may be seen, that is not so very far from the above-mentioned notions of "giving existence" and "conferring the right to exist." Here, however, the matter is seen, not from the lover's point of view, but from that of the beloved. Obviously, then, it does not suffice us simply to exist; we can do that "anyhow". What matters to us, beyond mere existence, is the explicit confirmation: It is *good* that you exist; how wonderful that you are! In other words, what we need over and above sheer existence is: to be loved by another person. That is an astonishing fact when we consider it closely. Being created by God actually does not suffice, it would seem; the fact of creation needs continuation and perfection by the creative power of human love.

But this seemingly astonishing fact is repeatedly confirmed by the most palpable experience, of the kind that everyone has day after day. We say that a person "blossoms" when undergoing the experience of being loved; that he becomes wholly himself for the first time; that a "new life" is beginning for him—and so forth. For a child, and to all appearances even for the still unborn child, being loved by the mother is literally *the* precondition for its own thriving. This material love need not necessarily be "materialized" in specific acts of beneficence. What is at any rate more decisive is that concern and approval which are given from the very core of existence—we need not hesitate to say, which come from the heart—and which are directed toward the core of existence, the heart, of the child. Only such concern and ap-

[1] *Being and Nothingness* (New York, 1956), 371.

proval do we call real "love". The observations of René Spitz[2] have become fairly well known. He studied children born in prison and brought up in scarcely comfortable outward conditions by their imprisoned mothers. These he compared with other children raised without their mothers but in well-equipped, hygienically impeccable American infants' and children's homes by excellently trained nurses. The result of the comparison is scarcely surprising: in regard to illness, mortality and susceptibility to neuroses, the children raised in prison were far better off. Not that the nurses had performed their tasks in a merely routine manner and with "cold objectivity". But it is simply not enough to be able to eat to satiation, not to freeze, to have a roof overhead and everything else that is essential to life. The institutionalized children had all such needs satisfied. They received plenty of "milk"; what was lacking was—the "honey". This allusion to the biblical metaphor of the "land flowing with milk and honey" (Ex 3:8) is to be found in the masterly essay by Erich Fromm, *The Art of Loving*,[3] which has had unusual success as a book. (That success may have had something to do with a misunderstanding assiduously furthered by the publisher's advertising,[4] which almost kept me from reading the excellent *opusculum*.) Milk, Erich Fromm says,[5] is meant as the quintessence of everything a person requires for allaying the mere needs of life; but honey is the symbol for the sweetness of life and the happiness of existing. And this is precisely what comes across when we are told what the children in the institutions apparently never heard: How good that you exist!

---

[2] "Hospitalism", in *The Psychoanalytic Study of the Child*, vol. 1 (London, 1945).

[3] *The Art of Loving* (New York, 1952).

[4] The cover of the American pocketbook edition (Bantam Books, New York) speaks of "the world-famous psychiatrist's *daring* prescription for love".

[5] Ibid., 41f.

Incidentally, Erich Fromm continues,[6] among people as a whole, not just children, we can very well distinguish those who have received only the milk from those who have received both milk and honey.[7]

When we consider this, what has been said about the creativity of human love also suddenly acquires a wholly new-found meaning. In human love the creative act of the Deity in establishing existence is continued—so that one who is consciously experiencing love can say, "I need you in order to be myself. . . . In loving me you give me myself, *you let me be*."[8] Put differently, "What being loved makes being do is precisely: be."[9] Of course, such language can be misunderstood, as we have said, and can be quite wrong if it is taken "absolutely". But what all such phrases quite rightly express is that man succeeds in fully "existing" and feeling at home in the world only when he is "being confirmed"[10] by the love of another. Above all, the ability to love, in which our own existence achieves its highest intensification, presupposes the experience of being loved by someone else.

Incidentally, Erich Fromm's little book also explicitly speaks of the creation of man by God—with that magnificent lack of embarrassment which it would seem a European achieves only under the influence of the intellectual climate of the American continent. According to Genesis, God did not

---

[6] Ibid., 42.

[7] My colleague Professor Paul Oswald has called my attention to the fact that similar wording is found in the works of Maria Montessori. In her last book (*The Formation of Man*), she sums up the education of children according to her convictions in the sentence: "The whole secret lies in two words: milk and love" (*Über die Bildung des Menschen* [Freiburg, 1966], 93).

[8] Robert O. Johann, *Building the Human* (New York, 1968), 161.

[9] Frederick D. Wilhelmsen, *The Metaphysics of Love* (New York, 1962), 139.

[10] Karl Marx in his youth used this very phrase. Cf. Karl Marx, *Texte zu Methode und Praxis II* (Hamburg: Rowohlts Klassiker, 1968), 180.

simply make the universe and man exist. He gave man instead a taste of the honey as well as the milk; that is, he specifically confirmed their existence and literally declared it "good, very good".[11] Now it cannot be altogether unimportant to man's being-in-the-world whether or not he is able to experience himself and his existence as something approved in so absolute a manner. To so experience it he must, of course, think of himself and the world as *creatura*. Whether this is an assumption that can be justified only by faith or whether it can also be supported and explained by rational arguments (which I happen to think it can be) is a question that need not be explored here.

In any case, the conviction that the universe has been created cannot possibly remain confined to any one special "sector" of existence—not if it is to be anything more than an abstract tenet carried around in the head. We cannot just file it away in a "philosophical-religious" pigeonhole. Once it has been thought through to the end, consistently and vitally, it inevitably affects our entire sense of being. For it then follows that all of reality (things, man, we ourselves) presents itself to us as something creatively conceived, something designed, hence something that had a distinct purpose from the start (an idea that, as is well known, Jean Paul Sartre passionately repudiated).[12] Above all we have then to view all reality, again including ourselves, as something creatively willed and affirmed, whose existence depends solely on being so affirmed and loved.

Once we perceive this context, we are awakened to the full meaning of a dictum that long ago degenerated into a sterile schoolbook text: the statement of the existential goodness of all things (*omne ens est bonum*). Augustine says in the last chapter of his *Confessions*, "We see things because they exist; but

[11] *Art of Loving*, 41.
[12] Cf. *L'Existentialisme est un humanisme* (Paris, 1946), 21ff.

they exist because Thou seest them."[13] There is an analogous principle at work in our context: Because God wills and affirms things, man and the universe as a whole, therefore and solely for this reason they are good, which is to say, lovable and affirmable, to us also.

We have, however, drifted once more into somewhat abstract and general realms. But instead of addressing ourselves to the enormous implications of this thought, let us rather consider what the concrete experience of being ourselves approved by the Creator might possibly mean. What really matters here is the living experience. In the example of René Spitz, the mothers' love, no matter how heartfelt, would be no help at all to the small children if they could not be reached in some way, if they did not "know" that they were loved. In the same way, of course, the Creator's approval can only really affect and change man's life when he "realizes" it believingly, that is, when he also "accepts" it. (In general, knowledge really becomes a part of our vital stock only when we want to perceive it.)

Perhaps at this point we have to refer to a possible counter-position, such as Spinoza's terrifying conception that "God, strictly speaking, loves no one",[14] in order to grasp the incredible alternative: that our own existence in fact testifies to nothing less than our being loved by the Creator. What this can specifically mean for man's relationship to the cosmos is movingly expressed by a remarkable, little-known writer with somewhat old-fashioned solemnity, "But insomuch as God loves me because I am I, I am truly irreplaceable in the world."[15]

---

[13] Bk. 13, chap. 38.

[14] "Deus proprie loquendo neminem amat" (*Ethica* 5, propos. 17, corollarium).

[15] Ladislaus Grünhut, *Eros und Agape. Eine metaphysisch-religionsphilosophische Untersuchung* (Leipzig, 1931), 20.

It seems clear to me that only through a conviction such as this can man achieve solid ground underfoot, within his own consciousness, as well. Presumably there exists something like a prime trustfulness by virtue of which one can live a "simple" life (in the biblical sense of "simple"),[16] that is, ultimately without complications (I am thinking of a character like the girl Chantal in George Bernanos' novel *Joy*). And if such prime trustfulness does exist, then it must consist in nothing less than the certainty of being so surpassingly, effectively and absolutely loved. I recall the words of a great student of human nature and a master of spirituality:[17] that simplicity, and he was referring here to the *simplicitas* of the New Testament, was at bottom nothing but "trusting to love". And with the peril of "loss of identity" so much discussed nowadays, it may be asked whether there is any other remedy for such dislocation than this experience of existing because of being absolutely, irrevocably willed by the Creator. Granted, only faith can provide anyone with that feeling. But compared with the absolute stability of this foundation, the oft-praised "basis in solid facts" is truly quaking ground.

Within man, however, there is also a tendency to fend off the creative love that unasked and undeservedly has given him his own existence.[18] At bottom all love is undeserved. We can neither earn it nor promote it; it is always pure gift. It is even, as the motto of this book puts it, the "prime gift" that makes all other gifts possible. But there seems to be in man something like an aversion for receiving gifts. No one is

[16] Mt 6:22.

[17] This is the Jesuit Stanislaus, Count of Dunin-Borkowski (1864–1934), known to scholarship chiefly by his work in several volumes on Spinoza (Münster, 1910–1936).

[18] Sartre, for example, interprets the idea that God "determined Adam's nature" as something in itself incompatible with human freedom. *L'Être et le Néant*, 622.

wholly unfamiliar with the thought: I don't want anything
for nothing! And this emotion comes uncannily close to the
other: I don't want to be "loved", and certainly not for no
reason! It was Nietzsche who made the acute remark that
"people addicted to honor", that is, people for whom their
own importance is what chiefly matters, are "resistant to being loved".[19] And C. S. Lewis says that absolutely undeserved
love is certainly what we need but not at all the kind of love
we want. "We want to be loved for our cleverness, beauty,
generosity, fairness, usefulness."[20] But the divine love of, as
Dante puts it, the "First Lover" does not find anything of the
kind to hand; as the possible object of his love nothing yet
exists: *nihil*. But C. S. Lewis also speaks of the shocking fact
of a (really or presumably or allegedly) "groundless" love of
human beings for one another. This fact is so well known
that people of ill will may even claim to love another person
with a love they call Christian—because they know that this
precisely will offend: "To say to one who expects a renewal
of Affection, Friendship or Eros, 'I forgive you as a Christian,' is merely a way of continuing the quarrel. Those who
say it are of course lying. But the thing would not be falsely
said in order to wound unless, were it true, it would be
wounding."[21]

But even if loving concern is innocently and gratefully experienced and accepted—whether this be the primal love of
God or the love of a loving person, which is our principal
theme here—the recipient is apt to feel something else besides encouragement and corroboration of his own existence.
There is also, quite understandably, a sense of something akin
to shame; being loved, one feels ashamed. It would seem that

[19] *Menschliches, Allzumenschliches* I, no. 603.
[20] C. S. Lewis, *The Four Loves* (London, 1960), 150.
[21] Ibid.

Plato first made mention of this truly curious fact. In the *Symposium*,[22] he has Phaedrus, the young man who is passionately stirred by the power of eros, speak at first of the fact that only lovers feel ashamed of doing anything shameful in each others' presence. But are they not ashamed because by loving each regards the other as better than he really *is*, objectively considered? The matter is somewhat more complicated than it seems at first sight.

First of all we must realize that the sense of shame we are dealing with here is a beneficial one; it has a "positive" aspect. For there also exists the contrary phenomenon of a destructive, "negative" sense of shame. This may also be bound up with the sense a person has that his real character by no means matches the opinion that people have (or had) of him. But because this shame is concerned principally with "exposure", such a feeling remains sterile; it obstructs the person affected instead of opening a path for him. In this connection we might well be reminded that the widespread practice of exposing a person to public ridicule, which has become standard fare for the "media" and is expected of them and greeted with amused interest, was once regarded in Occidental ethics as a specific form of injustice, the *peccatum derisionis*, a sin because it diminishes something that belongs to a man by right.[23]

On the other hand, the "positive" and fruitful shaming that affects us in the experience of being loved, and probably only there, has something to do with the anticipatory nature of all true love. Granted, the lover is one who approves and affirms what is. Nevertheless, this affirmation of the beloved is in no way an undifferentiated approval of pure factuality. And the beloved is well aware that loving approval cannot be intended in this sense. That is the source of a discrepancy that

[22] *Symposium* 178 d–179 a.
[23] Cf. II, II, 75, 1; 75, 1 ad 3.

repeatedly comes to light and that provides a very solid reason for feeling ashamed. Anyone who judges himself more or less without illusions knows perfectly well that what the lover tirelessly asserts simply is not true: How wonderful that you exist; it's glorious that you are; I love you! Perhaps others are saying bad things about you, but this person who loves you looks into your eyes and says, "I know you too well; you cannot possibly have ever done something like that!" In the Duc de La Rochefoucauld's *Maxims* there is the sardonic sentence: However people praise us, they are telling us nothing new. That is precisely the situation of lovers: Whatever the beloved is praised for comes as nothing new to the lover even though the beloved realizes that the praise is false and that he himself is far from glorious.

But that is only one side of the coin. The other side is that such praise of the beloved, although it may not correspond to actual facts, is not necessarily simply false. In saying this we are, it must be granted, making several assumptions. Above all we are assuming that a real lover is speaking in a truly human fashion, that we are not hearing the casually phrased "mating calls" of mere sensuality. Furthermore, the lover must be able to perceive what the "purpose" of the other's being is and what he is meant by nature to attain. This in turn seems to confirm the old dictum that where love is an eye will open[24] so that the lover alone may succeed in perceiving the beloved's very purpose in being. In spite of everything that is, the beloved feels neither mistakenly lauded nor unappreciated nor "misunderstood". Nicolai Hartmann in his *Ethics*[25] uses that word: "Instead of feeling misunderstood, he [the beloved who has been thus praised] feels rather understood

---

[24] "Ubi amor, ibi oculus." This maxim by Richard of St. Victor (Benjamin Minor, cap. 13) is also cited by Thomas Aquinas, for example, in the *Commentary on the Sentences* (3, d. 35, 1, 2, 1).

[25] Nicolai Hartmann, *Ethik*, 3d ed. (Berlin, 1949), 538.

in a basic manner—and at the same time strongly urged to be as the other sees him."

Whether he does feel so strongly urged and whether, as Hartmann adds,[26] he will really be "pushed beyond himself"—although within rational limits—is a question dependent on another assumption: that the beloved for his part accepts this shaming and challenging love and responds lovingly to it. Suddenly he too now knows, perhaps for the first time, that he really could be and would be so "grand", that he could really achieve this special style of fairness, of bravery—*if* he actually carried out what he was made for and what the lover's eye has intuitively perceived through all the shells of empirical inadequacy.

Oddly enough—we must interject this here—being loved, or, more strictly, *wanting* to be loved, has come in for a good deal of scorn in recent times. It certainly does not enjoy a friendly press, and I think that this fact, complex as is everything that has to do with the subject of "love", conceals something hard to fathom but rather important. Nietzsche[27] called wanting to be loved "the greatest of all presumptions". In psychoanalytical literature it is noted with disapproval[28] that most people see the problem of love as more one of being loved than of loving. Even Brecht comments that love is "the desire to give something, not to receive", and holds that the desire, or at any rate "the immoderate desire to be loved", has "little to do with genuine love".[29]

---

[26] Ibid. Franz von Baader also speaks of "that natural phantasmagoria as a consequence of which lovers mutually seem more beautiful, more lovable, more perfect and better than they are; but he adds realistically that the lovers ought to "take this rapture . . . only as an encouraging summons". *Sätze aus der erotischen Philosophie* (1828). Republished under the same title, ed. G.-K. Kaltenbrunner (Frankfurt: Sammlung Insel, 1966), 109.

[27] *Menschliches, Allzumenschliches* I, no. 523.

[28] *Art of Loving*, 1.

[29] *Gesammelte Werke* (Frankfurt: Suhrkamp Verlag, 1967), 12:407.

At first hearing all this sounds rather plausible; and to the extent that we keep our eye on infrahuman relations there is a good measure of truth in it. Plato, however, throws fresh light on the matter when he says that the lover is "more divine" than the beloved.[30] We might explicate the insight embodied in this phrase in a variety of ways, including the following: One would have to be God in order to be capable of loving without being dependent on being loved in return; it is a divine privilege always to be less the beloved than the lover; we (human beings) can never love God as intensely as he loves us; but above all: in his relationship to God it is quite appropriate for man to be loved more than to love. If we consider this last aspect, we may well wonder whether the general disparagement of wanting to be loved may not be a typically modern phenomenon, still another form of modern man's claim to equality with God.

Here, at any rate, is the point to remind ourselves of those thought-provoking phrases of Sigmund Freud, who speaks of the "part played by love in the genesis of conscience"[31] and defines "evil" as that "for which we are threatened with loss of love".[32] In all "guilt feelings", he argues, "fear of the loss of love"[33] is at work, the fear "that we will no longer be loved by this supreme power".[34] What "supreme power"? In his attempt to answer this question Freud misses the opportunity implicit in his magnificent beginning by defining that "supreme power" as the "mythical father of prehistoric times"[35] who, projected by way of the "Oedipus complex" into the collective and individual consciousness, engenders—as a "superego"—fear and guilt feelings. And in Freud's own view,

[30] *Symposium* 180 b.
[31] *Gesammelte Werke* (London, 1940–), 14:492.
[32] Ibid., 484.
[33] Ibid., 487.
[34] Ibid., 486.
[35] Ibid., 489f.

that, of course, is a wholly groundless, irrational reaction from which people ought to free themselves by bringing it to consciousness and "analyzing" it.

What Freud is calling for is clear: emancipation from dependence on the desire to be loved, which he views as founded on illusion, and therefore from the fear of losing love. Of course there is no denying what the researches of Sigmund Freud have compellingly demonstrated: that the conflict with the father (for instance) can be of enormous importance to psychic growth, to the formation of conscience, to the genesis of guilt feelings and also, sometimes, to the neurotically rampant growth of such guilt feelings. But can the Freudian explanation ultimately account for the psychological experience of *being* guilty? What if our existence itself really depended upon being wanted and being loved, not by an imaginary prehistoric father figure, but by an extremely real, absolute Someone, by the Creator himself? And what if at bottom being guilty ("sin") were really lack of being, resistance—to the extent that it is up to us—to that creative want and love of another in which, as we have already said, our existence literally consists? That, to be sure, is a totally different matter; and yet does not everything that Freud, with the penetration of genius, has to say about the part that love, including our own love, plays in the genesis of conscience and in the fear of losing love suddenly acquire a remarkable pertinacity within this framework?

When such thoughts are followed out, perhaps the familiar or even all too familiar Christian ideas of "a life pleasing to God" and of the "desire to please God" suddenly regain—or gain for the first time—something approaching the color of reality. As we have already said, in this realm words are constantly losing not only their sheen and their expressiveness but even their very meanings. The moment comes when they are nothing but sounding brass and can no longer be used seriously. (Consequently we must try to keep them alive and contemporaneous by special linguistic efforts!) Well, then: "desire to please"—surely that must mean much the same as desire to be loved? The word *eudokeín* (to be pleased with) occurs dozens of times in biblical Greek; from the purely semantic point of view, "of all expressions for choosing" it conveys "most strongly the emotional tone of the chooser's love", according to the Kittel.[36] At any rate, it once again becomes evident that the fundamental aspects of existence (desire to be loved, loss of love, guilt, conscience, being "pleasing to God") may be found in close proximity. Within the same context we will also find the concept of "glory" (*gloria*), which the ancients unabashedly defined as "clara cum laude notitia",[37] that is to say, as "fame", as being publicly taken notice of and recognized by God himself. At first it is actually a bit embarrassing, not to say shocking, to find the thing described so "naïvely". But the shock aims and hits deeper than we may think. For when we are asked to understand *gloria* as the supreme fulfillment of existence, as the "glory" of eternal life, we are expected to do two things. The first is to admit to ourselves that in our heart of hearts there is hardly anything we want so ardently as to be publicly "praised" and acknowledged. The second requirement is that we do not fall prey to the ideal of tight-lipped self-sufficiency, that gloomy resolve to take nothing as a gift, or fall into the infantilism of needing constant confirmation. In other words, we are asked to adopt an attitude that might best be characterized as "childlikeness": a way of leading our life so that we actually achieve *gloria*, that is, the acknowledgment by the "First Lover", who now "publicly", that is, in the presence of all creation, at once declares and sees to it that it is "glorious" to be the person we are.

[36] *Theologisches Wörterbuch zum Neuen Testament*, 2:738.
[37] Augustine, *Contra Maximinum* 2, 13; PL 42:770; similarly, 40:22.

IV

WE HAVE SEEN THAT LOVING CONCERN, although it actually confirms the beloved in his existence, can also have a shaming element. This fact—which seems paradoxical only at first glance—indicates that love is not synonymous with undifferentiated approval of everything the beloved person thinks and does in real life. As a corollary, love is also not synonymous with the wish for the beloved to feel good always and in every situation and for him to be spared experiencing pain or grief in all circumstances. "Mere 'kindness' which tolerates anything except [the beloved's] suffering"[1] has nothing to do with real love. Saint Augustine expressed the same idea in a wide variety of phrases: "Love reprimands, ill will echoes";[2] "the friend speaks bitterly and loves, the disguised foe flatters and hates."[3] No lover can look on easily when he sees the one he loves preferring convenience to the good. Those who love young people cannot share the delight they seem to feel in (as it were) lightening their knapsacks and throwing away the basic rations they will eventually need when the going gets rough.

But, it might be argued, doesn't "loving someone" virtually mean: taking him as he really is "with all his weaknesses and faults"? After all, what else is it supposed to mean when

---

[1] C. S. Lewis, *The Problem of Pain* (New York: Macmillan Company, 1967), 34.

[2] *In Epistolam Johannis ad Parthos* 7, 8; PL 35:2033.

[3] *Sermones de tempore* 49, 4; PL 38:322.

someone says, "It's good that you are; it's wonderful that you exist"? In response I would first of all suggest that "exist" signifies, not a purely static being-there, but something that is in process and that "continues". And of course the lover wishes it to continue *well*. But what about the weaknesses and faults? Are they not inevitably a part of actual existence?

To answer this question at all adequately, several distinctions must first be considered—above all, two. *First*, the distinction between, in brief, "weakness" and "guilt". "I'm a slow thinker and too quick to condemn; I have a tendency to fly off the handle—you'll have to take me the way I am!" This could, it seems to me, properly be said to one who claims to love us; this is not asking too much—even though, obviously, we can only be asking him to love us *in spite of* our weaknesses, not to love those weaknesses themselves. But compared with that, would it not be an entirely different matter if someone were to say, "I happen to be unjust, self-centered, dissolute (and so on)—and if you love me you'll have to take me the way I am"? Does not real love actually exclude that kind of acceptance and approval? Or, on the contrary, does real love perhaps begin only when faced with such faults?

At this point a *second* distinction proves essential, the distinction between two different ways of accepting something bad. One of these ways is proper to a lover; the other is not. I am referring to the distinction between excusing and forgiving.

As we all know, ordinary language does not draw too sharp a line between the areas of meaning covered by these two words. But their significance is fundamentally different. By "excusing" we mean discounting what is bad. We "let it be" although it is bad; we ignore the evil; we don't care; we are indifferent to it; we don't worry about it. Now there is very little if anything that a lover should "excuse" in the above sense—whereas he can forgive the beloved *everything*. In fact, forgiveness is one of the fundamental acts of love. But what specifically is meant by that? Certainly it does not mean "letting be" something bad, simply not regarding it as important—as though it were a mere oversight. We forgive something only if we regard it as distinctly bad, not if we ignore its negative aspect. And only forgiveness takes the other's personal dignity seriously; we are then not seeing him as a kind of apparatus that occasionally suffers functional disturbances and "breakdowns". Rather, we are seeing him as a person who has *done* something.

On the other hand, forgiveness seems to assume that the other himself condemns ("repents") what he has done and that he accepts the forgiveness. If we attempt to "forgive" someone although he stands by his wickedness and wants no forgiveness, we are in a very literal sense declaring him not of sound mind, not responsible for his actions. Moreover, strictly speaking, we can forgive and pardon only something that has been done to ourselves. But, as we have said, in all these matters ordinary language is not very precise and consistent, which is not to deny that it is expressive and valid.

Let us take as an example a man living under conditions of despotism who has saved his life (or his job or his fortune) by an act of betrayal. What he betrayed may have been his own convictions or even a friend. What is the situation of the woman who loves this man with regard to excusing and forgiving? Specifically, all sorts of possibilities are conceivable. Perhaps this man is deceiving himself, glossing over his own failure, twisting his account of it to make himself seem guiltless, in any case "excusing" himself. To reinforce his efforts along these lines would, of course, smack more of complicity than real love. The true lover will not want the beloved to persist in such self-deception. He necessarily wishes him to free himself from it—which, of course, is not to say how this

wish might be expressed or whether it would have to be expressed at all. But, in any case, love cannot accept what is bad;
love "excuses" *nothing*.

It is conceivable, too, that the man in question recognizes
the inexcusability of his action, does not try to find any ex-
tenuation for it and suffers because there is no longer a way
to make up for it. His wife, although she lovingly sympa-
thizes with his anguish, nevertheless could not wish him to
be unaffected by what has happened. And although the act of
injustice may not have involved her, she could grant him
something like forgiveness precisely because he is suffering—
although an outsider might scarcely be able to distinguish
between her forgiveness and a mere excusing of his fault
("Let it be; think no more about it").

The fact remains that to love a person does not mean to
wish him to live free of all burdens. It means, rather, to wish
that everything associated with him may truly be good. From
this point of view, the phrase about love's "inflexibility",
which comes up so frequently in Western moral philosophy,
loses some of its strangeness. To be sure, it is hard to determine once and for all the boundary at which love's severity
becomes loveless harshness, so that *in concreto* it can be almost
impossible to distinguish excusing from forgiving and weakness from guilt.

Sometimes it is instructive to take an extreme example
from which to read the answer to a difficult question. What
it means really to love another person is such a question.
Nor do we have to devise hypothetical cases for our purpose. A beloved person in the situation of a martyr is not at
all inconceivable; we may think either of the mothers of
young Christians facing the Roman proconsul or the wives
of persecuted innocent men before the "people's courts" of
modern dictatorships. Naturally these women do not want
to lose their beloved sons or husbands; naturally they are

horrified at the thought of what is facing them; and of course they hope with all their hearts that their men may in some miraculous manner escape their fate and be restored to them. But could these women in all seriousness, out of love, wish that the person they love so dearly would accept the opportunity, or even the offer, to buy their freedom by an act of baseness? We are concerned now, it must be remembered, not with the "casuistical" discussion of moral standards and certainly not with the question of how we ourselves might actually behave in such a situation. Our only point here is to bring to light by the exercise of our judgment on such an extreme case in what terms we desire everything to go perfectly well for a person close to us— which is to say, in what terms love operates.

I said "our judgment". For whether or not we are clearly conscious of it, our opinion of what love ultimately is reaches out far beyond the limits of our own direct experience. In the nature of things, everything we think about the world as a whole enters into this universal concept. And even those who declare human existence to be simply absurd, or who see it gloomily unfolding under the decrees of a blind fate, still have an inkling of that all-embracing love whose absence they lament or denounce. In the very manner of negation or mockery or perhaps even respect for the mystery of it all, there is present in the mind, whenever the world's evil is considered, some conception of *that* love which "turning moves the Sun and the other stars", as the last line of Dante's cosmic poem puts it. What I am saying is: an inevitable concomitant of thinking about love is some conception of what the love of God, the "First Lover", must be like.

And although, superficially considered, we would be quite pleased with a "senile benevolence who . . . liked to see the young people enjoying themselves",[4] we nevertheless know very well that the all-embracing love of him who desires everything to go perfectly well for the world and man cannot be of this nature. Certainly our occasional timidity is not altogether incomprehensible. We may well wish sometimes that "God had designed for us a less glorious and less arduous destiny". But in our hearts we surely do not deceive ourselves; we know that in that case we are wishing, "not for more love, but for less".[5] Incidentally, such a desire to escape the demands of love was so familiar to the thinkers of the past that they cited it among the seven "deadly sins" as *acedia*, that slothfulness of the heart to which Kierkegaard gave the name of "despair of weakness". By that he meant the despair of a man's not daring to be what he is. The upshot of all this indicates that our human understanding would never have found it so "unfathomable" that, as the mystics say, God's love can be "a thousand times sterner and harsher" than his justice.[6] We have been assuming that our concrete ideas about love (for a friend, for a sweetheart, for son and daughter) are partly shaped by an absolutely universal standard of "love" that is possibly hidden from "daylight consciousness". And if this is really true, it should not surprise us to find again in earthly human love the same stringent dispensation that combines affirmation and demand in a unity. Christendom's sacred book simply expresses what everyone has experienced: the bastards are pampered, but the sons are placed under discipline.[7]

Then what, ultimately and in terms of the whole, do we want when we truly love someone? The great tradition of

---

[4] *Problem of Pain*, 29.

[5] Ibid., 31.

[6] Georges Bernanos, *Die Freude* (Joy), 2d ed. (Cologne-Olten, 1953), 46.

[7] "If you are without chastening, then you are bastards and not sons" (Heb 12:8).

European theology has answered this question: "ut in Deo sit",[8] we wish that he may be in God. That is, to be sure, a very solemn response that voices the very limits of what we mean. But I venture to assert that it expresses the common view, even though, in a manner of speaking, it is a formal and solemn statement.

Now it is perfectly true that we cannot always speak this formally. Such excessive solemnity, such aiming at "the ultimate", as though something infinitely sublime and uncommon were constantly being asked of us, might even destroy love's essential reality among real people. It still remains true that all love directed toward a human being ("it's good that you exist") is a reflection of the Creator's creative love, by whose "approval" all beings, including this beloved person, exist at all. Nevertheless, we do not have to show our love by consciously "reenacting" the primal *creatio* in our own minds; we show it in the quite ordinary form of active helpfulness, in the friendliness of greetings and expressions of thanks, in a small word or even in a mere good-humored muttering—and, of course, in those infinitely difficult and yet wholly inconspicuous "acts" of which the New Testament[9] speaks: not being envious, not being boastful, not rejoicing at others' sorrows, bearing no grudges (and so on). On the other hand, we might well be reminded now and again that even the scarcely noted ill humor in our daily life would, were its intention carried out to its ultimate conclusion, amount to a negation of the created world, to the desire that the other person might not exist at all. I am afraid that we cannot escape from these truly fearsome interrelationships by an act of "the despair of weakness", perhaps by looking at things from an exclusively psychological or sociological point of view. On the contrary, the horizon

[8] II, II, 25, 1.
[9] 1 Cor 13.

against which human love, just like hate, occurs is enormous.

Normally we accept the fact of our own existence unconsciously, as a matter of course, until this vital self-assurance is shaken by outward circumstances. But when that does happen, it becomes clear that our acceptance of our own being, our assent to ourselves, our feeling at home in existence (and without self-affirmation, love for another person might not be possible at all)—this very courage for being is ultimately justifiable only by reference to the initial act of the Creator, who brought us into existence as a reality that henceforth can never be removed from the world, that is not susceptible to "annihilation", and who with absolute finality has declared it "good" that we exist. On what basis can anyone have such "courage for being"? Paul Tillich, who used this phrase as the title of one of his last books,[10] answers the question himself: "We consciously affirm that we *are* affirmed."[11]

But does not all that has been said about the severity and the challenge of love comport rather with the image of a moralistic schoolmaster than with that of a lover? Does not the wish that another person's situation may be "entirely good" seem a long way off from being real love? Can we not sincerely wish someone "all the best"—as we repeatedly do in leavetakings or in the complimentary closes of letters—without loving him? In fact, is there not an element of aloofness in this phrase, and do we not use it deliberately to keep him at a distance? All these objections, which I perfectly well understand, might be summed up in the one question: Does "good will", "benevolence", "wishing well", constitute the essence of love?

---

[10] *Der Mut zum Sein* (Stuttgart, 1954).
[11] Ibid., 131.

I would answer this question in three ways. *First*, it is certainly no small thing for a person to feel sincere good will toward another. *Second*, authentic love certainly requires that one person wish another well, or rather "the" good. *Third*, good will is not in itself enough to constitute what we mean by love.

Concerning this last point, we must mention a remarkable correction that Thomas Aquinas introduces into the famous Aristotelian definition that runs, in the Latin translation he cites: "Amare est velle alicui bonum",[12] to love means to wish someone the good. In the more complete text of Aristotle's *Rhetoric* it goes: "To love means to wish another everything we think good, and moreover for the other's sake, not for our own."[13] This clear and refined definition has rightly been repeated many times in classical treatises on the great subject of "love". Cicero, too, can find nothing better to say.[14] Thomas Aquinas, however, as we have said, explicitly takes up this point when he asks, "Is loving [*amare*] insofar as it is an act of *caritas* the same as wishing well [*benevolentia*]?"[15] He is speaking here, it must be realized, not of the *passio amoris*, not of the primarily sensual rapture kindled by the sight of the beloved, but of mental and spiritual love, which goes beyond mere fascination: *caritas*. Thomas asserts, then, that to equate *caritas* with mere well-wishing, *benevolentia*,[16] is to define it inadequately. Granted, no love can exist without such benevolence, but benevolence is patently something quite different from love.

---

[12] II, II, 27, 2; obj. 1.

[13] 2, 4; 80 b.

[14] "What else does it mean to love someone, if not that we wish him to receive the greatest goods?" (Cicero, *De finibus bonorum et malorum* 2, 24, 78).

[15] II, II, 27, 2.

[16] Incidentally, Aristotle himself said almost the same thing in the *Nicomachean Ethics* (9, 5; 1166 b).

But a qualification seems ready to hand. Of course well-wishing is not enough; the wish must be translated into doing good for someone. But that is not where Thomas takes issue with Aristotle's definition. And, in fact, to repeat the words of Karl Jaspers, it is perfectly possible for there to be "charity without love", a *doing* good that lacks something decisive to make it love. In her moving book *On Death and Dying*, in which the Swiss-American physician Elizabeth Kübler-Ross describes her experiences with dying persons,[17] she points out that in modern hospitals the moribund patient is an object of great medical interest, and incidentally also of enormous financial investments ("He will get a dozen people around the clock, all busily preoccupied with his heart rate, pulse, electrocardiogram . . . his secretions or excretions"),[18] but that the patient will not succeed, no matter how much he insists, in persuading a single one of these busy people to pause for a minute and listen to a question, let alone answer it. Those in attendance are very much concerned with physiological processes but not with the patient himself as a human being. If they paused, it is said, they might lose precious time that could be better spent saving the patient's life. Probably that is true, and we should try not to be too facile about criticizing anyone. But what the patient misses is being regarded as a person. Such concern for the human being himself need not necessarily be "love"; but it would be a first step toward love.

This is precisely what Thomas Aquinas implies when he says that something is missing to make well-wishing (and doing good) into real love. He calls the missing element the "unio affectus",[19] volition directed toward the other person, the wish to be with him, to be united with him, in fact to

---

[17] *On Death and Dying* (New York, 1969).
[18] Ibid., 8.
[19] II, II, 27, 2.

identify with him. When the true lover says, "It's good that you exist", he wants to be one with the person he loves.

This once again confirms, from another angle, that love's act of approval is not intended as a mere verification; rather, it is an impulse of the will that takes the person of the other as its partner and is involved in the other himself, an act of affirmation, or, as Alexander Pfänder somewhat dramatically phrases it, "a momentary, centrifugal striking out in the direction of the beloved person".[20]

But now this coin also has to be turned over once more so that we may see its reverse. "How wonderful that you exist"—certainly this impulse has more of an "impact" than a mere observation. Yet it obviously presupposes observation and verification! A necessary assumption is that *before* we have that impulse of the will we find it "good" and "wonderful" that this other, this beloved person, exists. In other words, we must previously have *perceived* that the other's existence, and the other himself, is something good and wonderful. Without such a preceding experience, no impulse of the will can exist in any meaningful way. That is, without such experience we cannot love at all, not anything or anyone. First of all, what is lovable must have revealed itself to our eyes, to our sensuous as well as mental faculty of perception: "Visio est quaedam causa amoris",[21] seeing is a kind of cause of love.

However, to find lovable and to love are two different matters. And the step from the one to the other need not necessarily be taken. If it is actually taken, that happens out of the spontaneity of volition; or, to say it another way: out of freedom. At any rate, love is in no way a logical conclusion that we can be compelled to draw. The situation is similar to the

---

[20] *Psychologie der Gesinnungen*, 370.

[21] I, II, 67, 6 ad 3. Thomas is here quoting Aristotle (*Nicomachean Ethics* 9, 5; 1167 a).

case of belief: the step from finding somebody trustworthy to really believing him is likewise nothing that can be determined by reasons, no matter how "compelling". "To believe someone" and "to love someone"—these are by their nature spontaneous acts in which, if we do not choose to call them simply "free", freedom certainly plays a part. Incidentally, that is the reason why both acts are peculiarly opaque and akin to mysteries. And yet in order for these spontaneous and opaque acts, whether belief or love, to be performed at all, there remains an indispensable prerequisite: the perception that someone is credible or lovable. We must have experienced and "seen" that the other person, as well as his existence in this world, really is good and wonderful; that is the precondition for the impulse of will that says, "It's good that you exist!"

But I do not mean to elaborate anything resembling an "epistemology of love". What concerns me is the previous step. Granted, it is true that one cannot love until he has seen and understood. But understanding is vain if it fails to grasp a reality—if, that is, it is wrong. In other words, if independently of our seeing, perceiving and thinking it is not *really* "good" that the beloved person exists, then all this approval is a deception, mistake, wishful thinking, a delusion. And then all love is an illusionary play of blind instinctual impulses, a trick of nature, as Schopenhauer[22] says, an unreal mirage and a self-deception striking at the heart of the "Lover's" own being.

"How good that you exist!"—well, yes, but must we not in some way be able to feel certain that it really is "good"? But on the basis of what can we feel certain of that? How do we know such a thing?

As a tentative answer I would suggest that for such a demanding process of ascertainment we would have to expect

---

[22] *Sämtliche Werke* (Leipzig: Insel-Ausgabe, n.d.), 2:1328f.

the whole person with all his powers of comprehension to be the organ of perception and that each of his "reflectors" must be "operative"—from the direct experience of the senses to the intellectual powers of thought and seeing and all the way to the insight, which only faith can bestow, into the nature of the universe and man as creations. And there are many indications that, when the senses no longer observe beauty and the intellect can no longer detect any meaning or value, what ultimately sustains love and remains believable as its real justification is the conviction that everything existing in the universe is *creatura*, creatively willed, affirmed, loved by the Creator and for that reason is really—in the most radical sense that the word "really" can possibly have—*really* good and therefore susceptible to, but also worthy of, being loved by us.

But isn't it clear that this exclamation, "It's good that this exists; how wonderful that you are", by its very nature does *not* refer to "everybody", let alone the whole of creation? In the ordinary course of events, doesn't it refer to a single "chosen" being?

In America the attempt has been made to trace the innumerable, widely different interpretations of the phenomenon of love that are to be found in the tradition of Occidental thought from Plato to psychoanalysis, to compare and discuss them, and to reduce them to a relatively comprehensible number of fundamental ideas. In the book[23] that sums up the results, a very few characteristics, to be numbered on the fingers of one hand, are found to recur in all characterizations of love. Among these is preference; "to be loved . . . is normally to be singled out."[24] Sigmund Freud regards this aspect of the phenomenon as so crucial that he specifically

[23] Robert G. Hazo, *The Idea of Love* (New York, 1967).
[24] Ibid., 39.

considers it an argument against the ideal of a universal human love. Incidentally, he mentions two such arguments; we shall come to the second in due time. He formulates the first reservation as follows, "A love that is not selective seems to us to forfeit part of its value by doing the object an injustice."[25] At first sight it seems as if this could scarcely be controverted. But a second glance shows us the matter in a somewhat different light. For if we look to the well-documented experience of great lovers, we learn that precisely this intensity of love turned toward a single partner seems to place the lover at a vantage point from which he realizes for the first time the goodness and lovableness of all people, in fact, of all living beings. This exceptional love offered to one single person who takes precedence over all others, this love that fills us so utterly that it would seem no room was left for any other love—this very love that is so restrictive evidently makes possible a universality of affirmation that prompts the lover to say, "How wonderful that all this exists!" "A heart that loves one person cannot hate anyone"—that is a Goethean dictum.[26] Dante says precisely the same thing in regard to Beatrice: When she appeared "no foe existed for me any more."[27]

I would not be disconcerted if someone were to say at this point: All very well, those are the statements of poets and mean nothing in regard to "concrete reality" (nor are they even meant to).[28] The authentic poet, of course, is not one who naïvely or intentionally—like the sophist[29]—embodies

---

[25] *Gesammelte Werke*, 14:461.

[26] *Die Laune des Verliebten*, scene 5.

[27] *Vita nuova*, chap. 11.

[28] We have here the familiar translation problem of *Dichter* and *Dichtung*. "Poet" is here used in the wider sense of creative writer, and "poetry" of imaginative writing.—TRANS.

[29] *Abuse of Language—Abuse of Power* (San Francisco: Ignatius Press, 1992), 43ff.

any wishful thinking that comes his way. The poet, to be sure, does not simply describe everyman's empirical reality; but he brings to consciousness something that this everyman in his better moments can recognize as what he had all along dimly sensed, what at bottom he has long known and can corroborate. With the aid of the poet's imagination we suddenly "know": Ah, yes, things could happen this way in the world of men if—of course *not* "if men were all angels", but if by a happy dispensation we were enabled to act out our true humanity, as happens in the case of love. It is no accident that from time immemorial poetry has glorified love!

In saying this we must be clear about two distinct matters. On the one hand, such universal human love cannot accomplish anything practical in the world; man's historical predicaments cannot be solved by love. But on the other hand—as we likewise know very well—ideal universal love is not simply an unrealistic fantasy. Rather, it is an innate potentiality reminiscent, as it were, of paradise, which is revealed for a moment solely in the exceptional figures of great lovers. (Freud speaks of Saint Francis of Assisi.)

The following sentence similarly rests upon the conviction of the *universal* goodness of all things by reason of their creation: "Good without evil can exist; evil without good cannot." [30] We cannot simply confirm such a proposition on the basis of our everyday experience; and yet we know that it is fundamentally true, that it is right.

All this has nothing whatsoever to do with any sort of naïve Pollyannaism. It is not to be forgotten that love also makes hate possible; one who cannot love also cannot hate. For the time being I shall leave out of consideration Catullus' famous couplet, "Odi et amo" ("I hate and love, and if you ask me why, I have no answer, but I discern, can feel, my

[30] I, 109, 1 ad 1.

senses rooted in eternal torture");[31] involved in that are the peculiarities of erotic love, which we shall not discuss just yet. I am referring now to hatred for everything that threatens to corrupt those whom we love; this is the hatred that accompanies love.

Jealousy is also quite close to our theme. But it must be remembered that there are two kinds of jealousy.[32] One kind is the jealousy of the covetous who want to keep something or someone for themselves alone but are not secure in their possession. Such jealousy in fact runs contrary to the idea of the universality of love. But it is quite another matter to be jealous, not "of" someone who is to be excluded, but "for" someone (or something), to feel angry, irreconcilable hostility toward everything (and to feel it selflessly rather than selfishly) that might possibly impugn the beloved subject. The English word "jealousy" is derived from the Latin *zelus*, which is used in that sense in the Psalter (Ps 69:9): "Zeal for thy house has consumed me." The disciples of Jesus remember this passage when he drives the money changers out of the temple (Jn 2:17). It is hard to say against what and whom that fierce antagonism is directed. But in any case we had better dismiss the thought that the call for universal love imposes a Pollyannaish view of the real world!

Sigmund Freud, I said, mentions two objections to the ideal of universal human love. His second is: "All men are not lovable."[33] At first this statement strikes us as more or less a commonplace, something we all discover every day. But as soon as we consider it in the light of principle, as soon as we radicalize it, so to speak, we realize what a monstrous assertion it is. For is it not tantamount to saying that there are

---

[31] *The Poems of Catullus*, trans. Horace Gregory (New York, 1956), 151.

[32] Cf. also I, II, 28, 4.

[33] *Gesammelte Werke*, 14:461.

people in regard to whom it would be impossible and unjustifiable for anyone to say, "It's good that you exist"? But who could possibly have the right even to think such a thought seriously?

Probably two matters must be more closely scrutinized here. The first has already been mentioned briefly: that *degrees* of approbation exist and that they are quite legitimate. Alongside the superlative of passionate praise for the beloved there are also varieties of less passionate but no less sincere and dependable affirmation. For example, anyone who seriously carried out what in colloquial speech is called "live and let live" would not be altogether remote from that "making be" which we have defined as one of the specific achievements of love. And even mere "acceptance" can be an extremely important matter, as an expression of affirmation. The point should be made, by the way, that the statements by poets cited above do not refer to any outpouring of universal brotherhood. They merely say, though with emphatic clarity, that "great" love enables a person to be nobody's enemy; great love keeps anyone from saying with regard to someone else, "You ought not to exist."

Probably even Sigmund Freud's remark that all men are not lovable was scarcely intended in any such drastic sense as we can take it in, when we regard it in purely abstract terms. Nevertheless, it brings us back to the question raised earlier: On what basis is man prohibited (and, psychologically speaking, what could stop him?) from saying in all seriousness of another person: He ought not to exist? Not: I wish he weren't here; and not: I wish he were dead; but: God ought not to have created him. It is this last and most radical formulation that once again presents the only cogent "reason" that could make it impossible for us to wish the nonexistence of a single created being or thing, were it only an atom of the material universe.

The second point that Sigmund Freud's comment forces us to consider is that "to call a person lovable or not lovable" can mean something entirely different from affirming or negating his existence. And in everyday language it may be that this other meaning is always the one intended, to wit, positive or negative estimation of a person's "qualities". The helpful neighbor is lovable; so are the pleasant coworker, the amusing companion, the fair fellow sportsman, the elegant dancing partner—and so on. A French writer proposes that in such cases we ought not to speak of "love" but of sympathy.[34] But if we ignore the question of terminology for the time being—a question that could give rise to endless disputes—we must at any rate concede that two different modes of concern for another person are involved. In the one case the affirmation is directed primarily to his existence, in the other case to his *essentia*, to the way he is. In the literature these two aspects are sometimes sharply opposed to one another; in fact each is used to counter the other. Thus it has been said that the true lover does not look to "qualities" at all, but only to the person.[35] Elsewhere it is even argued that according to experience "the attempt to love a person for his or her qualities—be they spiritual or physical, intellectual or temperamental—deteriorates into a kind of prostitution in which the person is used and valued for what he does and has. Relationships based on the mutual admiration of qualities end in disillusion and often in bitterness."[36]

At first hearing, such a formulation sounds odd and disturbing. It acquires somewhat more plausibility when we supplement it by a remark along the same lines by Emil Brunner. Brunner says, "The formula for love is *not*: I love you because you are *thus*—and we might add: *as long as* you

[34] Gabriel Madinier, *Conscience et amour*, 2d ed. (Paris, 1947), 95.

[35] Robert O. Johann, *The Meaning of Love* (Glen Rock, N.J., 1966), 26.

[36] Frederick D. Wilhelmsen, *The Metaphysics of Love* (New York, 1962), 37.

are thus."[37] It is precisely this addition that suddenly illuminates the matter; for it is evident to everyone that if a love ends the moment certain of the partner's qualities (beauty, youth, success) vanish, it never existed from the first. The test question, once again, is *not*: Do you find the other person likeable, capable, "nice"? Rather, the question is: Are you glad for his existence, or do you have anything against it; can you honestly say, "It's good that he exists"?

But of course, on the other hand, existence and the qualities of the existing person cannot be separated; there is no such thing as *existentia* without *essentia*. Even while the lover beholds the beloved[38] he naturally sees both; he cannot ignore the qualitative aspect, the rough sketch that the other person is destined to refine. This nature as a sketch, this perception of what the beloved was "really" intended to become, may be perceptible only to the lover's prophetic eye, as we have already said. And perhaps what also happens is that love, when it is taking its very first step, is kindled by the beloved's *essentia*. In other words, incipient love may after all be attracted by "qualities" (beauty, charm, flashing intelligence). But when it has become real love it will then penetrate to the core of the person who stands behind these qualities and who "has" them, to the true subject of that unimaginable act that we call existing, to the beloved's innermost self, which *remains* even when the lovable qualities long since have vanished, those same qualities that once upon a time, far back at the beginning, may have approximated a "reason" for love.

In this light the "formula" for true love that Emil Brunner likewise proposes, "I love you because you exist",[39] seems to me to be a quite unrealistic construction. No lover has ever said anything like that. He says, "It's good that you exist." But he has nothing to do with becauses and reasons. As I say, there may have been reasons in the incipient stages; but after love has developed, it no longer has need of them.

V

I T'S GOOD THAT YOU EXIST"—good for whom? So far we have not asked this question; but it is easy to see that it strikes to the heart of the matter. Obviously it makes a decisive difference whether we think it good for *our sake* that the other person exists (because we need him) or for *his sake* (because we want him to be happy and to arrive at the fulfillment intended for him). But if we find it good for *our sake*—can it be said that we love the other person?

In regard to love for the good things of this life, there is no problem at all. Of course we love wine (for example) for our own sakes. "It would surely be ridiculous", says Aristotle, "to wish for the good of wine (that is, to love it for its own sake); if one wishes it at all, it is that the wine may keep, so that we can have it for ourselves."[1] It has rightly been said, however, that it is possible for us to esteem beloved things in an entirely disinterested fashion and simply to rejoice "that such a thing exists"—like this choice Burgundy or these rare stones or fine jewelry.[2] Even in the narrower area of human sensuality, such an aloofness from mere desire is conceivable. Thomas Aquinas mentioned as something distinctively human the ability to experience sensual and sensuous concord, *convenientia sensibilium*, without the intervention of desire;[3] animals, he points out, observe only the possible object for

---

[1] *Nicomachean Ethics* 8, 2; 1155 b.
[2] Cf. C. S. Lewis, *The Four Loves* (London, 1960), 23.
[3] II, II, 141, 4 ad 3. Cf. also *Mal.* 8, 1 ad 9.

eating and coupling, whereas man, by disciplining his desires, is alone capable of enjoying sensuous beauty such as that of the human body *as* beauty.[4] But in digressing thus we have unexpectedly come back to the relationships of men to men. At any rate, what we want to remember is that there is nothing untoward in our loving things for our own sakes, in saying, "It's good that that exists—good for us!"

The difficulty begins when we love another person for our own sake. But that must be put more precisely. It is quite clear that the relationship of the sexes can include forms of sheer selfish use and abuse, as well as sexual subservience, that have nothing to do with love among men. Saint Augustine has expressed the matter as follows, "It is not permissible to love people in the same way as one hears gourmets say: I love carp."[5] There really is no serious dispute on this score. The real question, the one on which opinions divide, runs as follows: Whenever someone says, "It's good that you exist, good for me, because I cannot be happy without you", is this always a distortion of love? Is it unworthy for anyone, or at least any *Christian*, to love in such a fashion? Is it part of the essence of truly human love for the lover to want absolutely nothing for himself, neither joy nor happiness nor any other enrichment of his vital store? Is selflessness simply one of the essential characteristics of all human love that deserves the name? But, on the other hand, is not the longing for fulfilled existence actually and legitimately the root of all love? And is, in general, man capable of such absolute altruism that he would wish not to be happy?

Here it becomes apparent that in discussing the subject of "love", we must also consider the conception we have of man. It is always involved. In Plato's famous dialogue on this subject, after biology, psychology and sociology have put in

[4] Cf. Josef Pieper, *The Four Cardinal Virtues* (New York, 1965), 166f.
[5] *In Epistolam Johannis ad Parthos* 8, 5; PL 35:2058.

their word, Aristophanes arises to say: No one understands anything about love who has not considered the nature of man and what has befallen it, the *pathémata anthrópou*; and then he tells the myth of man's original perfection and his guilty loss of it.[6] The aforementioned American attempt to simplify and catalogue the multitude of theories of love likewise arrives at the same intermediate result: "How love is understood follows from how human nature is understood."[7]

The phrase "human nature" in such contexts should probably be taken more literally than is generally done. Strictly speaking, the problem at issue is not so much what kind of being man is but rather what he is "by nature". What is the character of and what happens with what man possesses and brings into the world with him by birth (*natura* comes from *nasci*, to be born)? We need only formulate this in such a bold fashion to find ourselves inevitably drifting, as happened to Plato also, into the realm of theology, and probably into highly controversial theology at that. As has been said, here opinions divide!

C. S. Lewis relates that when he began to write his book about love, which was published in 1960, he had intended pretty much without a qualm to sing the praises of pure, selfless, giving love, what he called "gift-love", and to speak more or less deprecatorily of craving, desirous "need-love".[8]

---

[6] *Symposium* 189f.

[7] Robert G. Hazo, *The Idea of Love* (New York, 1967), 160.

[8] This distinction between need-love and gift-love restates the well-known antithesis between *amor concupiscentiae* and *amor benevolentiae* (*amor amicitiae*), between desirous love and the well-wishing love between friends. As far as the subject goes, the distinction is probably as old as human reflection on the subject of love; and the terms, too, have been part of the textbook vocabularies in philosophy and theology for many centuries. Thomas Aquinas likewise employs this terminology, but at the same time he seems to hint at a slight aloofness from it. He himself apparently prefers to speak of "imperfect" and "perfect" love (e.g., *De spe* 3). But despite appearances he expressly does not intend these terms to be evaluative, at least not in any moral sense. Rather, in

But then he changed his mind. "The reality is more complicated than I supposed."[9] That such an attitude is assumed,
before reflection, reveals to what extent the collective consciousness and the atmosphere of thought, especially of
Christian thought concerning love, has already been molded
by a particular conception. We must now elaborate somewhat on that conception.

What is involved, to anticipate, is the antithesis of *eros* and
agape. Here eros does not stand primarily for love between
the sexes but for all demanding and needing love. Thus it
appears to be diametrically opposed to that love which alone
seems proper to the Christian, for which reason it has undergone an explicit and, we must say, a fateful defamation.
The phraseology may differ somewhat (*Eros and Caritas, Eros
and Agape, Eros and Love* are the titles of three books published in the thirties)[10]—but the common element is always
the deprecation of eros. The authors of those three books
are all theologians,[11] and their theses are based upon a particular interpretation of the sacred tradition, chiefly of the
New Testament. Inevitably, however, they imply a more uni-

---

a purely descriptive way, he means: if we "love" to drink wine for a festive
meal, obviously this "desirous" love directed toward the wine is imperfect insofar as the wine is not at all what is primarily and really loved. The real object
of our love is we ourselves; and understood in this sense the love directed
toward ourselves is "perfect"; which means nothing more nor less than that
the concept of "love" is realized in its full, unweakened sense. Normally, however, as indicated above, Thomas adopts the usual terminology but qualifies it
by saying that it is proposed or used *a quibusdam*, by certain writers (I, 60, 3).

[9] *Four Loves*, 10f.

[10] Heinrich Scholz, *Eros und Caritas. Die platonische Liebe und die Liebe im
Sinne des Christentums* (Halle, 1929). Anders Nygren, *Eros und Agape. Gestalt-
wandlungen der christlichen Liebe*, 2 vols. (Gütersloh, 1930, 1937). Emil Brunner,
Eros und Liebe (Berlin, 1937).

[11] Heinrich Scholz is better known for his later writings on philosophy and
logic; but he began his university career with a dissertation on the philosophy
of religion and systematic philosophy (under Adolf von Harnack).

versal, pretheological conception of man; and that is of concern to everyone who reflects upon the life of man.

The most radical and, in terms of intellectual history, the most provocative formulation of the thesis of "eros and agape" may be found in the two-volume book by that title, the work of the Swedish theologian Anders Nygren.[12] This book has had almost incalculable influence, although of course it itself may well spring from an idea that has probably always been present in Christendom as a subterranean current. For the moment I shall attempt here to present Nygren's thesis in a necessarily summary fashion, beginning with his characterization of the two basic concepts.

Agape, "the original basic conception of Christianity",[13] "above all others the basic Christian motif",[14] signifies primarily an almost entirely *unselfish* love, a yielding rather than self-assertive love, the love that does not seek to win life but dares to lose it.[15] Agape "has nothing to do with desire or lust";[16] it "fundamentally excludes everything that implies self-love".[17] Here Nygren cites Martin Luther's "Est enim diligere se-ipsum odisse",[18] to love means to hate oneself. Of course that is not to be taken altogether literally. Nevertheless, agape stands in irreconcilable opposition "to all eudemonistically founded action",[19] that is to say, to all motivation based on the desire for happiness, let alone "for reward".[20] At bottom there

---

[12] Nygren is regarded as one of the leading figures in modern Protestant theology. Professor at the University of Lund, later Bishop of Lund, he served from 1947 to 1952 as first president of the Lutheran World Federation. His principal work is *Eros und Agape*.

[13] Nygren, *Eros und Agape*, 1:31.

[14] Ibid.

[15] Ibid., 185f.

[16] Ibid., 2:12.

[17] Ibid., 1:192.

[18] Ibid., 2:533.

[19] Ibid., 2:548.

[20] Ibid., 2:549.

is no "motive" at all for agape; rather, it is explicitly "unmotivated".[21] Motivation, in the sense that something else is
"moving" it, would in fact signify a kind of dependence on
that something else; but agape "needs nothing at all from outside to set it in motion".[22] It is therefore "indifferent"[23] to
predetermined values. In conclusion Nygren uses the word
"spontaneity"[24] to define the decisive characteristic, the "up-
welling"[25] nature of agape. With similar significance he also
speaks of its "sovereignty"[26] and its "creative" character,[27]
since it creates values instead of assuming them.[28]

  Eros is, point by point, the counterpoise to agape. It is neither creative nor spontaneous, because it is essentially determined by its object, by the preexisting goodness and beauty
whose presence is first discovered and thereupon loved.[29]
Primarily, of course, eros is "love of a desirous, egocentric
kind".[30] "The starting point is human need, the goal is the
satisfaction of this need."[31] "Eros is fundamentally self-
love",[32] even in its most sublime form, even when it is conceived as a "way of man toward the divine".[33] Explicitly
included in this condemnation is Saint Augustine's well-
known phrase[34] that man's heart is restless until it reposes in
God. Here, Nygren argues, it becomes apparent that August-

[21] Ibid., 1:56; 2:549.
[22] Ibid., 2:551.
[23] Ibid., 1:60.
[24] Ibid., 2:548.
[25] Ibid., 2:551.
[26] Ibid., 1:185f.
[27] Ibid., 1:60.
[28] Ibid., 1:185f.
[29] Ibid.
[30] Ibid., 2:11.
[31] Ibid.
[32] Ibid., 1:192.
[33] Ibid., 1:154.
[34] *Confessions* 1, 1.

ine is fully under the influence of Plato's doctrine of eros, which has nothing to do with the Christian idea of love.[35] "No way, not that of sublimation either, leads from eros to agape."[36]

Yet in Nygren's opinion this very attempt at a "sublimation of desirous love or self-love into pure divine love"[37] began very early, by the incorporation of Platonic, which means pagan, ideas into Christian philosophy. As an example of this, Nygren mentions Gregory of Nyssa,[38] who speaks of the soul's rising to God, of the ladder to heaven, of the upleaping flame and the wings of the soul. This poor compromise, Nygren continues, which tries to unite incompatibles, was first developed into a system by Saint Augustine—the systematization resulting in the "*caritas* synthesis".[39] But it remained for Thomas Aquinas to carry the error to its logical conclusion. To be sure, Thomas reduced everything in Christianity to love but everything in love to self-love.[40] This wrongheaded harmonization of eros and agape by Thomas Aquinas falsified the original Christian intention, with the consequence that "the place where Christian agape-love . . . might have found a refuge has completely and finally vanished."[41]

Nygren goes on to interpret the end of the Middle Ages and the beginning of modern times as a shattering of that objectively unjustifiable "synthesis". On the one hand, it was smashed by Renaissance man's philosophy of life, which made an absolute of eros; on the other hand, by Martin Luther, who restored the idea of agape in its unadulterated

[35] *Eros und Agape*, 2:297.

[36] Ibid., 1:35.

[37] Ibid., 2:472f.

[38] Ibid., 2:244ff.

[39] Ibid., 2:255.

[40] Ibid., 2:465.

[41] Ibid., 2:467.

purity.[42] Nygren sees Luther's achievement as primarily one of destruction; and the phrases he uses are unusual in their vehemence. "Luther smashed to pieces" that false synthesis;[43] he "regarded it as his principal task to annihilate the classical Catholic idea of love, the *caritas* synthesis";[44] he was "the destroyer of the Catholic view of love built up essentially on the eros factor".[45] That is, assuredly, forthright and energetic language, which does not try to blur antitheses. The same may be said for Nygren's terse conclusion: "*On the one hand*—in Catholicism—desirous love is the bond that holds everything together. . . . *On the other hand*—in Luther—we are dealing with the religion and the ethos of agape."[46]

In this summary account, the wealth of argument and historical evidence that Nygren presents is, of course, barely suggested. Reading his book left me much perplexed—especially concerning the kind of love to be demanded of and expected of human beings. I found I simply could not accept the whole idea. Certainly this disparagement of eros, propounded with such force and held up as the only Christian view, has penetrated the general consciousness outside as well as inside Christendom. And I ask myself whether it may not be partly responsible for the disesteem directed against Christianity nowadays, precisely on the grounds of what nature really or supposedly accords to man as his due in the realm of eros.

It is not as if Nygren's thesis, especially its depreciation of needful, demanding love, represented only one special opinion on the radical fringe. I must add a word about that. For

---

[42] Ibid., 2:255.
[43] Ibid., 2:378.
[44] Ibid., 2:544.
[45] Ibid., 1:40.
[46] Ibid., 2:561.

me it was a saddening surprise to find Nygren seconded by a theologian of the rank of Karl Barth, of whom Hans Urs von Balthasar rightly says that we must "probably go back to Saint Thomas to find again such freedom from all tension and narrowness".[47] In fact, Karl Barth, in his doctrine of the creation, speaks with magnificently realistic candor of erotic love between man and woman, of the joys to be found in it, of mutual liking and deciding in favor of one another. He regards the moralistic rigor of Calvin, who "had his wife picked out by close acquaintances", as definitely not worth imitating. As for the German Reformer, he comments, "Let us hope Luther was not being entirely serious when he once remarked that he had married Katharina von Bora in order to deliver a blow to the papacy."[48] Here, evidently, clearly "erotic" love, kindling in the personal encounters of human beings with real bodies and by no means "unmotivated", is named by name and frankly defended. But when in his doctrine on redemption the same Karl Barth discusses "the problem of Christian love" and formally addresses the subject of "eros and agape",[49] he comes up with almost the same negative evaluation of eros as Nygren. Who influenced whom here (Barth is four years older than Nygren), and whether there is any dependence at all, seems to me of no importance. Still and all, in spite of his occasional rather sharp criticism of Nygren,[50] we find Karl Barth also discussing the "medieval" "*caritas* synthesis" and making the point that the opposition between "biblical agape" and "classical or Hellenistic eros" has remained "not outrightly unrecognizable but at this distance not unequivocally recognizable".[51]

[47] Karl Barth, *Darstellung und Deutung seiner Theologie* (Cologne, 1951), 35f.

[48] *Kirchliche Dogmatik*, vol. 3, pt. 4 (Zollikon-Zurich, 1951), 241.

[49] This is done in vol. 4 (pt. 2) of the *Kirchliche Dogmatik*, in a chapter headed "The Problem of Christian Love" (825ff.).

[50] *Kirchliche Dogmatik*, vol. 4, pt. 2, 834, 837.

[51] Ibid., 836f.

As we can see from this phraseology, Barth is not so doc-
trinaire as Nygren. Swiss realist that he is, Barth is simply too
close to an understanding of the average Christian's ordinary life
("As long as there are loving people they will, whether Christians or not, always live within the pattern of eros";[52] there is
"certainly no Christian who in more refined or cruder form
[and probably in both] does not also 'love' this way, by the standard of this entirely different mode of love",[53] that is, the mode
of eros). Nevertheless, Karl Barth again and again expresses his
fundamentally negative evaluation of eros. For him, too, eros as
"self-love",[54] as a "coarser or finer –appetite",[55] is "the diametri-
cal opposite of Christian love".[56] "Every moment of tolerance"
for eros-love "would be a decidedly unchristian moment".[57]
And even "the contention that it is a kind of preliminary stage of
Christian love"[58] is insupportable. "The whole strangeness of
Christianity within the world around it becomes apparent in the
divorce that also runs through the individual Christian—of
Christian love from that other love."[59]

Something else is revealed in this last, very fundamental sentence, just as we conjectured from the start. It is that in all this
talk about love in general and eros in particular a conception
of the nature of man is implicit, of what we might call man's
"pre-Christian" nature, as given to him when he was created.
Is it really something "strange", really "divorced" from Christianity? Or is it possibly the very ground without which the
Christian element, the supernatural, grace (or whatever else

[52] Ibid., 837.
[53] Ibid., 833f.
[54] Ibid., 833, 845.
[55] Ibid., 844.
[56] Ibid., 833.
[57] Ibid., 835.
[58] Ibid., 834.
[59] Ibid.

we may wish to call this new dimension) could not take root and thrive?

But, above all: If the natural man and that which he is and possesses by virtue of his creation has nothing to do with agape—then who, strictly speaking, is the subject of it? Who is really the lover here? Anders Nygren gives us a clear answer to this question. He gives it by interpreting a dictum of Martin Luther's. Luther's dictum runs as follows: "Whoso remaineth in love . . . is no longer a mere man but a god." Nygren's interpretation is: that means that "the real subject of Christian love is not man but God himself." And what about man? He is only "the conduit, the channel that conducts God's love".[60]

The answer is, as we have said, clear enough; but it also exposes the profoundly dubious nature, in fact the inherent impossibility, of the entire conception. For, on the one hand, agape, initially meaning not God's own love but the only kind of love that is proper for the Christian and requisite of him, is described as something independently sovereign in its absolute selflessness. It is characterized as spontaneous, overflowing, creative. It is, among Nygren's followers, hailed in the wildest terms: "The love that loves without reason and receives nothing";[61] "a love that is prepared to receive nothing at all but only to give".[62] That is, on the one hand, it imposes a tremendous demand upon man but also represents a tremendous demand by man. But, on the other hand, when we ask the question: Who is the subject that is supposed to perform such a love, the answer we are given is startling, for this same man is suddenly no longer involved. He himself is not the one who loves! On his side there is not only no creative sovereignty; there is absolutely nothing at all!

[60] *Eros und Agape*, 2:557.

[61] Ladislaus Grünhut, *Eros und Agape* (Leipzig, 1931), 20f.

[62] Erwin Reissner, *Glaube, Hoffnung, Liebe* (Hamburg, 1954), 44.

Before we go into the details of the argument, we had best present our own thesis without more ado. We contest both the nothingness and the sovereignty—and in so doing we are clearly in accord with the great tradition of thought in the Christian West (from Augustine through Thomas Aquinas to Francis de Sales, Leibnitz and C. S. Lewis, the great lay theologian of the present day). We are not in the least "nothing"; rather we are *creatura* and thereby have an existence that is our own—God-given, certainly, but for that very reason given to us to be truly our own. At the same time man, because of this same creatureliness, is by nature a totally needful being; he is himself "one vast need",[63] a thirst that must be quenched, "the hungry being pure and simple".[64] And both aspects, our being somebody and our needfulness, come most plainly of all to light when we love.

[63] *Four Loves*, 11.
[64] Georg Simmel, *Fragmente und Aufsätze* (Munich, 1923), 14.

VI

ANDERS NYGREN is concerned with the many ramifications and implications of man's "nothingness" and the insignificance of everything that man as a physical being brings with him into the world by nature and birth, which is to say, by virtue of his having been created. Because this is, strictly speaking, a theological subject, we will not go into it very deeply here. Nygren is also concerned with Plato's question about "man's nature and what has happened to it". That question involves the primal sin committed in inconceivably ancient times but whose effects still continue into the present. The important point here is how that sin has affected human nature and its power to love. The extent to which Nygren deals with these questions is indicated, for example, by his mentioning the Manichaean-Gnostic sectarian Marcion as one of the ancestors of his own doctrine of agape. The Church clearly and finally parted ways with Marcion in the second century. Marcion, says Nygren,[1] was one of the first advocates of the idea of agape. Marcion claimed that the Christian God "had nothing to do with the creation". Nygren takes up this argument and carries it further, contending that "the absolutely unmotivated" aspect of agape becomes understandable only upon the basis of such a denial "of all connection between creation and redemption".

[1] *Eros und Agape* (Gütersloh, 1937), 2:110.

The logic of all this seems sound, yet it brings to light once more, in almost alarming fashion, the whole dubiousness of Nygren's conception. But as we have said, this is all in the realm of pure theology, that is, a specific interpretation of sacred tradition and revelation. We, on the other hand, who wish to consider the question from the viewpoint of philosophy can scarcely contribute anything on our own. What we can do, however, and should do, is to state our own premises or, more precisely, what we believe or do not believe in regard to this matter. In so doing we are not ourselves engaging in theology, although we refer to and appeal to, perhaps inevitably, a theology we consider legitimate. For my part I have to cite what the great tradition of Christendom has held down to the present day: namely, that inherent in the concept of being created is the proposition that the *creatura* cannot itself dispose of the existence it possesses; that, therefore, even if it wanted to, it could neither change nor, certainly, destroy its own nature. Just because man had been summoned into existence by the absolutely creative power of God, he remains—possibly even *malgré lui-même*—what he is by virtue of his creation: a personal self and an individual. And it is this individual, man himself, who in love turns to another individual and says, "It's good that you exist!" In turning to another person with love, man is *not* a "channel" and "conduit". Then if ever he is truly subject and person. And in "supernatural" love also, whether it is called *caritas* or "agape", and although it draws its force from "grace"—in that kind of love, too, the lovers are we ourselves.

The second thing we know is knowledge gained far more directly, on the basis of our own inner experience: that our love is anything but "sovereign". Above all, moreover, it never creates "values" or makes anything or anyone lovable. Rather the same rationale is basic to it as that from which all human activities derive their character of being grounded in the real: that Being comes first, and then Truth, and finally Goodness. Applied to our theme, what this means is: What comes first is the actual existence of lovability, independently presented to us. Then this existence must enter into our experience. And only then, hence anything but "unmotivatedly" and "without reason", do we say in confirming love, "It's good that this exists!"

That precisely is the meaning of a sentence of Thomas Aquinas that Nygren singles out for disapproving and almost indignant comment. That Thomas Aquinas "did not shrink" from writing it down proves, to Nygren, that he reduced "everything in love to self-love"[2] and that, therefore, he could no longer open his mind at all to the original concept of pure agape. The sentence runs: "Assuming the impossible case that God were not really a good for man, there would be no reason for man to love."[3] What does this mean? Nothing less than that the emotion "It's good that you exist" has justification solely in the actual goodness of the beloved; that this is its basis in reality; and that this order of things applies not only to our love for material goods and our fellowmen but likewise to our love for God and still applies in the eternal life.[4]

How in the world could our love for God be "groundless" and "unmotivated", let alone "sovereign"? It would indeed be "a bold and silly creature that came before its Creator with the boast, 'I'm no beggar. I love you disinterestedly.' "[5] Our love of God cannot help being largely if not entirely need-love.[6] Is it consequently eros, that is, basically self-love? If we

[2] Ibid., 2:464f.

[3] "Dato enim, per impossibile, quod Deus non esset hominis bonum, non esset ei ratio diligendi" (II, II, 26, 13 ad 3).

[4] In fact the *articulus* of the *Summa theologica* (II, II, 26, 13) from which this proposition comes bears the heading: "Whether the order of love remains valid in the eternal life? (*Utrum ordo caritatis remaneat in patria*)?"

[5] C. S. Lewis, *The Four Loves* (London, 1960), 12.

[6] Ibid., 11.

do not forget that self-love is not necessarily "selfish" and that disinterested self-preservation[7] can exist, the answer to this question can only be: Yes.

But such need-love, whose goal is its own fulfillment, is also the nucleus and the beginning in all our loving. It is simply the elemental dynamics of our being itself, set in motion by the act that created us. Hence it is fundamentally impossible for us to control it, let alone to annul it. It is the "yes" that we ourselves *are* before we are consciously able to say "yes" (or even "no"). Here Augustine's idea, constantly reiterated in many forms throughout his entire work, acquires a perhaps unexpectedly precise meaning: "Pondus meum amor meus",[8] my love is my weight; where it goes I go. We can no more govern this primal impulse, which affects all our conscious decisions, than we or any other being can have dominion over our own natures.[9] And, once again, it is inevitable and incontestable that this natural urge for fulfillment and completion is basically *self-love*. "Angels like men by nature strive for their own good and their own perfection; and this means loving themselves."[10] Therefore, insofar as we are willing to accept the more or less established usage that defines eros as the quintessence of all desire for fullness of being, for quenching of the thirst for happiness, for satiation by the good things of life, which include not only closeness and community with our fellowmen but also participation in the life of God himself—insofar as we do accept this usage, eros must be regarded as an impulse inherent in our natures, arising directly out of finite man's existence as a created being,

[7] Cf. Joseph Pieper, *The Four Cardinal Virtues* (New York, 1965), 147f.

[8] "Pondus meum amor meus; eo feror, quocumque feror" (*Confessions* 13, 9).

[9] "Nihil habet dominium suae naturae" (I, 60, 1, obj. 2).

[10] I, 60, 3.

out of his creatureliness. And when Karl Barth insists that man must "choose whether he wishes to love this way or that",[11] either in the manner of eros or of agape, the question at once arises: Is man capable at all of so choosing? Choice implies being able to do otherwise. But can man do otherwise than, for example, want to be happy? Thomas Aquinas —whose importance here is less that of an individual writer than as the voice of humanity's traditional wisdom—answered this question many times with a decided "no": man cannot do otherwise. "By nature the creature endowed with reason wishes to be happy and therefore cannot wish not to be happy."[12]

In this formulation we should not ignore the explicit reference to man's creatureliness. Of course Thomas' dictum does not constitute a defense for every random whim and every asserted "need for happiness". Not at all. But still something has been said that is fraught with many consequences for the theme of eros and agape—especially, for example, that the call for an utterly disinterested, unmotivated, sovereign agape love that wishes to receive nothing, that is purged of all selfish desire, simply rests upon a misunderstanding of man as he really is. The error, it must be noted, consists not so much in mistaking man's empirical imperfection as in failing to recognize that the *conditio humana* is that of a created being. Thomas and the tradition of thought represented by him do not merely accept as a fact the idea of man's craving happiness by nature as a symptom of persisting human weakness. Rather, he holds that this desire, directed toward quenching the deepest of thirsts, is not only entirely "in order" but is the indispensable beginning of all perfection in love.

On the other hand, the denigration of the human desire for happiness, which is implicit in contempt for eros, clouds

[11] *Kirchliche Dogmatik* (Zollikon-Zurich, 1955), vol. 4, pt. 2, 835.
[12] *C. G.* 4, 92.

and distorts any clear view of the phenomenon of love. In fact, neither the one attitude nor the other can legitimately claim derivation from that Christian viewpoint which has shaped our thinking down to its barely conscious roots and down to our spontaneous forms of expression. This clarification, this recapture of an insight that the great tradition of European thought never lost, also clears the way for us to see once more the fundamental fact: that all love has joy as its natural fruit. What is more, all human happiness (which we instinctively desire, but not necessarily selfishly, and therefore with rightfully clear consciences) is fundamentally *the happiness of love*, whether its name is eros or *caritas* or agape and whether it is directed toward a friend, a sweetheart, a son, a neighbor or God himself.

The happiness of love, lover's bliss, happiness in love or even *happiness with love*—these are, as everyone knows, fairly ambiguous ideas. In ordinary language they have undergone a rampant growth of meanings and first of all need a bit of pruning. For the present we shall not go into the question of luck in love, that is, of the good fortune of finding the right partner. That certainly exists, and there is nothing whatsoever to be said against it—although it obviously makes a difference whether what a man is seeking and finding is the woman for the rest of his life ("until death do us part") or what Harvey Cox[13] calls a "Playboy accessory". But we are speaking of something else, of the essential relationship that connects happiness and joy with love, a relationship that, as will become apparent, is not so unequivocal as we might think on first consideration.

Joy is by its nature something secondary and subsidiary. It is of course foolish to ask anyone "why" he wants to rejoice;

---

[13] Harvey Cox, *The Secular City* (New York: Macmillan, 1965), 96.

and so it might be thought that joy is something sought for its own sake and consequently *not* secondary. But if we look into the matter more closely, it becomes apparent that man, if all works out as it should, does not want to plunge absolutely and unconditionally into the psychological state of rejoicing but that he wants to have a reason for rejoicing. "If all works out as it should!" For sometimes things do not work out as they should—for example, when in the absence of a "reason", a "cause" is brought to bear by a kind of manipulation, a pretext that does not result in real joy but artificially produces a deceptive, unfounded feeling of joy. Such a cause may be a drug or it may be the electric stimulation of certain brain centers. Julian Huxley has argued that "after all, electric happiness is still happiness";[14] but for the time being I remain convinced that Saint Augustine correctly defines the true state of affairs—as well, incidentally, as expressing the viewpoint of the average man—when he says, "There is no one who would not prefer to endure pain with a sound mind than to rejoice in madness."[15] Man can (and wants to) rejoice only when there is a reason for joy. And this reason, therefore, is primary; the joy itself secondary.

But are there not countless reasons for joy? Yes. But they can all be reduced to a common denominator: our receiving or possessing something we love—even though this receiving or possession may only be hoped for as a future good or re-

[14] In *Man and His Future*, ed. G. Wolstenholme (London, 1963), 12.

[15] *City of God* 11, 27. Still it must be considered that *in concreto* the boundaries between "genuine" justified happiness and a merely "caused" feeling of happiness are fluid. When we read in the Psalter (Ps 104:15): "Wine gladdens the heart of man", is not the reference to what may crudely be termed a chemically and physiologically caused "gladness"? I would comment: It depends whether what is involved is a heightening of an already joyous and festive hour or an artificial and deliberate substitute for gladness. Still, in Pascal's treatise on the passions there is the remarkable and, to my mind, rather dubious sentence: "What does it matter whether a joy is false if we are convinced that it is true?"

membered as something already past. Consequently, one who loves nothing and no one cannot rejoice, no matter how desperately he wishes to (this is the situation in which the temptation to self-deception by constructing "artificial paradises" gains force).

Up to this point the intimate connection between love and joy seems to be a clear, uncomplicated matter. We desire something that we "like" and "love"—and then we receive it as a gift. Something that we tried to bring about by loving effort—we call this "love's labor"—finally succeeds (a scientific proof, the breeding of a new variety of rose, a poem). Then there is the story of the two prisoners of war in Siberia who ask themselves when people are truly happy and what makes them so and who arrive at the conclusion: being together with those whom they love.[16] In all these examples the link between love and joy is direct and convincing. The much-cited "joy of being loved" is also a relatively clear though not entirely "pure" case—because some alien elements might well adulterate the joy of having someone else say, "How wonderful that you exist" (elements such as gratified vanity, confirmation of status, and so on).

But what about the joy of loving itself, that is, the joy that consists in loving? On the one hand, we have only to have the experience to affirm immediately, "Yes, this joy certainly does exist!" But then how can joy be something secondary, be the response to receiving or possessing something beloved? My answer to this question would be: Because we love to love! In fact, we actually are receiving something beloved *by loving*. Our whole being is so set that it wants to be able to say with reason, "How good that this exists; how wonderful that you are here!" The "reason", of course, the

[16] Cf. Helmut Gollwitzer, . . . *und führen, wohin du nicht willst* (Munich, 1951).

only reason that seems cogent to our own minds must be that the existence of those praised things or persons actually *is* "good" and "wonderful". As has already been said, in this is manifested the "solid" aspect of the context of life as a whole: that the indivisibility of love and joy is not a delusion, wherein two separate emotions or physiological stimuli only seem to merge, but is in fact a response to reality—primarily, of course, to the real suitability to one another of human beings who feel "good" toward each other. They were indeed created for one another. Once again we are reminded, in a fresh way, that love has the nature of a gift: not only being loved, but also loving. And the element of gratitude, which is already present in the first stirrings of love, now becomes somewhat more comprehensible. It is gratitude that we are actually receiving what we by nature long for and love: to be able wholeheartedly to "approve" of something, to be able to say that something is good.

We must not allow this perception, which reflects the way creation is fundamentally constituted, to be thrust off onto some innocuous, poetic sidetrack (although, on the other hand, Goethe's well-known lines "Happy alone / Is the soul who loves"[17] are incomparably precise and realistic). Perhaps if we look at the reverse of the coin we will come to a better understanding of this difficult matter. The reverse is the inability to love, fundamental indifference, "the despairing possibility that nothing matters".[18] The true antithesis of love is not hate but despairing indifference, the feeling that nothing is important.[19]

Despair is to be taken here more literally than it might seem. The radical attitude of "not giving a damn" in fact is in

---

[17] The last lines of the poem "Freudvoll und leidvoll".—TRANS.

[18] Rollo May, *Love and Will* (New York, 1969), 27. In the same book (111) may be found the sentence: "The most tragic of all, in the long run, is the ultimate attitude, 'It doesn't matter.'"

[19] Ibid., 29.

some way related to the state of mind of the damned. In
Dostoevsky's novel *The Brothers Karamazov*, Father Zossima
says: "Fathers and teachers, I ponder 'What is hell?' I maintain that it is the suffering of being unable to love. Once in
infinite existence, immeasurable in time and space, a spiritual
creature was given, on his coming to earth, the power of saying, 'I am and I love.'"

Should anyone find this too mystical or too theological,
perhaps he will be more impressed by what a German writer
of these present times, returned home from exile, has to report concerning his direct experience. Though phrased more
personally, it is basically no different from the Russian monk's
wisdom. "During this time I experienced two kinds of happiness", he writes in summing up his feelings upon his return
home. "The one was being able to help, to alleviate suffering.
The other, and perhaps it was the greatest and most blessed
happiness that has ever come my way, was: *Not to have to
hate.*"[20]

But is there not such a thing as "*unhappy* love"? And if so,
what light does that shed upon the seemingly plausible corre-
lation of love and joy?

Let us say, by way of leaping ahead somewhat, that unhappy love not only exists as a fact but that lovers alone can
be unhappy. "Never are we less protected against suffering
than when we love", says Sigmund Freud;[21] and an American
psychologist actually calls love itself "an experience of
greater vulnerability".[22] This has been known, and expressed,
forever and a day; we may find it said in Thomas à Kempis'

---

[20] Carl Zuckmayer, *A Part of Myself*, trans. Richard and Clara Winston (New
York, 1970), 396. The words "not to have to hate" are emphasized by italics in
the original.

[21] *Gesammelte Werke* (London, 1940–   ), 14:441.

[22] *Love and Will*, 102.

Imitatio Christi [23] and also, of course, in C. S. Lewis' book on love, which we have already quoted several times: "Love anything, and your heart will certainly be wrung and possibly be broken. If you want to make sure of keeping it intact, you must give your heart to no one, not even to an animal." [24] Obviously, only a lover can have the experience of not receiving or of losing something loved; and that means being unhappy. Moreover, the failure to receive or the loss can be experienced as something in the present, or it can be remembered, or it can even be anticipated in despair. The inability to mourn rests upon inability to love.

Of course, not receiving what we love can occur in a great variety of ways besides the one we are first inclined to think of: unrequited love in which the beloved turns away. The mystics likewise speak of this anguish: God is silent; he does not show himself. They call it "aridity" and "the sterile season". But another possibility is that the beloved being falls upon evil ways and commits wrongs. Then, too, the lover is bound to be unhappy, since loving another means wishing that everything will work out entirely well for the beloved, that the beloved will be "all right", not just happy, but perfect and good.

Then where do we stand? Do both principles apply simultaneously: love and joy belong together, but love and sorrow likewise—just as Thomas Aquinas says with his cool objectivity: "Ex amore procedit et gaudium et tristitia",[25] "out of love comes joy as well as sadness"? Is it a simple matter of both this and that? No, it is not quite so simple.

First: There can of course be love without pain and sorrow, but love without joy is impossible. Second, and this is

---

[23] "Sine dolore non vivitur in amore." Quoted from J. Guitton, *Vom Wesen der Liebe zwischen Mann und Frau* (Freiburg, 1960), 168.

[24] *Four Loves*, 138.

[25] II, II, 28, 1.

the main thing: Even the unhappy lover is happier than the nonlover, with whom the lover would never change places. In the fact of loving he has already partaken of something beloved. What is more, he still has a share in the beloved who has rejected him, been ungrateful to him, gone astray, or in some other way caused him grief. He has that share and keeps it, because the lover in some way remains linked with, remains one with, the beloved. Even unhappy or unrequited love has broken through the principle of isolation on which "the whole philosophy of hell rests"[26] and so has gained a solid basis for joy, a part no matter how small of "paradise".

In the light of this it becomes clearer why so many attempts to define love mention joy as an essential component of the concept. Here I am not thinking principally of that famous or notorious characterization, cast in the form of a geometrical theorem, to be found in the long list of definitions in Spinoza's *Ethics*: "Love is joy with the accompanying idea of an external cause."[27] This is a dubious, not to say disturbing, definition on a number of grounds. Suppose we were playing a guessing game and put this question: What is joy with the accompanying idea of an external cause? Who would ever guess that the answer was supposed to be love? And as a matter of fact Spinoza's definition has run into heavy criticism. Alexander Pfänder remarks that it indicates "very crude psychology"[28] and that "its complete wrongness" is easy to perceive.[29] Schopenhauer goes so far as to cite Spinoza's definition merely "for amusement, because of its extraordinary naïveté".[30] For my own part, I would point out

[26] C. S. Lewis, *The Screwtape Letters* (London: Fontana Books, 1969), 92.

[27] "Amor est laetitia concomitante idea causae externae" (*Ethica* III [Definitiones]; also *Ethica* IV, propos. 44).

[28] "Zur Psychologie der Gesinnungen", *Jahrbuch für Philosophie und phänomenologische Forschung*, 1 (1925), 357.

[29] Ibid., 355.

[30] *Sämtliche Werke* (Leipzig: Insel-Ausgabe, n.d.), 2:1325.

that this "definition" does not even make it apparent that purely in terms of elementary grammar "to love" is a transitive verb, that is to say, a verb that must be linked with a direct object. To love always implies to love *someone* or *something*. And if this element is missing in a definition, it has failed to hit its target.[31]

Leibnitz gives a magnificent characterization of love—and, moreover, in a context in which we would scarcely expect to find it. In his *Codex iuris gentium diplomaticus* he writes, "To love means to rejoice in the happiness of another."[32] But of course we must ask, "But what if the other is not happy?" And later, in his *Nouveaux essais*, Leibnitz offers a more precise formulation: To love means to be inclined to rejoice in the perfection, in the goodness or in the happiness of another.[33] That comes very close to the heart of the phenomenon and does not differ so greatly from the exclamation: How good that you exist!

A century earlier Saint Francis de Sales said almost the same thing, although his phraseology is just a shade more ex-

---

[31] This is true for quite a few "definitions" that may be found in philosophical writing. Here are only two examples: "The true essence of love consists in abandoning consciousness of oneself, forgetting oneself in another self, and yet for the first time having and possessing oneself in this fading and forgetting." Thus Hegel in his *Aesthetik*, vol. 1, 2d ed., (Frankfurt, 1955), 519. In this characterization, grandly impressive though it is, the "transitive" nature of love and "the other" scarcely appear. Still less do they in the following definition by Max Scheler, which holds that love is "the intentional movement in which from a given value A of an object the phenomenon of a higher value is attained"—*Wesen und Formen der Sympathie* (Frankfurt, 1948), 177; or that it is "a movement that proceeds from the lower to the higher value and in which any given higher value of an object or a person first flashes into being" (ibid.). In such descriptions the simple fact of love familiar to everyone is scarcely recognizable.

[32] "Amare sive diligere est felicitate alterius delectari" (*Opera Omnia*, ed. L. Dütens, 4.3:295).

[33] *Neue Abhandlungen über den menschlichen Verstand*, in G. W. Leibniz, *Philosophische Schriften*, ed. W. v. Engelhardt and H. H. Holz, vol. 3, pt. 1 (Darmstadt, 1959), 224f.

act. Love, he declares in his *Traité de l'amour de Dieu*,[34] is *the* act in which the will unites and joins with the joy and the welfare of someone else.

If we consider our own experience with people, we will in fact realize that shared joy is a more reliable sign of real love than shared grief, or compassion; it is also far more rare. We need not agree with the Duc de La Rochefoucauld's cynical aphorism that there is something not altogether displeasing to us in our best friends' misfortunes. But it is evident that a good many foreign elements having nothing to do with love may be involved in compassion—which, therefore, is not so "pure" a case as shared joy.

Immanuel Kant is so constituted that he basically mistrusts everything done out of "inclination", that is, out of joy. To him respect for duty is the only serious moral feeling.[35] ("Man is aware with the greatest clarity that he . . . must completely separate his desire for happiness from the concept of duty.")[36] For Kant "laboriousness" is the standard of all moral values. Yet even Kant is forced to recognize the relationship of love and joy: the fact of the matter is simply too compelling. His firm emphasis on doing as the true proof of love merits attention and respect, and we should not dismiss him too rapidly for his inflexible severity. After all, the New Testament contains some sentences that sound a similar note: "If you love me, you will keep my commandments" (Jn 14:15). And so there is much to be said for Kant's comment: "To love one's neighbor means to do all of one's duty toward him *gladly*."[37] But what is meant by this *gladly* (the emphasis is Kant's in the *Critique of Practical Reason*)? Of course it means nothing less than: with joy.

---

[34] 1:71.

[35] *Kritik der praktischen Vernunft*, in *Werke*, ed. W. Weischedel, vol. 4 (Wiesbaden, 1956), 208.

[36] Ibid., vol. 6 (Frankfurt, 1964), 138.

[37] Ibid., 4:205.

VII

IF LOVE, THE DESIRE FOR HAPPINESS, AND JOY are so closely intertwined, should it not be conceded that all love is a form, no matter how sublimated, of self-love? But how can that idea be reconciled with the other conviction, which likewise strikes us as self-evident, that genuine love never seeks its own?

In order to achieve some clarity on this question, we shall have to recall once more something difficult to grasp, that even the acts of man's mind, which means even his volition and not just his sensual desires, take place *by nature* and thus are not something at our own command. Rather, such acts happen over our heads, as it were; they are not left to our freedom of choice but have already *been* imposed. We find this difficult to grasp because we usually understand the terms "nature" and "mind" as mutually exclusive concepts. According to this habit of thought, for example, willing is either a mental act and consequently something not given by nature; or it is a natural event and consequently neither an act of volition nor a mental act at all. In contrast to this, the great teachers of Christendom unanimously insist that there is *one* being—that is in the strictest sense both mind and nature at once; and this being is the created mind.

We cannot repeat it too often: What happens "by nature" happens "by virtue of creation"; that is, on the one hand, it springs from the creature's inmost and most personal impulse; on the other hand, the initial momentum for this impulse does not come from the heart of this same created being but from the act of *creatio* that set in motion the entire dynamics of the universe. We might say it (the initial momentum) comes "from elsewhere"—if the Creator were not more within us than we ourselves. Anyone, therefore, who fully grasps and consistently applies the concept of creatureliness is forced to realize that at the core of the created mind and at the heart of its vital activity something happens that is entirely its own, and therefore a mental act, but simultaneously an event by virtue of creation and, consequently, a natural process.

The functioning of *eros* is exactly of this kind—insofar as we mean by eros the desire for full existence, for existential exaltation, for happiness and bliss: a desire that cannot be diverted or invalidated and that naturally dominates and permeates all our emotions and all our conscious decisions, above all our loving concern for the world and for other human beings. Once more, then: "Man desires happiness naturally and by necessity."[1] "To desire to be happy is not a matter of free choice."[2] Happiness can virtually be defined as the epitome of all those things that "the will is incapable of not willing".[3]

It is not in the least surprising that at this point, in regard to the interpretation and evaluation of eros, opinions differ. We should expect nothing else. Once more it is apparent that a conception of man must underlie any ideas about love. Anyone who maintains that man (and therefore he himself also) is an absolutely free, nonnecessitous,[4] autonomous being—at least in the life of his mind—must hold certain corollary views. He cannot regard the will as incapable of not

[1] I, 94, 1.
[2] I, 19, 10.
[3] I, II, 10, 2.
[4] "Man is a needy being insofar as he belongs to the sensual world" (Kant, *Kritik der praktischen Vernunft* [I, 1, 2], in *Werke*, 4:179.

willing its own completion and fulfillment—these being only alternative terms for happiness. Anything else would seem to him a degradation of the autonomous subject. On the other hand, one who comprehends man to the depths of his soul as *creatura* simultaneously knows that in the act of being created we are—without being asked and without even the possibility of being asked—shot toward our destination like an arrow. Therefore, a kind of gravitational impulse governs our desire for happiness. Nor can we have any power over this impulse because we ourselves *are* it.

Nevertheless, this does not mean that man is consequently "by nature" an impotent nullity for whom God, as ultimately the only self-motivating force, must leap into the breach. The freedom of our own personal choices emerges from the very ground of what is willed by nature; and in this very process of willing by nature it is we ourselves, from the heart of our hearts, as it were, who desire happiness, desire our own happiness, of course.

In saying this we have formally returned to our theme. This desire for existential fulfillment, acting in us by virtue of creation, is really "self-love". It is the basic form of love, on which all others are founded and which makes all others possible. At the same time it is the form of love most familiar to us from our inner knowledge of ourselves. Let us first consider this fact carefully. Then, perhaps, we may understand somewhat better why the love with which we love ourselves can be the standard for all other kinds of love. Granted, it sounds at first rather odd, and almost like a deliberate provocation, that self-love should serve as a paradigm from which we may read off what love in general is. But suppose we once more apply our "test" formula: It's good that you exist. To whom do we refer that expression, instantly and with sincerity, if not to ourselves? We do so even if at the moment we have been critically examining ourselves and do not find ourselves especially lovable. The spontaneous answer to this question seems to me so unequivocal that it hardly needs to be put into words. But of course it ill comports with the idea that love is equivalent to unselfishness.

Perhaps we are always engaged in somewhat repressing this truth, which strikes us as somehow unseemly. At any rate, we may be surprised by the blunt statements of the ancients on this point. Consider, for example, these sentences from Aristotle's *Nicomachean Ethics*: "The relations that serve to define the various kinds of friendship seem to be derived from our relations to ourselves."[5] And: "The highest form of friendship can be likened to self-love."[6] Thomas Aquinas, too, mentions loving friendship and self-love in one breath: "A friend is loved as one for whom we desire something; and man also loves himself in exactly this same way."[7] We might at first take this analogy as meaning that self-love is a kind of image of friendship, that we love ourselves as we love a friend. But Thomas means just the opposite: friendship is the image and self-love is the original; we love our friends as we love ourselves. The derivative[8] element is the love for others: "It proceeds from the similarity to the love we bear ourselves."[9]

As has been said, such a statement leaves us considerably puzzled and inclined to object that, strictly speaking, a man is not his own friend. After all, we do not feel friendship for ourselves! Thomas Aquinas agrees: "We do not feel friendship for ourselves but something greater than friendship. . . . Everyone is at one with himself; and this *being* one is more than *becoming* one (*unitas est potior unione*). Just as unity is

[5] *Nicomachean Ethics* 9, 4; 1166 a.
[6] Ibid., 9, 4; 1166 b.
[7] I, II, 2, 7 ad 2.
[8] 3, d. 28, 1, 6: derivatur.
[9] Ibid.

closer to the source than union, so the love with which a
person loves himself is the origin and the root of friendship.
For the friendship that we have for others consists in this, that
we behave toward them as we do toward ourselves."[10] Of
course, that statement is not intended, as it is in Voltaire,[11] as a
cynical unmasking of purported unselfishness. However, we
are being asked soberly to accept the fact that: "Everyone
loves himself more than others."[12] That is simply so, nor is
there anything wrong about it; it's not a matter of human
weakness. It is so on the basis of our creatureliness, that is, by
virtue of the immutable fact that in the act of being created
we were launched irresistibly toward our own fulfillment, toward our felicity too, toward the full realization of what was
intended for us—or, as it is put in Christendom's sacred
Book: "For God created all things that they might be" (Wis
1:14). Thomas cited this sentence and discoursed upon it
many times, showing that, in spite of the reference to the
Nicomachean Ethics,[13] he is not speaking simply as an Aristotelian (which, in fact, he never was, strictly speaking).[14] Augustine makes precisely the same point: "If you do not know
how to love yourself, you cannot truthfully love your neighbor."[15] And in *The City of God*[16] he says that the lover receives the standard, the *regula*, for love of neighbor from
himself, from his love for himself. Of course Augustine does
not refer to Aristotle, whose writings were scarcely known to

[10] II, II, 25, 4. Similarly: 3, d. 29, 1, 3 ad 3; *C. G.* 3, 153; *Quol.* 5, 6; *Car.* 7
ad 11.

[11] *Dictionnaire philosophique*, article "Amour-Propre". *Oeuvres Complètes*
(Paris, 1825), 51:326.

[12] I, II, 27, 3.

[13] Cf. II, II, 25, 4.

[14] Cf. Josef Pieper, *Guide to Thomas Aquinas* (San Francisco: Ignatius Press,
1962), 43ff.

[15] *Sermo* 368, 5; PL 39:1655.

[16] *City of God* 1, 20.

him, but to the New Testament, which likewise establishes self-love as the measure for all love among human beings: Thou shalt love thy neighbor *as thyself*!

Incidentally, we will sometimes find the realistic attitude underlying this idea expressed from an altogether different angle in British and American writing on the subject of love. Self-love, it is argued, may very well sometimes assume the functions of rational judgment and protect purported or truly disinterested love from hurling itself to destruction for the sake of some idol. Truly loving devotion, the argument continues, always presupposes that the self and its dignity are not really threatened; only then can the lover freely and unreservedly, without a backward glance, surrender himself.[17] The complexities of the problem, which are implicit in the matter itself, can scarcely ever be reduced to handy solutions and formulas. Our line of argument should make that quite apparent.

It is all the more important, therefore, to understand what is meant by setting "self-love" as the standard for the love directed toward all other human beings and perhaps even toward God himself. How then do we love ourselves?

It seems to me crucial that in loving affirmation of ourselves we always regard ourselves as *persons*, that is, as beings existing for their own sake. Even when we are finding fault with ourselves, we think and judge in terms of our own impulses, fears and goals, our inner motivations. And this is precisely what we do not do when, in a state of pure desire, we cast our glance upon another person like an object, seeing that person as a mere provoker of stimuli, a means to an end. This point, incidentally, was also formulated by Aristotle in the *Nicomachean Ethics*.[18] Above all, Aristotle says,

[17] Martin C. d'Arcy, *The Mind and Heart of Love* (London, 1945), 323, 325.
[18] 9, 4; 1166 a.

man really wishes the good for himself, whatever his concept of that good may be; he wishes it for himself and at the same time makes a reality of it for the sake of his own self. Moreover, we also wish the good as the persons we are now. In other words, we do not say: first I must change and become a different person, and then, when I "deserve" it more, I will wish good for myself. On the contrary, we say: I want it now, just as I am at the present moment—whether or not I happen to like myself right now. Loving, we remarked earlier, is not the same as liking. C. S. Lewis comments that for a long time he found it sheer hairsplitting that we are asked to hate sin but to love the sinner—until one day he realized that there was actually one person in the world toward whom he had followed that precept all his life, namely, himself.[19]

Another idea in the *Nicomachean Ethics* may at first appear too obvious: that in loving ourselves we like to spend time with ourselves, both dwelling on memory and looking to the future. But to translate these obvious facts, in practical terms, into relationships with fellowmen is just as difficult as—as love of neighbor (by which at this point we do not intend anything specifically Christian; what we mean is that attitude by which concern for another human being, including the partner in an erotic relationship, develops into "love").

It now appears that two separate ideas have crept into our discussion and become entangled: first, self-love, desire for happiness, striving for fulfillment as the root of all other love, the original source of love by nature. Second, self-love as the model and standard of love for others. But in both cases the question arises: How do we escape from love of ourselves—however much it may be the root or the model? How can we

---

[19] *Christian Behaviour* (London, 1943), 38f.

conceive this step to be taken? Or is it less a step than a leap, which sooner or later has to be taken, across the gulf that separates eros from agape?

After all, we do not have to accept Anders Nygren's extremist characterization of agape to realize that selfish love is not real love. And also to agree with Augustine when he states: "What is not loved for its own sake is not loved at all";[20] and: "When you love, love without recompense."[21] Everyone knows that from his own direct experience. Even Nietzsche, who spends a great deal of wit unmasking the "dreadful nonsense" that "love ought to be something 'unegoistical' ",[22] who calls love "this subtlest avarice"[23] and says of the lover that he is "more egoist than ever"[24]—even Nietzsche admits that when hearing the word "love" even "the slyest woman and the meanest man think of the relatively most unselfish moments of their entire lives".[25]

But precisely at this point the possibility of establishing a link appears, or at any rate a glimmering of what might be the nature of that step from self-love to disinterested or "selfless" love. Were not those most unselfish moments, of which both the slyest and the meanest persons think, also the happiest moments in their lives *because* of being the most unselfish? If eros, self-love, is basically the desire for happiness, then the question must be: What does happiness truly mean, and in what does it consist?

By way of a forewarning, we should say that no one can answer this question simply by giving a "positive" description of happiness. On this point Plato's view accords completely

---

[20] "Quod non propter se amatur, non amatur" (*Soliloquia* 1, 13; PL 32:881).

[21] "Si amas, gratis ama" (*Sermo* 165, 4; PL 38:905).

[22] *Ecce Homo*, in *Gesammelte Werke* (Munich: Musarion-Ausgabe, 1922–), 21:220.

[23] Ibid., 11:221.

[24] Ibid.

[25] *Menschliches, Allzumenschliches* II, 95, in *Gesammelte Werke*, 9:58.

with that of Thomas Aquinas. In Plato's *Symposium*[26] the point is made that the soul of the lover evidently craves something else besides sexual pleasure, a something "which she cannot tell and of which she has only a dark and doubtful presentiment". And Thomas declares, "By felicity everyone understands a state perfect to the highest degree; but in what this state consists is hidden."[27] Furthermore, we know from our own experience that we certainly are not made happy by receiving what at first glance we seem really to have longed for. Ernst Bloch's phrase about the "melancholy of fulfillment" is pertinent here.[28] Kierkegaard, too, says many times that one who insists upon pleasure has set his foot on the road to despair. On the other hand, if it is true that joy and happiness are our response to partaking of something we love; and if loving, simple approval, is something beloved in itself—then it must likewise be true that our desire for happiness can be satisfied precisely by such affirmation directed toward another, that is, by "unselfish" love. As Goethe puts it: "True happiness really consists only in sympathy."[29] At this point we must recall Leibnitz' definition that the essence of love consists in shared joy. This is how, he adds, "a difficult complication" is resolved, "namely, how disinterested love, *amor non mercenarius*, can exist. . . . For the happiness of those whose betterment gives us joy forms a part of our own happiness."[30]

Our initial question was how we might imagine the step from mere self-love to unselfish love that seeks nothing for itself. From all we have been discussing so far, we might draw

[26] 192 c–d.

[27] "Omnes . . . per beatitudinem intelligunt quemdam perfectissimum statum; sed in quo consistat ille status perfectus . . . occultum est" (2, d. 38, 1, 2 ad 2).

[28] *Das Prinzip Hoffnung* (Frankfurt, 1959), 221.

[29] To Sara von Grotthuss on April 23, 1814.

[30] *Opera Omnia*, 4.3:295.

the following conclusions: that no gulf separates the one kind of love from the other, at least not necessarily; that, on the contrary, it might be almost impossible to say where one's own desire for happiness ceases and unselfish joy in the happiness of others begins. Obviously there can be countless pretexts for self-deception, for covering up and for subtle falsification, but that only proves how fluid are the boundaries between eros and agape.

Even if *agape* (*caritas*) is explicitly identified as "supernatural", that is, as a "virtue" nourished not by our own strength alone but by some divine power communicated to us through grace, it still must not be thought of as strictly separated from nature-given self-love directed toward happiness and the fulfillment of existence. Such separation is possible only for one who holds, like Anders Nygren,[31] that creation and redemption have nothing to do with one another. Otherwise, on the contrary, we are rather prepared to find what is "by nature", that is, "by virtue of creation", strictly ethical matters and the supernatural so closely interwoven that the seam can scarcely be detected. Or at least it cannot so long as all three impulses, that which springs from nature, that which springs from ethical freedom and that which springs from grace are in harmony with one another. If you row your boat in the same direction as the wind is driving it—how are you to distinguish between the motion that is caused by your own efforts and what is caused by the wind?

Earlier I referred to Leibnitz' phrase "amor mercenarius". This phrase, mercenary love, with its implication of the lover's always eying his reward, has repeatedly been applied to need-love, that is, to eros, as a term of more or less summary

[31] *Eros und Agape* (Gütersloh, 1937), 2:110.

contempt. But as might be expected, here too we are dealing with a rather complicated matter; and once more the dividing line between the meaningfully possible and the perversion *in concreto* is often enough scarcely discernible. Augustine added an explanatory sentence to his dictum, already cited, about true love's not asking compensation: "If you truly love, your reward must be he whom you love."[32] Does Augustine maintain, then, that there is a reward for love? But there can be more than one kind of "reward". Here Augustine uses the word *merces* ("ipse sit merces, quem amas"). This is a rather coarse word that sometimes carries the faintly contemptuous connotation of a day-laborer's wages, of payment, of paying off. But it is likely that he might have used the word in quotation marks, so to speak, possibly because he was addressing this sermon to the fishermen of Hippo. Elsewhere he says *praemium* and not *merces*: "Praemium dilectionis ipse dilectus",[33] the beloved himself is love's reward. *Praemium* can also be translated by "reward" and "recompense", but, unlike *merces*, it also implies something not demandable, something that comes as a gift, even though it also comes as something intended and hoped for.

Of course we need not waste words making the point that what happens between the partners in "venal love", the kind that has its set price, has nothing to do with love. But what about the "reward" intended in real love, that reward which consists in the lovers' being together? Everyone who loves naturally wants this reward. But is that desire a selfish eying of compensation? Granted, the possibilities of illusion, self-deception and even of cynical misuse are, as we have said, legion. Even the reward implicit in lovers' being together can be misguidedly isolated so that eventually the embrace be-

---

[32] *Sermo* 165, 4; PL 38:905.
[33] *Enarrationes in Psalmos* 118, 22, 2; PL 37:1563.

comes, perhaps unintentionally, a means to a selfish end. When that happens, the "lover" sets out on a course that ends with the alleged or supposed "beloved" no longer being regarded as a person at all but as a thing, "as a machine to be used for his pleasure".[34]

For the present, however, we are speaking of the reward that comes with real love or, rather, that is present along with it and it alone, as an immanent fruit. No one, it seems to me, has stated this matter so well as Bernard of Clairvaux. It is perhaps equally characteristic of him that his formulation comes from a treatise on the love for God[35] and that it does not so much as mention the name of God. The sentence reads: "All true love is without calculation and nevertheless is instantly given its reward, in fact it can receive its reward only when it is without calculation. . . . Whoever seeks as the reward of his love only the joy of love will receive the joy of love. But whoever seeks anything else in love except love will lose both love and the joy of love at the same time."

The paradoxical structure (and it is truly paradoxical) described here with magnificent simplicity recurs in all fundamental existential contexts. The indispensable goods of life can be acquired only by their being "given" to us; they are not accorded to us when we directly aim for them. One of the most important lessons of modern psychotherapy, for example, is that nothing so hampers the attainment of psychic health as the deliberate or exclusive intention to achieve or retain good health. As spiritual and ethical persons we must want to be "all right"; then such health will be given to us.

That love, insofar as it is real love, does not seek its own remains an inviolable truth. But the lover, assuming that he is disinterested and not calculating, does after all attain his own,

---

[34] Cf. C. S. Lewis, *The Problem of Pain* (New York: Macmillan, 1967), 64.

[35] *De diligendo Deo*, ed. W. W. Williams (Cambridge, 1926), 32f.

the reward of love. And this reward, in its turn and in view of human nature, cannot be a matter of indifference to him.

I try to imagine the pleasure Augustine must have felt in arriving at this dialectical formulation (modeled on the biblical sentence about that special love which loses what it tries to keep): "If you love your soul, there is danger that it may perish. Therefore you are not permitted to love it, since you do not want it to perish. But in not wanting it to perish, you love it."[36]

---

[36] *Sermo* 368, 1; PL 39:1652. In the same sermon (cap. 5) there is the formulation: "Whoso loves his soul will lose it because he loves it. You do not want to lose it? Then you are incapable of not loving it."

VIII

HOWEVER DIFFERENT OUR DEFINITIONS of love and however different in fact its manifold forms are, one element recurs in all descriptions of it and in all actualizations of
it: the tendency toward union. Love is, as Dionysius the Areopagite puts it, a "vis unitiva et concretiva" [*henotiké kai synkra-
tiké*].[1] What happens in love among human beings is that two
persons become one, so to speak. "So to speak"—for of
course no one can actually become as closely united with any
other person as he is with himself. Moreover, union in love
presupposes that the elements of this new unit nevertheless
remain distinct and independent: "Unio est aliquorum dis-
tinctorum."[2] Or, as Jules Michelet elegantly puts it at the end
of his famous though on the whole rather barren book:
"Pour s'unir il faut rester deux",[3] in order to become one,
they must remain two. The matter can also be expressed, with
reversed accenting: Although the pair remain two, they become one. The paradox is unresolvable; it is inherent in the
thing itself.

We have already cited C. S. Lewis' *The Screwtape Letters*, in
which the argumentative devil pronounces it the sum of in-
fernal philosophy that one thing is *not* the other and especially

---

[1] *De divinis nominibus* 15, 180. Cf. also Thomas Aquinas, *In div. nom.* 4, 12;
no. 455.

[2] II, II, 17, 3.

[3] Jules Michelet, *L'Amour*, 4th ed. (Paris, 1859), 398. Similarly, Erich
Fromm, *The Art of Loving* (New York, 1952), 17.

that one self is *not* another self—whereas the philosophy of the "Enemy", that is, God, amounts to nothing else but an incessant effort to evade this obvious truth. "He aims at a contradiction. Things are to be many, yet somehow also one. The good of one self is to be the good of another. This impossibility, He calls *love*." [4] That is something that does not exist in hell; in fact, as Dostoevsky's Russian monk says, its absence is precisely what makes up the essence of hell. Incidentally, the word "hell" need not necessarily imply something in the hereafter. If we may properly speak of heaven on earth,[5] then why not also of hell on earth?

But if this is so, if every form of love really and essentially seeks oneness and has union for its fruit,[6] then it must be said that such union, such merging of subjects who are nevertheless different from one another and remain so, finds its most complete realization in what is called erotic love. Consequently, love between the sexes becomes a paradigmatic form of love in general. Nevertheless, the concept of sexuality, which comes to mind as soon as love between man and woman is discussed, gives rise to a certain misunderstanding. For that reason we must speak somewhat more precisely.

Although obviously sexuality always plays a part in erotic love; although the human being, through all the levels of his individual life, up to and including the style of his intellectual activity, is either man or woman; although the biblical phrase about two who are made one flesh applies particularly to sexual union—it is nevertheless important, I think, to keep in mind something else that is likewise obvious and familiar to everyone. On the one hand, the sexual act can take place without love and even without love in the narrower erotic sense. On the other hand, love between man and woman,

---

[4] C. S. Lewis, *The Screwtape Letters* (London: Fontana Books, 1969), 92.

[5] Ernst Bloch, *Erbschaft dieser Zeit* (Frankfurt, 1962), 157.

[6] "Unio est consequens amorem" (I, II, 26, 2 ad 2).

understood as the closest imaginable union of persons, includes in addition to sexuality many quite other things—so
much so that a sexuality set apart and therefore "absolutized"
tends rather to block love, even erotic love, and to alienate
people from one another as personal beings.

In the following discussion we are not, strictly speaking,
dealing with what is usually described in "love stories" as
amour-passion. Ortega y Gasset remarks in his essay on love
that in all such stories "usually everything happens except the
one thing that deserves to be called love in its proper sense."[7]
However, we want to speak here of love in its proper sense,
which we define as the power that can produce a passionate
merging not merely for the duration of an episode or an affair but for a whole life ("till death do us part"), a union and
communion embracing and permeating all the dimensions
of existence. Integrated into that union and communion are
all the forms and aspects of love among human beings—from
sexual desire to supernatural agape. The decisive factor, as I
see it, is precisely that all these elements enter into it; this,
too, is what makes it paradigmatic: in such a communion of
love there is no separation of eros and agape.

Incidentally, man does not wish to be loved "purely un-
selfishly". Not at all. Of course he wants to be affirmed and
loved as a person, not just as the holder of certain qualities
and abilities. In short, he wants to be loved for himself. But
he is also concerned with being of value to the other and
with being "used". Moreover, he definitely wants to be desir-
able, and certainly not just as an object of love unmotivated,
value-neutral and solely-desirous-of-giving (the qualifica-
tions, we will recall, of that agape-love which Anders Nygren regards as the only kind appropriate for a Christian).

But erotic love can be and actually has been discredited in

[7] *On Love* (New York, 1957), 51.

other ways besides being pitted against theologically inter-
preted agape. We need only cite the grotesque terms in
which Immanuel Kant, during the period he was writing the
Critique of Pure Reason, disparaged the "sexual inclination":
"Man certainly has no inclination to enjoy his fellowman's
flesh, and where that is done, it is more an act of revenge in
war than an inclination; but there remains one inclination in
man that can be called an appetite and that aims at enjoyment
of his fellowman. This is the sexual inclination." And he
adds: "This cannot be love but appetite."[8]

I have posited that the separation of erotic from ethical-
supernatural love was a fateful thing fraught with many consequences. I have said that it was unrealistic because it ignores
man's nature, that is, the condition imparted to him by virtue
of his creation. And I have related the rift thus created between the two kinds of love to certain contemporary attitudes. This hypothesis might be extended. We might, for
example, wonder whether the separation of eros from agape
might not lead, almost of necessity, to that other aberration
of love: namely, the isolation of sex from eros. It has been my
observation that the integration of all aspects of the many-
faceted phenomenon known as love, as it is experienced in
the lifetime communion of man and woman, if everything
goes as it should—that this integration is brought about and
sustained by eros. In other words, to sum it up in an epigram,
erotic love is the clamp that alone can hold together sex and
agape. "He who despises eros succumbs to sex." That is another epigram (from Walter Schubart's sometimes problem-
atical book *Religion und Eros*).[9] But it seems to me that what
is conveyed by these two pointed phrases calls for the most
serious reflection. While we reflect, it is important to keep in

[8] *Eine Vorlesung Kants über Ethik,* ed. Paul Menzer (Berlin, 1925), 204f.
[9] *Religion und Eros* (Munich: C. H. Beck, 1941), 251.

mind the naturally *mediate* character of eros. Plato, too, laid stress on this aspect of eros in the *Symposium*:[10] Love "is intermediate between the divine and the mortal . . . ; he is the mediator who spans the channel that divides them, and therefore in him all is bound together." There is much to suggest that if this clamp that is called eros should fall away and be denied, the meaningful wholeness of human potentialities for love would instantly disintegrate.

But now the time has come to seek for a more precise meaning of eros and erotic love. Kant, Nygren and Karl Barth place their emphases differently, but on the whole they are of one accord in saying that eros is really mere self-love, is "appetite".

I feel safe in going back to Plato, whom the above-mentioned writers also claim to be following. Plato tends first of all to say that erotic love is something akin to poetic rapture and, in fact, to artistic enthusiasm in general, a state of being carried out of the normality of everyday existence. In ordinary experience this quality is apparent in what we call infatuation: Ortega y Gasset wittily calls it an abnormal state of attention in a normal man.[11] But infatuation is not love; at most it is the beginning of love. Erotic love, too, is a kind of transport and rapture—the latter word literally meaning, as suggested above, being carried away by force out of the soul's normal state. The slang phrase, that a person is "gone on" someone, gets at the heart of the matter. This rapturous departure from the normality of everyday equilibrium happens, furthermore, upon encounters with physical beauty. Erotic love is kindled first and foremost by beauty—that is a commonplace.

---

[10] *Symposium* 202 c.
[11] *On Love*, 51.

But what does *beauty* mean? The old definition, which at first glance seems abstract and vague, is that *beautiful* means pleasing to look at. Yet the definition is apt insofar as it avoids pinning itself down. Beauty cannot be objectively defined or measured like any other "quantity". Is there any need to belabor the point that the "measurements" used in beauty contests are sheer commercialized idiocy? Nevertheless, beauty is something distinctly sensual or, at any rate, something that comes to the fore in the realm of the senses. But, as we have said, it escapes precise definition. When we try to characterize the beauty of a face that does not conform to any set pattern, we may speak of its charm; or we may call a certain way of speaking or moving "charming". But these words really mean no more than enchanting, enrapturing, transporting.

The difficulty, if not the impossibility, of a positive definition is perhaps connected with the fact that in experiencing sensual beauty we are being referred to something that is not simply present and discernible. What takes place within us at the sight of beauty is not really that we experience satisfaction of any sort but rather something like the awakening of expectation. We do not see or partake of a fulfillment but of a promise. Goethe summed it up in a marvelously succinct phrase that, incidentally, reiterates Plato's view: "Beauty is not so much performance as promise."[12] That erotic love responds to just this promise-aspect of beauty has been recognized and expressed again and again. Paul Claudel has said: "[Woman is] the promise that cannot be kept; but it is precisely in this that [her] grace consists."[13] And as might be expected, C. S. Lewis is quite familiar with the concept: "Eros is driven to promise what Eros himself cannot perform."[14]

[12] *Campagne in Frankreich* (Münster, December 1792).

[13] Paul Claudel, *The City*, II, end of act 3.

[14] *The Four Loves* (London, 1960), 131. Similarly in *They Asked for a Paper* (London, 1962), 200.

What happens in erotic love is thus not "gratification" but an opening of the sphere of existence to an infinite quenching that cannot be had at all "here". Naturally, this interpretation of eros is not to be taken as a simple description of the average situation, as though that is what actually happens at every encounter between Jack and Jill. But it is certainly not mere romanticizing. Rather, it indicates that we are vouchsafed something in all erotic emotion and rapture that we would otherwise never know—that we are drawn into something that goes infinitely far beyond what seems at first hand to be meant.

Naturally, sexuality is always present in the erotic love of man and woman, and sexual union is also kept in view. Nevertheless, the specifically *erotic* quality of the relationship is of an entirely different kind. Perhaps we may even cast doubt on what Sigmund Freud[15] seems to be asserting: that the sexual relationship is "primarily intended" and is only set aside or merely glossed over temporarily. In this connection Rollo May[16] refers to the example of Antony and Cleopatra in Shakespeare's tragedy. Undoubtedly, May says, there were plenty of courtesans in the Roman army to satisfy the general's "sexual needs". But in the encounter with Cleopatra something wholly new suddenly happened; only then "Eros entered the picture, and Antony became transported into a whole new world." And in Goethe's novel *Werther* we are shown two persons who are clearly lovers and altogether man and wife; and yet Werther can say, "All desire is stilled in their presence."

Of course, sensuality is involved, and so is sexuality; but these urges are neither isolated nor primary, at least not as

[15] Freud calls all nonsexual love "goal-inhibited love"; it "was originally fully sensual love and still is in the person's unconscious" (*Gesammelte Werke*, 14:462).

[16] *Love and Will* (New York, 1969), 76.

long as the mediative daimon Eros reigns. All this has nothing whatsoever to do with "puritanism", "bourgeois morality", or any kind of ascetical disparagement of sexuality. Once more we may quote Goethe, who is hardly open to the charge of prudishness. Yet he makes this very distinction several times, even in his autobiography when he reports on his own earliest erotic experiences. Thus he writes in *Dichtung und Wahrheit*[17] (*Poetry and Truth*), "The first erotic leanings of unspoiled youth take an absolutely spiritual turn. Nature seems to desire one sex to perceive goodness and beauty sensuously embodied in the other sex. And so the sight of this girl, because of my affection for her, opened up to me a new world of beauty and excellence."

That is, as we see, not so very distant from what Plato says about eros. But neither Goethe nor Plato deceives himself into thinking that he has thereby said everything there is to say about love, and certainly not everything about what constitutes the lifelong communion of man and wife. Plato especially—whom we late-born and enlightened readers all too soon suspect of speaking too academically, that is, "platonically", about love—Plato is actually quite free of illusions and hardly apt to slip into unrealistic attitudes. We need only read carefully what he puts into the mouth of Socrates concerning the brutality of the many or concerning the cultivated sensuality of a rationalized, technical approach to living—both attitudes fundamentally aiming at nothing but pleasure.[18] It is also true, however, that in the same dialogue, *Phaedrus*, we find the statement that that eros which renounces sexual pleasure is the most blessed form of love.[19] Here is where doubts arise as to whether this is not a romantic, sentimental exaggeration. Still and all, Paul Claudel says,

[17] Pt. 1, bk. 5.
[18] *Phaedrus* 256.
[19] Ibid., 256 b 3.

"Human love is beautiful only when it is not accompanied by gratification."[20] That is a profoundly problematic sentence, one that at any rate raises a number of fresh questions. But it can do no harm, I think, to consider from time to time that the man who could seriously hold this idea was a person of a certain stature.

To return to Plato for the moment: he knows perfectly well that the heroic form of love is a rarity that cannot be required of the average human being. Nevertheless he remains convinced that only the mediative power of erotic rapture can humanize naked desire and that only such self-forgetfulness can preserve men from "the dark pathways". On the other hand: "He who is not a lover can offer a mere acquaintance flavored with worldly wisdom, dispensing a niggardly measure of worldly goods; in the soul to which he is attached he will engender an ignoble quality."[21] But the same mediative daimon that alone can prevent the isolation of *sexus* from love is also able to keep allegedly pure ethical or spiritual "love" (which likewise is in constant danger of degenerating into inhumanity) from repressing the capacity for sensual upheavals and thus becoming a gloomy, an inflexible "charity without love".[22]

It is therefore not altogether incomprehensible that eros, viewed in such terms, should embody in its overall purest form the essence of love—*as long as it reigns*. But we must add this qualification: Granted, the word "forever" is quintessentially native to the vocabulary of eros. And it is by no means just "sounding brass". In the festive being-beside-oneself of erotic rapture, time really stands still; there emerges

[20] Paul Claudel/Jacques Rivière, *Correspondance 1907–1914.*

[21] *Phaedrus* 256 e 4.

[22] Cf. Josef Pieper, *Divine Madness: Plato's Case against Secular Humanism* (San Francisco: Ignatius Press, 1995), 53–55.

something of that "suspended present" which, in fact, is an element in the concept of eternity. Yet even if we grant this, erotic love seems to unfold to the full blossoming of its beauty only for a short span of time, especially at the beginning, during the "first" encounter of lovers. Eros, it has been said, is "a preface by nature".[23] But if all goes well this preface will not be forgotten. It has set a standard, has established a stock that can never be used up. On the other hand, undoubtedly it is only realistic to call erotic love the notoriously "most mortal form" of love.[24]

But, once more: as long as eros reigns, it embodies in purest form the complete essence of love. Then, above all, the "wonderful that you exist" springs most intensely from the heart, most blessed and blessing, and least contaminated by other elements.

In contrast to that statement we find, in Werner Bergengruen's posthumous autobiography, the elegiac sentence: "Love for children is perhaps the most intense love; for it knows that it has nothing to hope for."[25] But as a kind of response we might consider the words of Lacordaire: "It is an honor for you to find again in your children the same ingratitude you showed toward your own fathers and thus attain to the perfection of loving, like God, without self-interest", with a *sentiment désinteressé*".[26] But the father's as well as the mother's love is naturally always mingled with other elements, such as concern and anxiety. Pure, unadulterated affirmation is, it seems, attained only in erotic love. Nowhere else, moreover, is the gift-nature of being loved as well as of loving and

---

[23] George Santayana, "Friendship", in *The Birth of Reason and Other Essays*, ed. D. Gory (New York, 1968), 83.

[24] *The Four Loves*, 130.

[25] Dichtergehäuse (Zurich-Munich, 1966), 40.

[26] Quoted in Jean Guitton, *Vom Wesen der Liebe zwischen Mann und Frau*, 313.

being permitted to love so intensively experienced. For the first and perhaps for the only time you spontaneously and effortlessly love another person truly "as yourself".[27] And that is why such lovers cannot conceal their joy; they actually radiate it—very differently from mere sex partners who, as everyone has observed, tend to walk about looking rather frustrated and sullen. For a moment in erotic love the world of man is whole, hale, holy, and life has turned out good and happy. For that reason everyone is well-disposed toward lovers; "all mankind loves a lover."[28] Erotic love is also the theme of Georg Simmel's melancholy epigram that music and love are the only undertakings of mankind that are not hopeless from the start.[29]

If we consider all this, it will scarcely seem surprising that eros has repeatedly been deified. Of course, the biblical sentence "God is love" (1 Jn 4:8) has nothing to do with such deification—quite aside from the fact that the New Testament text does not use the terms *eros* or *amor*, but *agape* and *caritas*. Nevertheless, the Christian tradition of European thought shows a constantly recurring stress on the "erotic" elements even in the love of God. I think it significant that the idea, first expressed by Dionysius the Areopagite, that the noun *eros* is "more divine" (*theióteron*) than the noun *agape*[30]

[27] Cf. Lewis, *The Four Loves*, 131.

[28] R. W. Emerson, *Essays*, 1st series (London, 1903), 128.

[29] *Fragmente und Aufsätze*, 9.

[30] Thus in the book *On the Divine Names* (4, 12; 164). But like so much in the history of Dionysius the Areopagite's influence (on this subject, cf. Josef Pieper, *Scholasticism* [New York, 1960], 46ff.), this idea also rests upon a misunderstanding, specifically upon misinterpretation of a sentence in the *Epistle to the Romans* of Ignatius of Antioch. There it is stated (7, 2): "My love [*eros*] is crucified." Dionysius, as Origen had done before him, understands this to mean that Christ is referred to in the sense of *eros*, beloved. But the context clearly shows that what is meant is: my erotic love (for worldly things) has been nailed to the cross with Christ. Long before Anders Nygren (*Eros und*

should be taken over centuries later by Thomas Aquinas in his famous textbook for beginners. To be sure, Thomas immediately offers an interpretation: because *amor* primarily means being carried away, he says, it is somewhat more divine than *dilectio*, which contains more of an element of rational selectiveness: "Divinius est amor quam dilectio."[31] And Saint Francis de Sales also appeals to Dionysius the Areopagite[32] when he defends the title of his treatise on the love of God; quite rightly, he says, the love of God is given the more excellent name of *amor*.[33]

We are dealing with something quite different when we consider the apotheosis of eros such as is to be found in, for example, Walter Schubart's already cited book *Religion und Eros*, which Karl Barth has called a "frightening book".[34] Schubart argues not only that "eroticism is a religious category",[35] which, in a sense, might still be considered acceptable, but also that: "Religion and eroticism have the same goal",[36] and: "Love between the sexes when impelled by the urge to redemption, and the love of God, are the same in their essence."[37] Here, clearly, we have a romantic obliteration of boundaries between two entirely different realms, and the result does justice to neither. On this point we must agree fully with Karl Barth's criticism, just as we agree with his sharply ironical condemnation of Schleiermacher's embarrassing "Intimate Letters concerning Friedrich Schlegel's

---

Agape, 2:409ff.), Fr. X. Funk pointed this out as early as 1901 in his edition of the Apostolic Fathers (*Patres Apostolici*, vol. 1 [Tübingen, 1901], 261).

[31] I, II, 26, 3 ad 4.

[32] *Traité de l'amour de Dieu*, 1:53.

[33] "Le nom de l'amour, comme plus excellent, a été justement donné à la charité" (ibid., 73).

[34] *Kirchliche Dogmatik*, vol. 3, pt. 4 (Zollikon-Zurich, 1951), 140.

[35] *Religion und Eros*, 123.

[36] Ibid., 278.

[37] Ibid., 123.

Lucinde" and of Schlegel's own nonsense about the "sacredness of sensuality" and the "priests and liturgists" of the religion of eros.[38] But it remains completely incomprehensible to me how a man like Karl Barth could have hit on the idea that the Catholic doctrine of the sacramental nature of marriage is in any way related to such deification of eros.[39]

But let us consider something of greater importance and greater contemporary relevance than discursive theory. There seems nowadays some strong imperative to conduct ourselves as though eros really were a kind of absolute authority. There are those who feel that they are in the right, are carrying out a kind of religious duty "in the service of eros"—even though they may be deceiving a spouse, betraying a friend, abusing hospitality, destroying the happiness of others, or abandoning their own children. Then everything appears as a "sacrifice" painfully offered upon the altar of love.[40] C. S. Lewis with his magnificent metaphysical common sense has framed two memorable warnings in this connection. The first is: "When natural things look most divine, the demoniac is just round the corner."[41] And the second: "Natural loves that are allowed to become gods do not remain loves."[42]

In conclusion, nevertheless, we must say one word more in favor of erotic love. When people graced with mystical insight search for the figure of speech to communicate their directly incommunicable experiences in their dealings with the personal ground of their own existence, that is, with God, they evidently can find nothing more appropriate than comparison with the ecstatic raptures of eros. Thus we find the language of love in both the Canticle of Canticles and in

---

[38] *Kirchliche Dogmatik*, vol. 3, pt. 4, 134.
[39] Ibid., 135f.
[40] Cf. *The Four Loves*, 130.
[41] Ibid., 128.
[42] Ibid., 17.

the writings of such mystics as Hugh of St. Victor. In his small book *On the Love of the Bridegroom for the Bride*,[43] Hugh writes, "I will speak, He said, with my bride. . . . And when I speak to the bride, ye shall know that I cannot speak of anything but love."

---

[43] *De amore sponsi ad sponsam.*

IX

THERE IS AN IMPLICATION to calling eros a mediative power that unites the lowest with the highest in man; that links the natural, sensual, ethical and spiritual elements; that prevents one element from being isolated from the rest; and that preserves the quality of true humanness in all the forms of love from sexuality to *agape*. The implication is that none of these elements can be excluded as inappropriate to man, that all of them "belong". The great tradition of Christendom even holds that those aspects of man which derive from his nature as a created being are the foundation for everything "higher" and for all other divine gifts that may be conferred upon him. "It is not the spiritual that comes first but the sensuous-earthly and then the spiritual"—if one were unfamiliar with this quotation, one would scarcely guess that it comes from the New Testament (1 Cor 15:46).[1] Furthermore, Thomas Aquinas, the last great teacher of a still undivided Western Christendom, says that were natural love (*amor*), or eros, not something good in itself, then *caritas* (*agape*) could not perfect it.[2] Rather, agape would have to discard and exclude eros (which Anders Nygren asserts that it does). That same tradition we call "Western" in the specific sense of being not unworldly but rather characterized by a "worldliness" founded on a religious and theological ba-

[1] Translated from the German translation by Otto Karrer, *New Testament* (Munich, 1959).
[2] I, 60, 5.

260

sis[3]—that tradition speaks with complete matter-of-factness of sexuality as a good.[4] It says, with Aristotle, that there is something divine in the human seed.[5] And unresponsiveness to sensual joy, *insensibilitas*, is treated not only as a defect but also as a *vitium*, a moral deficiency.[6] On the other hand, the underlying conception implies that all of man's powers, and especially sexuality, can remain "right" and "in order" only in their natural place, which is to say, within the wholeness of physical-spiritual-mental existence. Once again we call to mind the mediative and integrating functions of eros.

Everything that is intermediate naturally runs the risk of ambiguity; it can be misinterpreted in two directions. In the case of eros this emerges in a characteristic semantic instability of the words associated with it. *Desiderium*, for example, means both "longing" and "wanting"; significantly, "I want" can mean both "I lack" and "I wish for". The word *desire*, which is derived from *desiderium*, means both "longing" and "lust". *Appetitus* may at one time mean a "striving toward", at another time "appetite". And from here it is only a step to the deprecatory judgment that eros is only a "coarser or subtler appetite".[7] With which we return to the subject of "disparagement of eros". This time it is disparagement from "above", from the viewpoint of a spiritual or supernatural conception of man. Eros is regarded as basically a more or less obvious disguise for purely selfish desire. A similar charge may also be made from "below", from the viewpoint of blunt instinctuality. Then too, eros appears to be merely a mask, a wholly superfluous furbelow, sheer romantic affecta-

---

[3] Cf. Josef Pieper, "Was heißt 'Christliches Abendland'?", in *Tradition als Herausforderung. Aufsätze und Reden* (Munich, 1963), 36ff. Cf. also by the same author the article "Scholasticism" in the *Encyclopedia Britannica* (1972 ed.).

[4] *Mal.* 15, 2.

[5] Ibid.

[6] II, II, 142, 1; 153, 3 ad 3.

[7] Karl Barth, *Kirchliche Dogmatik*, vol. 4, pt. 2 (Zollikon-Zurich, 1955), 844.

tion needlessly covering up what is really meant: a simple gratification of the instinctual drive.

Now that we have discussed the danger of separating agape from the wholeness of existence, we should have something to say about that other perversion which, as everyone knows, is especially prevalent today: making isolated sexuality into an "absolute".

A word of warning, though. Let us not exaggerate the gravity of "sexualization" as it supposedly affects the public nowadays. Too much of it comes down to commercial motives and the techniques of advertising. And although there has been talk of a "wave"—if there is one, we should conceive of it not so much like the natural waves of the ocean as like the mechanically produced movement of the water in a swimming pool. On the other hand, of course, the isolation of sexuality, as a form of potential human degeneracy, has always been with us. And it should be pretty apparent that it has existed both as a practice and as an outlook.

We come upon just such a situation in the Platonic dialogue that we have already cited several times. Young Phaedrus, who crosses Socrates' path, has an air of being dazzled and perhaps somewhat dazed. He has just come from a gathering of avant-garde intellectuals. Plato sees this group as marked by a speciously reasoned negation of traditional values, by a sophisticated life style, by a deliberate surrender to instinctual drives. And Phaedrus, fascinated by the modernity and the eloquence of "the ablest writer of our day",[8] who had done the talking, tells Socrates about the pattern of action they propose. In briefest summary this pattern might be reduced to the following points: Lust without love. The aim should be a maximum of pleasure with a minimum of per-

---

[8] *Phaedrus* 228 a.

sonal involvement. The erotic emotion, the *passio* of love, is considered a romantic disease that unnecessarily complicates everything. Refusal to let oneself be deeply affected is declared to be the sole "rational" kind of behavior; what is more, it is also extolled as really "decent", as *areté*.

As we can see, perhaps with some astonishment, these attitudes are uncannily topical today. Or, more precisely, they are attitudes human beings have evidently been able to form and adopt throughout the ages.

Socrates listens to it all for a while, at first pretending to the credulous Phaedrus that he too is enthralled by these ideas. Then, suddenly, he abruptly drops the mask and puts an end to the game: Don't you see, my dear Phaedrus, how shameful all this really is?[9] Suppose a truly noble man had been listening to us now, one who loved another person as generous and humane as himself. Would not such a man surely think that we had been brought up among galley slaves and had never known love among free men?[10]

I trust we need not point out that this contrast between free men and galley slaves does not, despite appearances, have anything to do with the social reality of the Greek "slave-holders' society". What is meant here by slavery is a concept that no social changes, no emancipation, can wipe off the face of the earth. What is meant is something that, as the example of the Athenian upper crust shows, can quite naturally occur in all social classes: the ethically vulgar, plebeian quality of such an attitude and the barbarous crudity and brutality concealed behind all its civilized subtleties.

And now Socrates summons up before the astonished eyes of this ignorant young know-it-all, Phaedrus, the picture of the mediative daimon Eros. Much of what he says scarcely speaks directly to us nowadays; we can approach it only by a

[9] Ibid., 243 c 1.
[10] Ibid., 243 c 2.

detour, employing the interpretive tools of intellectual history. The crucial lesson is that in eros sensuality fuses with spirituality and morality and, moreover, with what must be reckoned the gifts of God, into a unity. Here too, it must be granted, Plato's mythic imagery ("the soul acquiring wings") sounds somewhat sentimental and strange to us. But in reality something entirely realistic is meant. It comes pretty close to what Goethe was saying in his reference, cited above, about "the first erotic leanings of unspoiled youth": that nature seems to be desiring it.[11]

I wonder how Socrates would have treated this Goethean statement, how he would have taken it into his hand and turned it round and round. Well, friends, what shall we say: Does uncorruptedness really exist? And what might be the difference between an uncorrupted and a—let us put it cautiously—a not uncorrupted youth?

For my part, I would answer this truly socratic question by drawing attention first of all to the fact of the word's *passive* form. Youth does not simply spoil the way butter turns rancid or milk sour. But—unfortunately—youth can be spoiled by someone else; that can very well happen. For example, it can be spoiled by seduction and commercial manipulation, which, contrary to the natural course of things, acquaint it sooner with isolated sexual lust than with falling in love and love—so that sex enters youth's consciousness and life before eros does, and in such a way that experiencing real love is hampered if not blocked permanently.

Precisely this is what is so bad and so inhuman about sexual activity separated from eros: it frustrates the very experience that constitutes the meaning of the erotic encounter within the whole of existence. That experience is the escape from

---

[11] *Dichtung und Wahrheit*, pt. 1, bk. 5.

one's own limitations and egotism by union with another person. The mere sex partner does not come into focus as a personal being, that is, as a living self with an individually cast human countenance. An American has put the matter very wittily, remarking that where the "playboy" is concerned, the fig leaf has merely been moved to another place; it now covers the human face.[12] Actually, the man who is merely lustful does not, despite the usual phrase, want "a woman" at all. It is eros that wants a beloved woman and wants being together with her. Sex, on the contrary, seeks a neuter, something material and objective, not a "you" but an "it", the thing in itself (as the partners in Orwell's *1984* explicitly tell one another); the desire is "to do the thing" (as the phrase is in a novel by Heinrich Böll).[13] The encounter that is sheer sex and nothing else has rightly been called deceptive in character. For the moment, an illusion of union arises; but without love this apparent union of two strangers leaves them more remote from one another than they were before.[14] Thus it should cause little surprise that "in a society that makes sexuality the prerequisite for love and not love the condition for the gift of physical union", sex paradoxically "rather separates than unites man and woman, leaving them alone and lonely precisely where they thought they would surely find each other".[15] As such sex consumption increases, this effect is intensified

[12] Rollo May, *Love and Will* (New York, 1969), 57.

[13] *The Clown*, chap. 7.

[14] Erich Fromm, *The Art of Loving* (New York, 1952), 45f.

[15] Joachim Bodamer, *Liebe und Eros in der modernen Welt* (Hamburg, 1958), 40. In an essay, "Ich und Du", published as long ago as 1925, Martin Buber says, "If we deduct from the much-discussed eroticism of the age everything that is essentially egotistic, that is, all relationships in which one is not present to the other, not summoned to mind by him, so that the one is only enjoying himself—what would be left?" (*Werke*, vol. 1 [Munich-Heidelberg, 1962], 108).

and the sexual encounter becomes increasingly disappointing. The result, says Paul Ricoeur,[16] is not what Sigmund Freud's generation expected from the abolition of sexual "taboos" but rather the "forfeit of value by making intercourse free". Ricoeur points out, "Everything that makes the sexual encounter easy simultaneously speeds its collapse into insignificance." At bottom that is hardly surprising. It might be called an iron law. What can be had on demand and almost gratis, and almost at once as well (Americans use the robust expression "short-order sex"),[17] necessarily loses both its value and its attractiveness. The head of the health center at an American state university, a psychiatrist by profession, reported that some of the more promiscuous female students replied in answer to an inquiry, "It's just too much trouble to say 'No'."[18] At first hearing, that may sound like sheerest freedom, but clearly it also means: I don't really care; it doesn't matter. The wholly inevitable result is already implicit: "sexuality not only without joy but without pleasure";[19] "so much sex and so little meaning or even fun in it".[20]

As I indicated, a universal law is operating here. Goethe in later life once put the matter thus, in a quite different context, "Every century... tries to make the sacred common, the difficult easy, and the serious amusing—to which there really could be no objection if it were not that in the process seriousness and amusement are destroyed together."[21] That's just it: the fun goes out of it, too. And so it is grimly apt that

[16] Paul Ricoeur, *Sexualität. Wunder—Abwege—Rätsel* (Frankfurt: Rischer Bücherei, 1967), 15.

[17] *Love and Will*, 282.

[18] Seymour L. Halleck, "The Roots of Student Despair", in *Think* (published by IBM) 33 (1967): 22.

[19] Jean Brun, in Ricoeur, *Sexualität*, 129.

[20] *Love and Will*, 40.

[21] To Zelter, March 18, 1811.

the article by the university psychiatrist should be entitled: "The Roots of Student Despair".

We are certainly not dealing here merely with the consequences of a wanton abuse of freedom, at least not with that alone. The matter is not so simple. Along with the discussion of the devaluation of easy sex, Rollo May also speaks of its nearly compulsive nature.[22] In the grayed world of a work-oriented society geared to output, sex seems to be the only remaining green thing.[23] David Riesman's well-known phrase has been echoed many times: Sex is the last frontier, that is, the last still accessible realm of adventure, excitement and unregimented life. But once we fix our gaze upon this "sociological" aspect of the matter, we have to ask whether a kind of vicious circle has not formed here, and one almost impossible to break out of. On the one hand, "the one green thing"[24] in the midst of a world of labor that is more and more completely dominating man is love alone, eros, the rapturous affirmation of the beloved that makes for forgetfulness of self (or even the affirmation of any thing loved disinterestedly). And this true overstepping of the bounds of all functionalism aimed solely at utility and gratifying needs is also implicit, more or less obscurely, in sexual craving. On the other hand, this very thing that is truly longed for cannot be attained by detached, easy sex.

Max Horkheimer's remark in an interview, "We must pay for the pill with the death of erotic love",[25] raised a good many hackles, but it contains an almost undeniable truth. However, it seems to me that the decisive factor is not, as

[22] *Sexualität*, 16.

[23] Gerald Sykes, *The Cool Millennium* (New York, 1967). Cited in May, *Love and Will*, 59.

[24] Ibid.

[25] *Die Sehnsucht nach dem ganz Anderen* (Hamburg, 1970), 74.

Horkheimer implies, the destruction of longing. What is more decisive is that something in principle not freely available is to be made available at will, and "without risk". But of course this easily available thing cannot be what was really sought.[26] What is really sought, human closeness, overcoming of loneliness, union with another personal being—all that can be had only in real love. But at this point we see a further segment of the vicious circle. For love—above all, eros—is by nature something that cannot be fitted smoothly and easily, without problems, into the functional context of utilitarian plans. "Eros is the one element in man that most intensely resists assimilation by the technological system."[27] On the other hand, detached sex as a "consumer good", as a "ware", can be smoothly installed and planned into the great utilitarian organization—as has been persuasively described in a number of important literary visions of the future, such as Aldous Huxley's *Brave New World*.

But now another "on the other hand" must be considered, one that seems to close the vicious circle. Human personality forbids being "used" for the ends of others. Yet in consumer sex, which deliberately fends off love, the partner is regarded purely as a means and instrument. Hence the human face is not seen at all (this ignoring of the other may be quite mutual). Complete absence of human warmth is almost requisite. Consequently, in such detached sexuality there is hidden, despite all the outward show, a measure of frigidity[28] in the clinical sense of the word. There is also, insofar as the relationship of person to person is concerned, an element of violence and a tinge of exactly that same "totalitarian cold-

[26] I am speaking here of the "pill" only to the extent that it is a means for making sex consumption easy. The extremely complicated problem of birth control and family planning would, of course, involve far more discussion.

[27] Joachim Bodamer, *Sexualität und Liebe* (Hamburg, 1970), 20.

[28] Bodamer, *Liebe und Eros*, 40.

ness"[29] which pervades the atmosphere of dictatorships and of purely technocratic societies—in which there is no room for the "green thing" called love, so that again the human being is driven to the one seemingly open but, in fact, deceptive escape route of isolated sex consumption.

It is highly significant that in serious modern writing on the subject, for all the variety in philosophical or scientific approaches, the idea of the *demonic* comes up more or less explicitly. This idea has, of course, nothing to do with the Platonic conception of the "mediative daimon Eros"; on the contrary, it refers to an evil power that aims at dehumanization and destruction. Karl Barth has expressed it in a phrase that for him is unusually forceful: "Coitus without coexistence is a demonic affair."[30] Harvey Cox, equally unexpectedly, actually brings up the obsolescent concept of exorcising demons and driving out devils, although the word "exorcism" has already vanished from several theological dictionaries.[31] Because the dehumanization of life nowhere appears in more devastating form than in the modern sex industry, he says, nowhere else is "a clear word of exorcism more needed".[32] Physicians and psychologists speak of the underlying tendency to self-destruction involved in detached sexuality.[33] Only eros can preserve men from that, they say.[34] And C. S. Lewis puts a verse of John Donne as the terrifying motto of his book on love: "That our affections kill us not, nor dye."[35]

[29] Ibid., 35.

[30] *Kirchliche Dogmatik*, vol. 3, pt. 4 (Zollikon-Zurich, 1951), 148.

[31] For example, the entry "Exorcismus" (and also "Satan" and "Teufel") does not appear in the German theological dictionary *Kleines theologisches Wörterbuch* edited by Karl Rahner and Herbert Vorgrimler (Freiburg, 1961).

[32] Harvey Cox, *The Secular City* (New York: Macmillan, 1965), 192.

[33] Cyrill Koupernik, in Ricoeur, *Sexualität*, 246.

[34] *Love and Will*, 317.

[35] *The Poems of John Donne*, ed. Sir H. J. C. Grierson (London: Oxford University Press, 1933), 317.

Now, it is part of the nature of the demonic power (in the strict sense of the word) that it never shows itself in its true form. Rather, it masquerades as sheer amusement and, above all, as an almost obligatory modernity—which, of course, magnifies its destructive effect. If only eros can give what is sought in sex, then this is precisely what "the shamans of sales" and "the sorcerers of the mass media and the advertising guild"[36] will try to deceive men about. The lie consists in this: that with an enormous expenditure of money (the whole thing is big business, after all), but also with the investment of tremendous psychological knowledge, with a maximum of skill in dealing with words and pictures, and with impressive subliminal use of music, color, form (and so on), the consumer is made to believe that sex is the same thing as eros and that all the gifts of eros, all the joyful raptures of "togetherness" can be had in sex consumption. It isn't offered for free, certainly not, but still it is basically available to everyone.

The production of such deceptions has from ancient times been the business of the sophist, whom Plato in one of his late dialogues[37] described as a maker of fictive reality. The sophistic "art of persuasion" by flattery and propaganda creates the image of mass idols, or the illusion that smoking a particular cigarette will bring one "the pure joy of life" and "the fragrance of the great wide world". In the erotic realm the range of such sophistry extends from the suggestive slogans of advertising[38] to the department of *haute littérature*, as, for example, in the novels of D. H. Lawrence, who has already become rather old-fashioned. Of a couple celebrating

[36] *The Secular City*, 192

[37] *Sophistes*, 236ff. Cf. also Josef Pieper, *Abuse of Language—Abuse of Power* (San Francisco: Ignatius Press, 1992), 43ff.

[38] According to the report in the *Frankfurter Allgemeine Zeitung* (September 6, 1969) on the Teenage Fair in Düsseldorf, the advertising slogan of a furniture factory there read: "Make your table sexy and youthful!"

the sexual act in the woods, Lawrence solemnly says: "They let themselves be carried away by the wave of life." On which C. S. Lewis dryly remarks: Since in these novels the characters never speak of possible fertility, in the terms neither of hope nor of fear, it must be assumed that they will allow themselves to be carried away by the wave of life only just so far as seems useful to them and no farther.[39]

Such realistic reminders of what's what can serve as a form of "exorcism", as can the corrective irony of sober language. Socrates, as everybody knows, constantly made use of such techniques. But he also knew that such opposition was not sufficient. And so, thinking of the danger to young men of the type of Phaedrus, he asked the disturbing question,

> When they huddle together in groups—in the theater, in court, in the camps—and express their displeasure or approval with tremendous noise, with clapping and shouting, and everything resounds with disapproval and applause—how do you think the young person will feel then? What an extraordinary education he will have had to receive in order to put up resistance and not be carried along with the current wherever it happens to be going. Ought we not to say: If he really liberates himself and thrives in healthy growth—that is owing to divine providence and is pure gift?[40]

That is, as we can see, not so very different from a call to prayer. So, too, I have not the remotest notion of how Harvey Cox imagines that an "exorcism" is to be carried out in concrete form. But in using this word, he is introducing a clearly religious category and is indubitably right in doing so. He too is suggesting that the realm of sex and eros needs both purification and perfection by a superhuman power.

[39] *Studies in Words* (Cambridge, 1967), 298f.

[40] This is a compression of the Platonic text and therefore not quite literal, but it is, I think, a faithful rendering of the meaning of a passage in the *Politeia* (492 b–493 a).

X

So far we have spoken not at all about several aspects of the phenomenon known as "love". One such, for example, is friendship or, more exactly, the love of friends. That is, in fact, a special form of love, though one that nowadays, oddly enough, comes in for little praise, whereas Aristotle devoted to it one entire book of the ten books that make up his *Nicomachean Ethics*. Friendship takes time, he says there;[1] it is normally kindled, not just by the sight of the other, but by the surprise at discovering that here is someone else who "sees things exactly" the way one sees them oneself, someone of whom one can say happily, "It's good that you exist!" Friends do not gaze at each other, and, totally unlike erotic lovers, they are not apt to talk about their friendship. Their gaze is fixed upon the things in which they take a common interest. That is why, it has been said, people who simply wish for "a friend" will with fair certainty not find any. To find a friend you first have to be interested in something.[2] Although, therefore, real intimacy does not exist in friendship, a friend is perhaps the only human being in whose presence we speak with complete sincerity and "think aloud"[3] without embarrassment.

So far we also have not spoken directly of the distinctive

---

[1] *Nicomachean Ethics* 8, 4; 1156 b.

[2] Cf. the illuminating chapter entitled "Friendship" in C. S. Lewis' *The Four Loves* (London, 1960).

[3] R. W. Emerson, *Essays*, 1st series (London, 1903), "Friendship", 151.

qualities of maternal love. It has always been said that mothers, as those who love most intensely, seek less to be loved than to love.[4] A mother's love for her children is "unconditional" in a unique fashion; that is, it is not linked with any preconditions. Because of that it corresponds to the deepest longings of children and, indeed, of every human being.[5] Maternal love does not have to be "earned"; and there is nothing anyone can do to lose it. A father, on the contrary, tends to set conditions; his love has to be earned. But that likewise repeats a fundamental element peculiar to all love: the desire that the beloved not only "feel good" but that things may in truth go well for him. A mature person's love must, as has rightly been remarked,[6] contain both elements, the maternal and the paternal, something unconditional and something demanding.

And so there may well be an untold number of possible ways for human beings to feel good toward one another, to like each other, to feel closeness and affection for one another. But varied as these forms and unsystematic as these degrees of fondness, attachment, liking and solidarity obviously may be, they all have one thing in common with friendship, parental love, fraternity and specifically erotic love: that the lover, turning to the beloved, says, "It's good that you are here; it's wonderful that you exist!" (Unexpectedly we see once more that mere sex partnership cannot be included in this category—because in such partnerships there is no trace of a "you"; there is an ego, and maybe there are two egos, but there is no "you" involved!)

The fundamental affirmation that recurs in identical form in all real love is, as we said at the very beginning of our reflec-

[4] II, II, 27, 1.
[5] Erich Fromm, *The Art of Loving* (New York, 1952), 35.
[6] Ibid., 37.

tions, by its nature and quite apart from the lovers' awareness of it, the reenactment of something else that precedes it. It is an imitation of the divine creative act by virtue of which the human being we have just encountered, who suits us and who seems "made for us", exists; by virtue of which, in fact, all reality exists at all and is simultaneously "good", that is, lovable.

But this aspect of the phenomenon of love, which admittedly points beyond empirically knowable reality, must be considered more closely once more—in order for us to be able to name and grasp another special form of love that we have hitherto said nothing about, at any rate not explicitly, but that most certainly cannot be overlooked. Not that we have any intention of going into theology! A theological book on love, that is, one interpreting the documents of the sacred tradition and revelation, would undoubtedly have to deal with entirely different matters from those we are now about to discuss. No, we shall keep our eyes fixed upon the phenomenon of love as we encounter it in our experience. The question is, however, whether we may not, by dint of including in our considerations something that belongs to the realm of belief, be able to clarify and interpret a fact of experience that would otherwise remain obscure and uncomprehended.

There is, for example, to pitch our discussion in concrete terms at once, the quite empirical contemporary phenomenon of Mother Teresa,[7] the Yugoslav nun in Calcutta who has recently been receiving a considerable amount of publicity. She taught English literature in her order's high school for girls. One day she could no longer endure seeing, on her way to school, deathly ill and dying people lying in the street without receiving any humane aid. She therefore persuaded

[7] In January 1971, Pope Paul VI made her the first recipient of the John XXIII Peace Prize, which had been founded in 1963.

the city government to let her have an empty, neglected pil-
grims' rest house and in it established her subsequently famous Hospital for the Dying. I have seen this shelter, which
at the beginning was a most dismal place. Of course people
die inside it likewise—but now they need no longer perish
amidst the bustle of the streets. They feel something of the
presence of a sympathetic person.

On the one hand, what can we call this work of mercy but a
form of loving concern, nourished by the fundamental impulse of "It's good that you exist" and affecting the loving
person not just on a supernatural or spiritual level detached
from all natural emotions. Rather, it affects him through all
the levels of his being. *On the other hand*, something new and
fundamentally different is taking place here or, at any rate,
something that cannot so easily be reduced to a common denominator with friendship, liking, fondness, being smitten—
and so on.

I should like to try, step by step, to make this new element
seem plausible, to show how it is something lying within
man's potential or, more precisely, something that has been
put within the scope of human feeling. The first step, without our knowing it, has already been taken. It consists in our
reenacting, whenever we love, the primal affirmation that
took place in the creation. But it would also be possible
that—taking the second step—we "realize" deliberately this
iterative aspect of our loving. When we find something we
see good, glorious, wonderful (a tree; the structure of a dia-
tom seen under the microscope; above all, of course, a human face, a friend, one's partner for the whole of life, but also
one's own existence in the world)—when we see something
good, I say, when we love something lovable, we might become aware of our actually taking up and continuing that
universal approval of the creation by which all that has been
created is "loved by God" and is therefore good. It would be

a further step, beyond the mere recognition of this truth, to wish to observe it expressly, as if we were joining in with the Creator's affirmative and allying ourselves with it in a sort of identification—joining with the primordial act of affirmation and also with the "Actor". We might, in other words, for our part also love the "First Lover". Obviously that would change our own love for things and people, especially for those whom one loves more than all others; our own love, that is, would receive a wholly new and literally absolute confirmation. And the beloved, though still altogether incomparable, still someone personally and specially intended for us, would at the same time suddenly appear as one point of light in an infinite mesh of light.

Yet even after we had taken this step, we would still not have attained the stage of *caritas* and *agape* in the strict sense. The true motives of that remarkable nun in Calcutta would not yet have come into view. Incidentally, when a reporter remarked to her in astonishment that he would not do "anything like that" if he were paid a thousand dollars a day for it, she is said to have replied, tersely and magnificently, "Neither would I." Anyone who seriously asked her, "Why are you doing this?" would probably receive the reply—if she did not choose to remain silent—"For the sake of Christ!" At this point Anders Nygren is undeniably right; love in the form of agape is "the original basic conception of Christianity".[8] It rests upon the certain faith that the event that in the language of theology is called "Incarnation" conferred upon man the gift of an immediate and real participation in God's creative power of affirmation. Or, as we might also put it: participation in the divine love, which is what creates the being as well as the goodness of the world in the first place. As a conse-

---

[8] *Eros und Agape* (Gütersloh, 1930), 1:31.

quence of that, man can turn to another person in a way that otherwise he would be utterly incapable of doing and, while remaining altogether himself, can say to that other, "It's good that you are." And it is precisely this more intensive force of approval, operating from a wholly fresh basis, that is intended by the word *caritas (agape)*. But because like God's own love it is universal, at least in intention, excluding nothing and no one, we find we can use the word meaningfully without explicitly naming an object, saying, for example, that someone is "in love" (1 Jn 4:18). Such love, no matter how "forlorn"[9] it may seem, possesses that imperturbable nonirritability of which the New Testament speaks: "caritas non irritatur" (1 Cor 13:5). Likewise other hyperboles, such as that in love a maximum of freedom is attained[10] and that it gives the heart perfect peace,[11] prove true only with regard to *caritas*.

It is really self-evident that the images hitherto employed of a succession of steps and stages do not quite accord with the radical newness and otherness of that participation in the creative love of God that has been given to man—what in the New Testament is called grace. Nevertheless, the great tradition of Christendom has always insisted that this new thing is indeed tied to what man is by nature and by virtue of creation with an inseparable, though almost indescribable, bond.

Above all, *caritas* in the Christian sense does not invalidate any of the love and affirmation we are able to feel on our own and frequently we do feel as a matter of course. Rather, *caritas* comprehends all the forms of human love.[12] For, after

[9] The magnificent formulation that agape is essentially "lost love" comes from Anders Nygren, who in support of it quotes Luther's phrase "amoris est falli" (*Eros und Agape*, 2:554).

[10] Thomas Aquinas, *In duo praecepta*, no. 1134. *Opuscula Theologica*, vol. 2 (Turin, 1954).

[11] Ibid., no. 1150.

[12] "Dilectio caritatis sub se comprehendit omnes dilectiones humanas" (*Car.* 7).

all, it is our own natural, native will, kindled at the creation and by virtue of this very origin tempestuously demanding appeasement, that is now exalted to immediate participation in the will of the Creator himself—and therefore necessarily presupposed.[13]

Anyone who considers and accepts this principle cannot find it surprising that the whole conception of *caritas* is dominated by felicity. If happiness is truly never anything but happiness in love, then the fruit of that highest form of love must be the utmost happiness, for which language offers such names as felicity, beatitude, bliss. Nor should this be in any way confused with "eudemonism". In the first place, *felicity* means not so much the subjective feeling of happiness as the objective, existential appeasement of the will by the *bonum universale*,[14] by the quintessence of everything for which our whole being hungers and which we are capable of longing for in (only seemingly paradoxical) "selfless self-love". Moreover, *felicity*, as has already been said, cannot be defined positively at all in regard to its content; it is a *bonum ineffabile*,[15] toward which our love ultimately directs itself, a good that cannot be grasped in words.

At any rate, although we may find the fact startling and troublesome at first, the great teachers of Christendom always considered the concepts of *caritas* and felicity as very closely linked. "*Caritas* is not just any kind of love of God, but a love for God that loves him as the object and the author of happiness."[16] And in the world, we are told, we can love in the mode of *caritas* only what is capable of sharing happiness,

---

[13] Perfection presupposes perfectibility; cf. I, 2, 2 ad 1.

[14] Cf. Josef Pieper, *Happiness and Contemplation* (New York, 1958), 39ff.

[15] Augustine, *Sermo* 21, 2; PL 38:143.

[16] "Caritas non est qualiscumque amor Dei, sed amor Dei quo diligitur ut beatitudinis objectum" (I, II, 65, 5 ad 1). "Diligendus est ex caritate Deus ut radix beatitudinis" (*Car.* 7).

or beatitude, with us.[17] This includes our bodies, into which happiness will "flood back";[18] but above all our fellowmen, insofar as they will be our companions in beatitude[19] (or ought to be).[20]

Of course it is possible to ask skeptically just what it means to love another as the possible companion of future beatitude. Would love of this sort alter matters at all? I think that, in fact, a great deal would be altered if we succeeded in regarding another person (whether friend, beloved, son, neighbor, adversary and rival or even an unknown who needed our help) truly as one destined like ourselves to share in the perfection of bliss, as our "socius in participatione beatudinis".[21] That other person would then, in my view, simply enter into a new dimension of reality. Suddenly we would realize that "there are no ordinary people."[22]

It is no accident that almost all the above has been written in the conditional tense, the *modus irrealis*. In fact, it happens very seldom, and only to a few persons, to see the extraordinariness of everyone ("wonderfully created and even more wonderfully re-created"),[23] let alone to respond to it with the exclamation of love: It's wonderful that you are! This is, as we see, not so very far from the vocabulary of eros. And truly, if anyone has asked what in the world the mutual rapture of lovers has to do with the work of a nun who wishes to succor dying beggars—precisely this is the point at which the hid-

---

[17] *Car.* 4 ad 2.

[18] *Car.* 7; II, II, 25, 5 ad 2.

[19] *Car.* 7.

[20] *Perf. vit. spir.*, cap. 2.

[21] *Car.* 7.

[22] C. S. Lewis, *They Asked for a Paper* (London, 1962), 210.

[23] "Deus qui humanae substantiae dignitatem mirabiliter condidisti et mirabilius reformasti . . ."—such is the wording of a prayer in the "oldest books of the Roman Mass" that has recently been deleted from the Ordo Missae. Cf. J. A. Jungmann, *Missarum Solemnia* (Vienna, 1948), 1:77ff.

den common element becomes visible, as if seen through a tiny crack.

It also becomes immediately apparent that the act of *caritas* is not simply a farther step on the road of eros, and that what is involved is something different from mere "sublimation". It is true that *caritas* can be incorporated into the most common-place forms of expression in men's dealings with their fellows. In fact, that is usually what will be done with it—so that possibly, to the uninitiated eye, there will be scarcely anything noticeable about its outward appearance to set it off from the usual conduct of people reasonably well-disposed toward one another. In other words, the natural forms of love are presupposed to be intact; and no special, solemnly sublime vocabulary is needed to describe the operations of *caritas*. Still, the classical statement of the relationship of grace and nature speaks not only of presupposition and intactness but also of the perfecting of what man by nature is and has.[24] And when I said that the bond between eros and *caritas* exists but is almost indescribable, the difficulty of description in practice consists in this question: "What is the meaning of *perfecting*?" This is one of those concepts which probably can never be known and defined before it is experienced. It is simply in the nature of the thing that the apprentice can have no specific idea of what the perfection of mastery looks like from inside or of all that is going to be demanded of him. Perfection always includes transformation. And transformation necessarily means parting from what must be overcome and abandoned precisely for the sake of preserving identity in change.

"Perfection" in *caritas*, therefore, may very well mean that eros, in order to keep its original impulse and remain really love, above all in order to attain the "foreverness" that it

[24] Cf. I, 1, 8 ad 2; 62, 5; I, II, 99, 2 ad 1; III, 71, 1 ad 1.

naturally desires, must transform itself altogether, and that this transformation perhaps resembles passing through something akin to dying. Such thoughts are, at any rate, not unfamiliar to mankind's reflections on love. *Caritas*, in renewing and rejuvenating us, also brings us death in a certain sense: "Facit in nobis quamdam mortem", says Augustine.[25] The same thing is conveyed by the familiar figure of speech that calls *caritas*, because it consumes everything and transforms everything into itself, a fire.[26]

Thus it is much more than an innocuous piety when Christendom prays, "Kindle in us the fire of thy love."

[25] *In Ps.* 121, 12; PL 37:1628.
[26] *In Isa.*, cap. 30.

ABBREVIATIONS

Quotations from the *Summa theologica* of Saint Thomas Aquinas are identified in the footnotes only by numerals. For example, I, II, 3, 4 means: Part I of Section II, quaestio 3, articulus 4. The same method is used for references to his commentary on the *Sentences* of Peter Lombard. For example, 2, d. 3, 4, 1 means: Book 2, distinction 3, quaestio 4, articulus 1. The titles of the other works of Saint Thomas are abbreviated as follows:

C. G.	*Summa contra Gentiles*
Car.	*Quaestio disputata de caritate*
Comp.	*Compendium theologiae*
Contra Graecos	"Declaratio Quorumdam Articulorum Contra Graecos, Armenos et Saracenos"
De spe	*Quaestio disputata de spe*
In Div. Nom.	Commentary on Dionysius the Areopagite's *De divinis nominibus*
In Hebr.	*Expositio super S. Paulo epistolam ad Hebraeos*
In Isa.	Commentary on Isaiah
In Trin.	Commentary on Boethius' *De Trinitate*
Mal.	*Quaestiones disputatae de malo*
Perf. vit. spir.	*De perfectione vitae spiritualis*
Pot.	*Quaestiones disputatae de potentia Dei*
Ver.	*Quaestiones disputatae de veritate*
Virt. card.	*Quaestiones disputatae de virtutibus*
Virt. comm.	*Quaestiones disputatae de virtutibus in communi*

INDEX